Bamaga

Batavia
Downs

Merluna

Coral Sea

Coen

Alice

Mitchell

Koolatah

Dunbar

Palmer

Drumduff

Laura

Cooktown

River

River

Highbury

River

Gamboola

Wrotham
Park

Van Rook

Chillagoe

Mareeba

Cairns

Gilbert

Einasleigh

River

Mt Garnet

Woodleigh

Innisfail

SOUTH PACIFIC

OCEAN

Croydon

River

Mt Surprise

Herbert

Kirrama

Georgetown

Rosella Plains

Forsayth

Einasleigh

River

Esmeralda

Robin
Hood

Greenvale

Kilclooney

Ingham

Oak Park

Mt Full Stop

Burdekin

Townsville

Somerset

River

Charters Towers

Mt Ravenswood

Strathalbyn

Dalbeg

River

Maxwelton

Richmond

Hughendon

Strathmore

Collinsville

Bowen

River

Mackay

Archer

River

caroni

aten

Gilbert

anda
owns

BAGMEN
MILLIONAIRES

BAGMEN MILLIONAIRES

LIFE AND PEOPLE IN OUTBACK QUEENSLAND

JOHN ANDERSEN

VIKING O'NEIL

Viking O'Neil
Penguin Books Australia Ltd
487 Maroondah Highway, PO Box 257
Ringwood, Victoria 3134, Australia
Penguin Books Ltd
Harmondsworth, Middlesex, England
Viking Penguin Inc.
40 West 23rd Street, New York, N.Y. 10010, U.S.A.
Penguin Books Canada Limited
2801 John Street, Markham, Ontario, Canada L3R 1B4
Penguin Books (N.Z.) Ltd
182-190 Wairau Road, Auckland 10, New Zealand

First published by Lloyd O'Neil Pty Ltd 1983
Reprinted 1984
This edition published by Penguin Books Australia Ltd 1988

3 5 7 9 10 8 6 4 2

Produced by Viking O'Neil
56 Claremont Street, South Yarra, Victoria 3141, Australia
A division of Penguin Books Australia Ltd

Printed and bound in Hong Kong through Bookbuilders Ltd

National Library of Australia
Cataloguing-in-Publication data

Andersen, John, 1953-
Bagmen Millionaires.

ISBN 0 670 90062 1.

1.Country Life—Queensland. 2. Queensland—Social
life and customs—1976-   . 3. Farm Life—
Queensland. I. Title.

994.306'3

For Robyn

Contents

Acknowledgements

This book was written without any form of financial assistance in the way of grants. There were, however, some business houses which helped and offered assistance. I would like to thank Neilsen Toyota of Townsville for supplying me at cost price with a Toyota Hilux 4WD. This vehicle covered 16 000 kilometres over some of the worst roads in the country and never let me down once. I would also like to thank the *North Queensland Register* newspaper which regularly published my feature stories and so helped keep the wolf from the door. Thanks also to Air Queensland and TAA. Both organisations offered me cut price and free air travel while the book was in preparation. Special thanks to my wife Robyn, who became my secretary, critic, manuscript typist and cheer leader on those horrible 'off' days.

Information used in telling of the history and wild days of the Bowen River Hotel was gleaned with kind permission from *The Bowen River Saga*, a booklet written and published by Mr E. Cunningham. Thanks are also due to the family of Mary Ada McDowell for permission to publish extracts from her journal of reminiscences.

But it was the people of the bush, the people on the stations which I visited, who made this book possible. I wish to thank them from the bottom of my heart for their kindness and infinite patience. I know it's hardly an original phrase, but they ARE 'a race apart'.

'So many people from the towns and cities don't have any idea what life is like on a station . . . people talk about wealthy grazier snobs and it's so wrong. They think we're all millionaries. If we are, we're bagmen million-aires.'

(Nancy Sheahan,
Kilclooney Station, Mt Fox.)

Introduction

With this book I hope to promote a better understanding of the way life is lived on back country cattle stations in north Queensland. I would like to stress right from the outset that the text concentrates on contemporary lifestyles and not on the history of the northern cattle industry. Many of the people I met while researching and writing the book assumed it was going to deal with the historical chapters of some of the north's better-known stations. This was not my intention at all. Although I have the utmost respect for the pioneers who expanded the boundaries of the northern frontier, I had no intention of dwelling on them in any length, at least in this book.

To my way of thinking too much is made of the hardships which faced our pioneers. It has become popular, particularly in the Australian film industry, to romanticise the pioneering past. Most Australians fail to realise that there are people living in remote areas of northern Australia today who live lifestyles little different from those of our early pioneers. The pioneer of today who lives in rugged geographic isolation often does not have access to either television or telephone. The only communication link in situations such as this is the radio telephone or two-way radio.

The Royal Flying Doctor Service and the School of the Air have changed outback living. But there is still, I think, that loneliness which comes from being cut off from the majority of the population. It is a life lived close to the bosom of the earth, away from outside influence and the zany natterings of the world. It is a life which breeds, if you like, that lost paragon of the Australian idiom — the Rugged Individual.

It is wrong to say that the pioneering era is past. Women and men are still out there today battling as they always have against Mother Nature, cruel cattle prices, and governments which are scarcely aware of their existence.

In this book I have covered a cross-section of stations from large company-owned operations to smaller holdings run by the battlers. My belief is that many Australians, when they think of a big northern station, think of Brunette Downs in the Northern Territory. They don't think of the battler who lives in a tin hut and runs a thousand head of cattle. Glamorous as it is, Brunette Downs remains a blonde in a field of brunettes.

After reading *Bagmen Millionaires* I hope at least you can say, 'Jeez, those poor bastards have got it tough up there'.

Phil Schaffert

Although he lived in Cairns, during his twilight years Phil Schaffert remained one of north Queensland's best known cattlemen and bush identities. He was known the length and breadth of the Gulf country and remained one of its most respected sons until his death in May 1983. Station owners and managers, grizzly old head stockmen, hardcase ringers, and wet-behind-the-ears jackeroos who worked under him all have one thing in common: Phil Schaffert, they say, was a Good Man.

He was born in Georgetown in 1906 and at thirteen was given the choice by his father of either going to school in Cairns or going droving. Phil went droving, and commenced what was to become a remarkable career on the land. He managed Gregory Downs for thirteen years and Miranda Downs for twenty-eight years. He was a bushman's bushman. And he was a wizard of a story teller, with a remarkable head for dates and occurrences. His stories, as often as not, were filled with the poignant drama of the outback and its unabashed humour.

Below are three of Phil Schaffert's adventures which he related to me when I visited him in Cairns in 1982.

The crash of the Liberator at Moonlight Creek

It was a few minutes before 2 am in a black Gulf of Carpentaria sky in 1942. An American Liberator bomber was flying in a southerly direction towards the Australian mainland. The pilot was fighting to keep the crippled plane in the air. Neither he nor the other nine men in the plane knew what lay below. Was it the waters of the Gulf or was it land? If land, then who did it belong to? Would it be Australian soil or would it be an island?

At 2 am the pilot could no longer hold the heavy bomber in the sky. He called to his crew to brace themselves for a crash landing. The plane screamed earthwards. Sometime about then one of the airmen must have panicked and jumped from the bomber, pulling the ripcord on his parachute. His mangled body, which had been caught in the propellers, was found tangled in the parachute not far from the crash site by searchers some months afterwards. The plane tore through the low ti-tree scrub and, when it finally came to rest, the survivors who stepped out could only guess at their position. Inside the plane were the bodies of three men killed in the crash. Outside was the decapitated corpse of the parachutist.

The survivors then, it seems, plotted their course of action. Two elected to head east and four decided to go west. But to where? Unknown to them, they had come down in the featureless scrub country at Moonlight Creek, north of the Doomadgee Aboriginal Reserve. Either way, east or west, they would be lucky to chance upon some form of civilisation.

Nine days later, Fred Waldren of Escott Station, west of Burketown, was out mustering horses with two Aboriginal stockmen on a large salt flat. Far ahead Waldren spotted two figures crossing the bare expanse. Thinking they were Japanese soldiers, he started to gallop away, but drew rein when one of his stockmen heard the men shout in English: 'Come back! Come back!'

The two men were the airmen who had elected to travel east. They were in a shocking state, as they had been walking and living off what they could catch with their bare hands during the days since the crash. Waldren took them to the Burketown hospital and the search got under way for the remainder of the survivors.

There were sixteen bushmen in that search party, one of whom was Phil Schaffert, who had travelled from Gregory Downs to help locate the plane and the survivors. For ten days they rode the country around Moonlight Creek, but no trace could be found of the plane. On the tenth day they found six parachutes which they spread out over high ant hills to create some sort of landmark in the featureless country. One of the searchers found a set of goggles, along with a jacket, some bullets, fishing lines, a compass and some compressed dried fruit. That night the searchers were confident that the next day they would locate the plane.

But heavy rain set in and it became apparent that, unless they hurried, they themselves would be trapped by floodwaters in the low-lying country. A radio message was sent to the Royal Flying Doctor Service asking for a plane to help locate the bomber. The next day the search plane appeared and after circling for some time the pilot dropped a note tied to a spanner to the horsemen below. He had located the Liberator bomber. The search party set off, but was still unable to find the plane from the ground. The RFDS plane had meanwhile returned to base. The searchers combed the country for another two days, but the rain was showing signs of settling in and all further efforts were unanimously called off.

Some months later Jack Kiernan, the owner of wild Seven Emus Station near Borroloola in the Northern Territory, was mustering coastal country with three Aboriginal stockmen. He sent the natives on to a bark hut used as a mustering camp on the coast, and told them to unpack the pack horses and cook some corned beef while he went and checked the water level at a nearby spring. When he had finished, he started to ride back to the camp, but found his stockmen more than a kilometre from the hut. They were talking animatedly and were obviously distressed about something. Kiernan, angry that none of the chores had been done, shouted at them for not unpacking the horses.

'Mr Jack,' one of the stockmen sang back. 'Big mob of Japanese up there. You can see him tracks.'

Gulf residents during the war thought a Japanese invasion from the northern coastline was inevitable. To many it was just a matter of when, and exactly where? Kiernan unholstered the pistol he always carried and, taking one stockman with him, made for the coast. When he neared the hut he instructed his companion to wait. 'If I don't come back, ride for home and tell everyone the Japanese are on the coast,' he instructed.

With that Kiernan began to crawl forward, pistol at the ready. Not far from the hut he saw two feet sticking out from under a bush. A heavy smell hung in the air, telling him the man was dead. Kiernan, still cautious, approached the hut and found a note written on a clam shell. It read: 'If anybody should come please do not leave. Just about on my last. Been hunting for food.'

Kiernan realised he had stumbled upon one of the missing airmen, one of the four who had headed west.

The Aboriginal stockmen set to work and tracked the note-writer through the bush. They found him alive, a walking skeleton who had not had a proper meal for months. He had lived on insects and dead fish he found and whatever else he could catch with his bare hands. Apart from the dead man at the hut he was alone.

Kiernan slowly took the sick man back to his homestead where he was nourished back to health. He later told Phil Schaffert that all through the first night back at the homestead the only sound that could be heard through the house was that of a spoon rasping across a tin plate as the starving airman devoured meal after meal. Only guesswork can be used to try and determine what happened to the two airmen who did not make it to the hut. Possibly they were taken by sharks or crocodiles as they swam the numerous coastal channels they would have encountered on their horror journey through to the Northern Territory. Even today, some forty-one years after the crash, it takes an experienced bushman to find the site where the crippled Liberator and its crew went down.

The perishing doctor and the insurance salesman

It was in the dry season one year while Phil was manager at Gregory Downs. He and his brother Charlie were driving an old Dodge utility from the station to Georgetown. The trip took them through some of the driest country in the Gulf. This is known as the 'forest' country and some of its most arid examples can be found in the Yappar River area south of Croydon. The two brothers planned to cross the Yappar and then make for Iffley Station via Croydon. The Yappar, like most watercourses in the area, only runs for a few short months during the wet season. After this it becomes a bed of dry sand, a trap for the unwary. Phil and Charlie, being experienced bushmen, were carrying enough water to sustain them even if they should run into trouble lasting several days.

When they came to the lonely crossing across the dry river, they found the track blocked by a vehicle hopelessly bogged to its axles in the sand. There was no sign of anyone, but a note tied to the steering wheel advised that the occupants had gone in search of water as their supplies were almost exhausted. There was no date on the note.

Phil and Charlie set off to search for whoever it was, and by sheer luck found two men lying in the shade of a tree not far from the car. Their water had run out and they had not had a drink for two days. They were suffering from dehydration and must have been close to death. They drank some water and began to talk. As soon as Phil introduced Charlie and himself, one of the stranded men let out an exclamation. He leapt to his feet and threw his arms around Phil in an embrace. 'I brought you both into the world. And now by good fortune you save me from going out of the world. I am Dr Taylor,' the man shouted.

It was indeed the doctor who had attended the births of both Phil and Charlie. The second man was an insurance agent who had invited the doctor to accompany him on a business trip through the outback.

'How about that for a coincidence,' Phil laughed when he finished telling me the story in the comfort of his Cairns living room.

Smiler White and Karadue

In 1930 a rascal by the name of Smiler White bought a horse called Karadue from the late Scamp White, another well-known rogue. The horse apparently had a dark history, and it was necessary for Smiler to take him to a property outside of Croydon to fake his brand before nominating him in a scheduled race meeting at Mareeba. Smiler registered the horse as Wood King. He set off for Mareeba with Wood King (*nee* Karadue) and another horse. Wood King was covered in mud, his coat was rough and his mane was tangled with burr. The second horse, King Hound, was a dud, a real turtle on the race track; but he was groomed and clipped and made to look like a winner.

Smiler's plan worked to perfection. King Hound crawled around the track while the disreputable and lightly backed Wood King romped home, winning his race by fourteen lengths. A headline in the *North Queensland Register* proclaimed: A NEW PHAR LAP HAS BEEN FOUND IN NORTH QUEENSLAND. It is doubtful that this was the sort of publicity Smiler was looking for. Some diligent official might decide to check this wonder horse, and things might be discovered which would put Smiler in a very tight predicament.

Smiler next raced Wood King at Charters Towers, where once again the horse bolted home an easy winner. It so happened that a distinguished racing personality from the south was at the Charters Towers meeting, who remarked to his hosts that the horse Wood King reminded him of a top galloper called Karadue. Word got to the stewards, who examined the horse and then told Smiler to appear before them the following morning, with the horse. Smiler told them that certainly he would do that. Then he saddled Wood King and rode to Einasleigh, more than 300 kilometres to the north; far away from the hand of the law, at least for a time.

In 1932 Phil Schaffert was managing Gregory Downs Station. One night his men returned from the hotel just across the Gregory River, which runs past the homestead, and told him there was a man camped at the crossing who said he knew him. The next morning, curious, Phil went down. He saw a man sitting beneath a calico fly, but the man's face was obscured by a white handkerchief. They exchanged formalities for some time and Phil still had no idea of the masked man's identity. It wasn't until the stranger pulled away his mask that Phil saw who it was—Smiler White, a man he'd known for years.

'I read in the *Register* where you'd doctored a race horse and had been disqualified for ten years,' Phil exclaimed. Smiler told Phil it was all true. But he added that he'd had to get out of the Einasleigh and Georgetown districts and was hoping Phil could give him a job as a stockman. He explained he was unknown in the district and would like to be known as Bill Edwards. Phil agreed to this, and Smiler started a new life.

Smiler stayed on the station for seven years and was a top class stockman and jockey. He eventually bought his own droving plant which operated through the Gulf, and then purchased Bowthorn Station on the Northern Territory border. In his time he became a respected cattleman, although there are still some today who say that Smiler was for a time the King of the Gulf's poddy-dodgers. Race horses, though, were in his blood and eventually led to his death. It happened when he was putting a galloper through a time trial at Normanton. He fell from the horse and was kicked in the head as it thundered over him.

One of north Queensland's best known bushmen, the late Phil Schaffert.

An old newspaper photograph taken of Edna Jessop as a young girl during a trip in the Northern Territory.

Aboriginal woman and her children on Planet Downs Station.

Brazilian billionaire and Australian land owner, Sebastiao Maia, pictured in front of the Lawn Hill homestead.

Holding the plant horses while they have a drink on the way out to a mustering camp on Robin Hood Station. Note the pack horses.

Closing the gates on the portable steel yard after yarding-up on Doomadgee.

Edna Jessop

No book which purports to paint a picture of the north Queensland cattle industry would be complete without a portrait of Edna Jessop—Australia's legendary female boss drover and prima donna of the Plains. She's the toughest, hardest talking female in the Queensland back country, and around Mt Isa, where she lives today, she is known simply as 'Edna'.

''Ow 'ya going Edna? Alright?' A passing station hand might ask.

'I'm all right, matey. And yourself?' she will inevitably reply.

How many Australian women can boast of being on a droving trip from Wave Hill Station in the Tanami Desert of the Northern Territory to Morestone Station north of Camooweal in Queensland, when they were only fourteen years old? Edna Jessop can.

Edna thinks she was born in 1926. Her father was the gargantuan boss drover Harry Zigenbine. When Edna was six years old, the family moved from their home at Thargomindah, in the Queensland southwest, to a spot between Duchess and Dajarra, in the dry northwestern part of the State. While living here, Edna learnt the fundamentals of droving while her father supported the family by droving Kidman cattle down into the Channel Country.

When she was fourteen, Edna made her debut on the droving track on the Wave Hill to Morestone trip. From that trip on, Edna Jessop was hailed as the belle of the Northern Territory stock routes. Many a young drover with romance in his head was smitten by the beautiful young woman, dressed in jodhpurs and heavy cotton shirt, with a bold bandana knotted around her neck and a felt hat low over her eyes.

Edna had no schooling, and only in recent years has she taught herself, with the help of friends, how to read and write. She told me in her tough, matter-of-fact voice that as a youngster she couldn't even say the ABC.

'But I can say it now okay,' she said, without the hint of a smile. Edna Jessop doesn't smile much.

Now, as pound keeper on the 32 000 hectare Mt Isa common, Edna's only criticism of her droving life is that she never had any education.

In 1950 she captured the imagination of every Australian when she took charge of 1500 Bedford Downs bullocks in the Kimberleys and walked them to Dajarra, south of Mt Isa. The trip took six months, and journalists from all over Australia made a point of meeting this romantic heroine. One reporter, agog with the enormity of it all, filed this patronising report back to his Sydney office:

> The only literature she knows is the camp fire folklore of the north. Her favourite poem is The Condamine, a rollicking Territory song in which a departing drover tells his wife why she can't accompany him.

> > *Your delicate constitution love,*
> > *Ain't equal unto mine,*
> > *And you couldn't eat the damper*
> > *Down on the Condamine.*

Harry Zigenbine made Edna the boss over his own sons on the Bedford Downs to Dajarra trip. He told veteran Territory correspondent, Douglas Lockwood: 'Don't worry about Edna, mate. She's the best man I've got and what's more she's a drover.' In his report Lockwood wrote:

> Edna, aged 23, small but wiry, brunette and blue-eyed, will be in charge of one mob and a gang of men both black and white. She will, we believe, be Australia's first female boss drover.

By the time she was put in charge of the Bedford mob, Edna was already adept at the tricks of the drover's trade, such as pinching grass from stations along the track. This was something drovers were expected to do; if grass was scarce along the stock route they would hide the mob on a station till they had eaten their fill. Doing this meant the difference between arriving at the rail head with a herd of cattle in good condition or arriving with a herd of walking skeletons. A drover who reached his destination with his cattle in good condition was never short of work. More often than not a drover would get a contract from a station he had 'stolen' grass from the year before, only because the manager or owner of that station knew that he would go to great lengths to keep his charges fat and healthy.

Edna remembered the time she walked a mob of cattle across the Georgina River at Headingly Station on the Queensland-Northern Territory border. She had a big mob of cattle and grass was scarce. Edna let the cattle graze along the river for three days, letting them eat their fill of Headingly grass. Meanwhile, the manager of Headingly knew she and her mob were somewhere on the station, but try as he might he could find neither hide nor hair of them. Nevertheless, the following year Edna was offered the Headingly droving.

There was one hazard that Edna had to dodge which the male drovers didn't have to worry about—marriage proposals while on the track. In the 1950s love-struck sundowners, drovers, and adventure-seeking file clerks in faraway cities vied for Edna's hand. Letters arrived from all parts of the country, written by men who were only too eager to walk the aisle with the woman from the Murranji Track. One hopeful groom who wrote from Norway went so far as to include a photo of himself so Edna could get an eyeful of what she would be getting.

'He was a good looking guy, too,' she explained rather wistfully.

Competition among rival suitors sometimes reached epidemic proportions. Wild young drovers with romance in their heads would appear at the Zigenbine camp at night under the pretense that they were just passing by while looking for water or strayed stock. Harry Zigenbine once told a reporter: 'I grinned up my sleeve and reckoned that if Edna could handle cattle she could handle young men.'

Competition for Edna's interest once become so intense that the orderly comings and goings along the entire east-west stock route were thrown into utter confusion. The usual practice in droving was for the different mobs to be kept thirty kilometres apart. This allowed the cattle to graze as they travelled and prevented congestion at watering points. It also saved cattle from getting 'boxed' with another drover's herd in a 'rush'. On this occasion the drovers behind the Zigenbine herd were speeding up so they could go a-courting at night, while the drovers in front were slowing down for the same reason. Harry Zigenbine said at the time: 'It looked like the whole annual turn-off of Territory cattle was going to hit Anthony Lagoon in one great mob.'

Enough was enough for Harry Zigenbine. He gave the swooning young drovers a dressing down and told them to save their courting until they reached Camooweal. Edna probably didn't realise at the time how close she came to causing one of the greatest cattle mix-ups in Australia's history.

One drover was not to be put off so easily. He left his herd in charge of a subordinate and rode hell for leather to the nearest telegraph office, where he ordered a hand-carved saddle from Brisbane. When the Zigenbines arrived at Camooweal, the dashing young overlander presented Edna with the saddle. 'She was more thrilled than if he'd given her twelve mink coats and a thousand orchids,' Harry Zigenbine was reported as saying in the Sydney papers.

When Edna told me about the hand-carved saddle incident in 1982 I said to her: 'He must have been well and truly struck by you, Edna, to ride off like that and spend all his money on an expensive saddle.'

'Yes, I suppose he was a bit keen on me,' she replied, with just a tiny hint of embarrassment, as she leafed through some old newspaper clippings.

Eventually it was a young Queensland drover by the name of Johnny Jessop who stole Edna's heart. The couple were married in 1952. Johnny Jessop died in 1981.

Edna still tells stories of how the Aboriginals were tortured and sometimes shot on the lonely Territory stock routes. She named one drover who shot two of his Aboriginal drovers in the 1950s. Very rarely, of course, was anyone ever brought to justice over incidents such as this. It was nothing, she said, for Aboriginals to be beaten and starved and made to walk for miles behind the boss drover's horse.

In 1960 Edna decided to make the move to Mt Isa. She had a young son and wanted him to have an education. In Mt Isa she hoped to be able to give up horses and cattle and get a job in the mine. Somehow, though, the mining job never materialised, and now she is as much involved with stock as ever. For the past fifteen years she has been of invaluable service to the Mt Isa Rotary rodeo committee, mustering stock from the arena and collecting the

Edna Jessop pictured at Mt Isa in 1982.

Pat Carrington (right) and her sister-in-law Nancy Carrington.

kicking straps fallen from the bucking stock. Rodeo time in 'The Isa' is a special occasion for her; not only does she enjoy the work in the ring, but also she gets to have a jaw-wag with the rough riders who, she thinks, are a pretty good bunch. The cowboys in return treat her with the respect deserved by any outback matriarch.

As we sat at the kitchen table in her small Mt Isa home I watched as she lifted a can of beer to her lips and drank deeply; her large, dirt-ingrained fingers were slung hard around the flimsy aluminium. She leaned back in the chair and stretched one Levi-clad leg over the table. Her bosom pushed at the press-stud buttons on the rodeo shirt, and her straight, brown hair hung like a mane over her saddle-weary face. She looked like a cross between Ma Baker and a middle aged Janis Joplin.

'Edna, do you think that in your life you've missed out on much?' I asked. 'While you were a young girl droving cattle, others your age were wearing pretty dresses and going out on dates. Your home was under your hat and you lived in jodhpurs and double pocket shirts. Do you regret any of that?'

She scratched around the table for a while and then answered with her eyes averted.

'As a young girl I was happy. It wasn't a bad life, even though, you know, droving isn't all that it's been cracked up to be. It's not as romantic as some people like to make out. It's just damned hard work, bloody hard work. No, I don't think I missed out on anything. I'd do it all again if I had my time over, except I wouldn't mind a bit more of an education next time round.'

And with that the Prima Donna of the Plains cupped her palm around a flaring match as she lit a smoke. 'You want a cup of tea, mate? Yeah, I think we need a cup of tea.'

She walked bow-legged to the stove and switched on the kettle. She stood there drawing on the smoke, and I couldn't help but think of Slim Dusty's song 'Give My Regards To Edna'.

When you're passing through Mt Isa
Don't forget to take the time
To go around old mate and meet
A real good friend of mine
Do not look in beauty parlours,
Or the modern fashion stores,
You'll find her at the saleyards,
Loading fats or dipping stores . . .

Planet Downs

Since Henry Lawson wrote his classic short story 'The Drover's Wife', the lot of the Australian woman living in the outback has improved dramatically. About most of these women, though, there is still a lingering atmosphere of loneliness, coupled with that same resolute acceptance of things so aptly demonstrated by the protagonist in Lawson's story.

'The Drover's Wife' has not really died. She has changed her ways somewhat in keeping with the times. She now lives in a world of 32 volt and 240 volt power generators, two-way radio communication and School of the Air correspondence lessons. In most cases she has an electric or gas stove in the kitchen and there is nearly always a deep freeze unit stocked with supermarket goods in some corner of the house. Being a true-blue woman of the eighties, The Drover's Wife today is more likely to tell her man to go to hell should he take off on too many long-distance droving trips, leaving her at home to mind the kids.

Outback women have not got much that they did not fight for themselves. They are still battling for better education standards for their children, improved medical care, and the right to live as comfortably as possible in the hard environment of the outback.

One such woman is Pat Carrington of Planet Downs Station, south of Burketown. She is a fighter for a better deal for bush women, but at the same time she is a humorist whose wit and appreciation of things farcical allow her to roll with the many blows dealt to the people of the outback.

As a young woman of twenty-three she found herself teaching school in the northwest Queensland township of Richmond. It was here, she said, 'in true Mills and Boon fashion that I discovered a dashing, good looking, and even more importantly, single cattleman. His fate was sealed'.

Not long after, Pat married that 'dashing, good looking, single' cattleman. His name was Alec Carrington. But before the marriage took place Pat faced her first moment of truth about the bush, when the wedding arrangements had to fit in with the mustering programme on the Carrington family's property at Planet Downs.

'The wedding was held in the wet season when the mustering was over, and it rained and rained. All but the most determined would have abandoned any plans of a wedding,' she said, grinning, obviously delighting in the memory.

After the honeymoon the fun really began as Pat settled into the routine of station life. Things were different from the comfortable home life she had been accustomed to in Sydney. There were no outings now to theatrical shows or cinemas; there was none of the music or repartee of Gilbert and Sullivan which she had loved so much; nor was there the vital appeal of Sydney.

Pat Carrington and Planet Downs came face to face soon after the honeymoon was over when she was put in charge of the cooking.

'Competent in a minor sort of way to prepare a meal for an average suburban family, I had not the slightest idea of how to deal with the kitchen or the cooking which faced me. I was used to buying meat in neat slices from the butcher, and here I was confronted with an enormous lump of meat, an equally enormous frying pan and an even more enormous double-oven wood stove. And it was out.

'My beloved lit the stove and then found me hacking away at the meat. Naturally, I had cut it the wrong way, so he had to take over. Then, after a while, he had to take over the cooking of the meal. I was allowed to make the gravy, which I burned.

'But indeed,' Pat went on, 'I had begun to discover the real outback life. I don't think that many people realise how basic it is. When it comes to cooking meat you should follow the sort of steps Mrs Beeton lays down in her cookery book. First, catch your beast and then kill it. Then dress it and store it and render from it four to eight gallons of fat and then salt the corned meat, remembering of course to turn it twice daily until it has cured.

'Bread, too, is something you don't take for granted out here. Although now we can buy large quantities of bread and preserve it in deep freezers, most of us still prefer to bake our own. On our place we make eight loaves three times a week. It isn't really hard, just time consuming. It *was* hard. We used to have to sift the grubs out of the bags before we could use the flour, but the forty pound drums now in use have put a stop to this.

'Not only do freezers allow us to keep bread if we want to, but we can also store large amounts of butter. Formerly we could only have tinned butter, which was just delectable after a summer of being melted and reset time and time again before being opened.

'They say the west has mighty men. They ought to be, they eat enough. Three large meals a day supplemented by a couple of big smokos in between to keep their strength up. As they eat, so do they work—long hours, early rising, and hard, demanding work. And guess who trails along beside them?

'So many people think that cattle and sheep are just turned out to grass to get fat and left to grow until they are ready to sell or shear. But their care is constant and demanding. And the weather is King. Rain is needed but droughts are dreaded. Fires are fearful and putting them out is hazardous. Floods are a veritable disaster. I once watched over a hundred goats being swept away in a raging flood and though we tried we could do nothing to save them. Five survived, that time. Once a cyclone wiped out fifteen hundred cattle in one night. Mostly they died from suffocation caused when they piled on top of each other for protection.

'At the back of all this, and behind all the work the men do, are the women, mostly wives, daughters, and sisters who work with the men because they are needed.'

Although Pat lives in one of the more isolated shires in the State, she believes that everyone has the right to the sorts of amenities taken for granted by people living in more settled areas. Burke Shire, which covers an area of 42 000 square kilometres, has only sixteen kilometres of bitumen road. Often there are no mail services or only weekly services to the stations. During the wet season mail deliveries can be cut for weeks on end. There are no telephones on the stations, only two-way radio, and of course television may as well be in another galaxy. Pat thinks that not having television could be a blessing in disguise, but she defends the right of bush people to have it if they wish. Even today, in the latter part of the twentieth century, most Australians don't realise that people living in the real outback don't have access to television.

This was demonstrated to me in 1982 when a Richmond woman told me about a crew from the popular television series *Sixty Minutes*, who visited the property where she lives. Her husband, at the time of the crew's visit, was away at another property and could only be contacted by two-way radio. The *Sixty Minutes* team refused to believe that he could not be contacted by telephone. They simply could not digest the fact that a large number of Queenslanders were still without a telephone service. And, further, they refused to believe that she had to drive her children a number of kilometres to catch a school bus which took them the last fifty-five kilometres to town. Neither could they believe that, if her children wanted to complete their secondary schooling, they would have to attend a boarding school hundreds of kilometres away from their home. This woman and her husband live in a fairly 'civilised' part of the northwest. Conditions here are almost 'suburban' compared to the more remote areas.

Pat Carrington has nothing but praise for the work done by the Royal Flying Doctor Service. On different occasions members of her family have been flown to Mt Isa suffering from snake bite, illness, or broken limbs received in horse accidents. The doctor sees young women through their pregnancies and a sister supervises the immunisation programmes. Access to specialists and X-ray services is still extremely difficult in the outback, but not impossible. All medical problems have to be discussed over the two-way radio with the doctor, who is hundreds of kilometres away at his base in Mt Isa. All through the network area people are standing by their radios, either waiting to get a call through themselves, or simply listening in to the session for the lack of something constructive to do.

Pat Carrington recognises the humorous side of these public, on-air, out-patient clinics.

'Can you imagine holding a discussion with your doctor over the air, well aware that it could be heard by everyone for hundreds of miles around? It's not too bad when Billy has a sprained ankle, but when Mum has to discuss Dad's urinary tract infection or her own developing milk abcess the whole thing can become a bit embarrassing,' she laughed.

This reminded me of a story about a bloke way out in the back country who was suffering from haemorrhoids. He suffered and suffered, flatly ignoring the pleadings from his wife to hop on the radio and speak to the doctor. There was no way he was going to let the whole Gulf country know he had 'piles'. In the end his wife got on the radio herself and explained his problem to the doctor, who promptly told her what to do, and in no time at all hubby was leading a perfectly normal life. Proof that everyone in the Gulf knew of his condition came when a few of his wag mates called up on the radio to inquire about Fred's 'err . . . ahh . . . (chortle, chuckle) condition'.

Pat is a staunch supporter and a creative innovator in the Country Women's Association. The popular hayseed image of the ladies in their hats and gloves drinking tea and eating pumpkin scones while they get their claws into Lady Di's latest millinery acquisition and her anorexia nervosa does not fit Pat Carrington's style. She is a determined campaigner and sees the CWA as an important social outlet for isolated women, and as a potentially powerful lobby. She helped form the Burketown branch of the association. This branch has been solely responsible for the implementation of some much-needed change and innovation. The branch formulated and got into motion plans for refresher courses to be introduced for governesses working in isolated conditions. Before this happened, governesses had to keep up with the rapidly changing trends in education the best way they could. The branch was also responsible for bush children being able to keep up with their schooling while they were staying at Bush Children Homes throughout Queensland. Prior to this, outback children were deprived of lessons when they were forced for medical or other reasons to spend long periods of time at a home.

In 1979 Pat was invited by the National Women's Advisory Council to address a meeting in Mt Isa on the subject of women living in isolation. The following year she travelled to Canberra as an elected delegate to the much publicised National Women's Conference. Once again she was asked to speak on the topic of women in isolation.

This conference, according to Pat, did not do for Australian women what its chief organisers would have everyone believe. The 'trendy' element was very much in evidence and dominated most of the proceedings. There were, Pat said, too many secretive little groups, each with an axe to grind. There was no unity, no common goal, only different factions of women pushing their own conference carts.

'There was the lesbian faction, the Aboriginal faction, and the this and that faction. No one was interested in women as a whole,' Pat said. 'They were only interested in what they as a group or as an individual wanted.'

Pat, the straight-shooter from the bush who went prepared for almost anything, said many of the conference leaders suffered from desperate personality disorders. This prevented them keeping the problems of Australian women in a balanced perspective. One such delegate strolled around the conference complex wearing a badge which proclaimed: I HATE MEN. This mentality was not conducive to enlightened discussion, Pat explained.

The topics to be dealt with by the handful of delegates from the truly remote areas of the nation were relegated to the end of all agenda programmes. No agenda was ever completed and the bush women didn't get a chance to have their say. The city girls stuck their stilleto heels fair square in the faces of their country cousins. The outback women went home, not surprisingly, somewhat disillusioned about the whole thing.

Pat's sense of humour, although put to the test, carried her through the farcical machinations of the entire affair. There is, though, a note of sad disappointment in her voice when she discusses the futility of the conference. Despite the media ballyhoo, nothing terribly earth-shattering was achieved.

Bowthorn

Finding Bowthorn Station — 183 kilometres from Burketown, 177 kilometres from Gregory, eighty kilometres from Doomadgee, and 483 kilometres from the nearest supermarket at Mt Isa — is no easy matter. A maze of bull dust tracks made by mineral exploration crews weaves through the bush south and southwest of Doomadgee. Picking the right one to Bowthorn is largely a matter of luck. Usually when driving through strange country to a station it is safe to stay on the track which looks as if it gets the most use; this is usually the one that leads to the homestead. But in the case of Bowthorn, where the tracks all look the same and all head in roughly the same direction, the matter becomes confusing. Travelling with me was Townsville journalist Blair Roots. We turned what was usually a ninety-minute drive from Doomadgee into a three-hour marathon through the backblocks. This was annoying, as it was an unnecessary waste of fuel. We were carrying four jerry cans of reserve fuel and hoped this would get us through to Lawn Hill and into Camooweal after leaving Bowthorn. I did not want to have to depend on any stations for petrol. Not only do they have to pay dearly for petrol and can ill afford to squander it on passing motorists, but also most stations have now converted to diesel and carry little or no petrol.

Kerry McGinnis of Bowthorn lives alone for the greater part of the year while her sister, Judith, and brother, David, work from the mustering camps scattered around the 1295 square kilometre station. When I walked into the homestead the first thing I noticed was a large dining table covered with anthologies by Blake and Tennyson and scattered pages of foolscap paper. It wasn't hard to guess that there was a university assignment in the air. Kerry McGinnis is, in fact, an external student of the Arts Faculty at Queensland University. Living where she does near the Northern Territory border, eighty kilometres southwest of Doomadgee, must make her one of the University's most geographically isolated external students.

As a young girl she had limited opportunities for education and in 1980, keen to take advantage of the openings available, she enrolled in the Arts Faculty. Since then, in between her chores around the station, she has managed to complete three English units a year. By 1988 she hopes to have majored in English literature. One gets the feeling that there is a book

16

A sign at a gate on the track to Bowthorn.

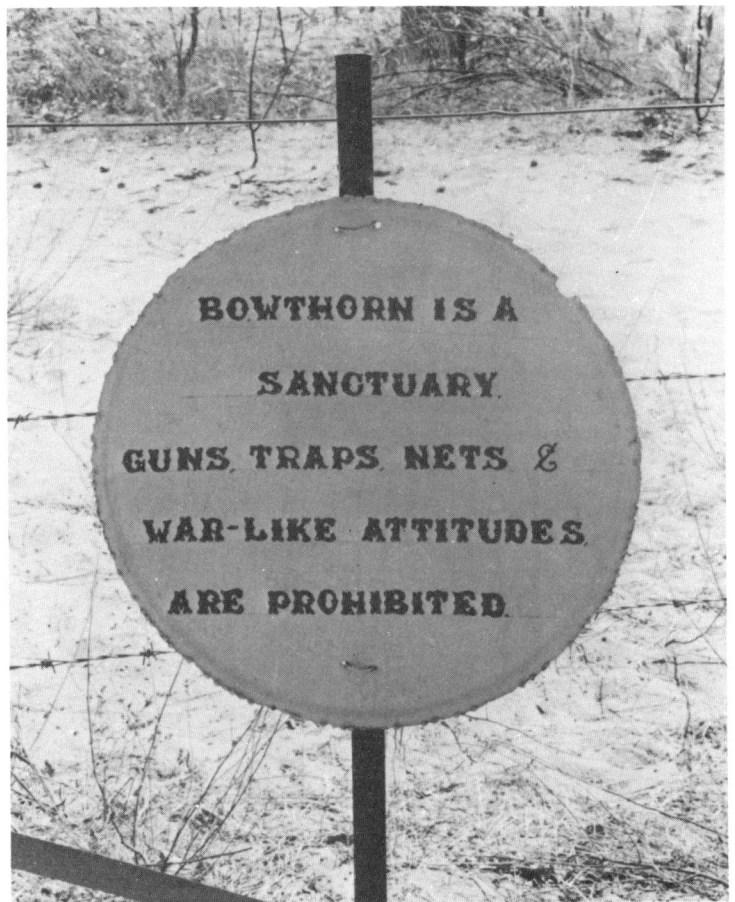

BOWTHORN IS A
SANCTUARY.
GUNS, TRAPS, NETS &
WAR-LIKE ATTITUDES,
ARE PROHIBITED.

Judith McGinnis well protected from sun and dust at the start of a day's mustering.

working its way out of Kerry, and if and when it does arrive it will inevitably be set in the Queensland bush. Already she has to her credit several stories published in American magazines such as *Western Horseman.* These stories have dealt with such diverse topics as 'hanging' dogs, pack horses and broncoing.

Given her lifestyle and academic inclinations and an obvious appreciation of bush life from a writer's point of view, I had hoped that Kerry could offer some insight into the subject of women in isolation. But to her it was cut and dried. Women either liked the life and stayed or they hated it and left. Women from families who owned stations were more likely to stay on in the bush. These women have the obvious advantages of being part of a station's progress and development, and therefore achieve a certain amount of satisfaction and fulfillment. But, she said, the life could be hard on women married to men who worked on stations. These women were more prone to disenchantment because they could not get that feeling of belonging or contributing to a station's progress.

Kerry enjoys the life of intense solitude she leads, and admits that she enjoys looking after the house and tending to the garden while David and Judith spend the long months out in the camps. Kerry's main form of communication is the two-way radio. Occasionally she might chat with a woman on a neighbouring station, and these 'chats' occur sporadically for several years without the two women ever meeting. Kerry talks to Francine Gould at Westmoreland Station quite often and has been doing so for a number of years, but the two women have never met face to face.

The McGinnises have built Bowthorn from its bare bones. They built the homestead themselves from homemade bricks. The station itself is a fine example of the principles of self-sufficiency as laid down by devotees of alternative lifestyle practices, except that this one is away over in the dry country on the Northern Territory border. The rainforest children of the northern New South Wales coast and far north Queensland, searching for dhama in the damp jungle and on the rolling green hills, would be hard pressed in this land of spinifex, rock and snappy gum.

The homestead garden grows all the station's fruit and vegetable needs, and towards the end of each year, when the heat kills all but the hardiest plants, Kerry starts making preserves. She bottles enough vegetables to keep them going until the garden once again begins to bear after the wet season.

David is considered by many people in the district to be a genius with machinery. Give him a spanner and a screwdriver and he'll get the biggest wreck in the world going, some say. He has built an all-terrain vehicle from bits and pieces which can tackle the most rugged parts of the station and can 'swim' across waterholes.

He has an old crawler tractor powered by an engine taken from a conventional wheeled tractor. This engine is mounted out in front of the crawler and the drive components are powered by a system of cogs and belts. The end product vaguely resembles free-form modern art, and it would sit just as nicely in the gardens surrounding the new National Gallery as it does in its shed at Bowthorn. The crawler is a high powered work horse and is responsible for the many dams which have been built on the property since the McGinnis family bought Bowthorn in 1966.

Judith has taught herself saddlery and makes all the saddles and harness equipment used on the station. The two sisters and the brother, each in their own way, have skills which are injected into the property. Combined, these skills represent a formidable talent.

The three McGinnises, all unmarried, lead a very reclusive life. They make about three trips a year to Gregory for race meetings and the like, and two trips a year to Mt Isa. Judith and David usually make a mid-year trip to 'The Isa' for David to do business while Judith shops for birthday presents. Kerry and David do another trip at the end of the year, and while David runs around seeing solicitors and accountants and all the other nasties associated with the administration of a cattle station, Kerry does the Christmas shopping.

The trip to Mt Isa over rough roads usually takes about two days, but it is looked on as a social outing; a time to call in on station people along the way and to visit friends in the northwestern mining city.

The McGinnis family have all been around stock since an early age. Their father, Paddy McGinnis, was a scrub runner in the Dawson River area of Central Queensland and a jack-of-all-trades before starting up a droving plant when his children were old enough to help. Paddy made the move into Queensland in 1957, and in 1958 he started to buy horses and equipment for his droving plant. While the children were still young he taught them to ride and handle stock, preparing them for the time when they would take to the stock routes droving cattle.

Late in 1958 the family moved into the Northern Territory with their horses, a flock of sheep and some goats. They carried their worldly possessions in a wagonette and travelled mainly around the Alice Springs area, tailing-out their stock on the stock routes. Their income came from the wool taken from their sheep.

In 1960 the sheep, goats and wagonette were sold and the family moved back into Queensland. Paddy had decided that his children were old enough to help him with the droving and contract mustering work.

They spent 1960 mustering Walgra Station on the Georgina River. Walgra was then a bullock depot for Victoria River Downs Station in the Northern Territory. The following year they mustered Ardmore Station west of Mt Isa, but it was a dry year and most of the Ardmore sheep had been sent away on agistment to a property near Boulia. Late in the year they shifted camp to the Boulia property to muster these sheep, which had to be taken to a neighbouring property for shearing. The owners of the two properties were feuding and Kerry remembered one chasing the other with an axe, and another time when a rifle was brought into play. They were both so old and crazy they were incapable of doing much harm to each other. They were, Kerry said, both as queer as 'Dick's hatband'.

When they finished the Boulia muster they walked their plant north to escape the grip of the drought. They stopped in the Gregory district when rain began to fall and began droving again. In 1962 Paddy McGinnis bought Yeldham Station near Gregory. Yeldham was a dry block, which means it had no natural water or bores. The 518 square kilometre station became the family's base, and they were able to work it slowly in between droving trips. Most of these trips involved taking bullocks from Lorraine Station to the rail head at Kajabbi north of Cloncurry. Sometimes they took bullocks from Thorntonia and Neumayer Valley Stations to places further west.

The Lorraine droving contract occupied most of their time and the family was split into two camps so that, while one plant was returning north to Lorraine to collect another mob, the second plant was on its way down to Kajabbi.

The trip from Lorraine to the rail head took nine days, with the cattle being trucked on the ninth day. As all the McGinnis family were teetotal (Kerry, Judith and David still are) there was no time wasted going on a spree in Kajabbi when a mob was delivered. It was straight back to Lorraine for another mob. For a young girl in her early teens it was a hard life, but Kerry said that more than anything it was monotonous and at times boring work. The Lorraine to Kajabbi run was the same time after time; the same drab bush, the same lifeless track. The only relief came when a contract was scored in new country; this meant a change of scenery and a change from the routine. While droving, Kerry always did the cooking chores and, like any drover's cook who has crossed the open Downs country in either northwest Queensland or the Northern Territory, Kerry's main complaint was the lack of firewood. In some areas she had to scrounge and hoard wood and hide it from the rest of the camp in case someone might extravagantly burn a piece; the success of a batch of bread or damper might depend on the coals from that piece of wood. Small wonder that cooks, when crossing the open country, become mighty hard to live with.

She knows what it is to be lying in a swag at night listening to the bush sounds and then jumping at the sound of the thunder as the restless mob, scared by a strange noise or movement, 'rushes' in the dark. This is what the Americans call a stampede. Then there is a scramble from the swag to the horses and a mad gallop in the night to turn the mob. Sometimes cattle are lost in these 'rushes' and days are spent in tracking them and getting the mob together again.

Bullocks and spayed cows are most likely to rush in the night and, with fat bullocks which always have to be camped down out in the open, the risk of losing some in a rush is high. Any drover who yards fat bullocks under his care would be laughed out of the game. Yarding the 'fats' would result in bruising and knocking about in the yards, which would mean dollars lost at the meatworks when the damaged meat would have to be generously trimmed. No, any drover worth his salt always camps his bullocks down in the open; if they rush that's his problem—he has to find them.

The family bought Bowthorn in 1966 after selling Yeldham, which by that time they had equipped with three bores. When they arrived at Bowthorn it had very little internal fencing and no boundary fence. Now it has some internal fencing and the boundary has been fenced where possible. In some parts the country is so rough that it is not worth fencing because cattle would not voluntarily travel over it.

The McGinnis family thrives on hard work and is tempted by few of the extravagances lifes has to offer. While Judith and David spend six to eight months a year in the mustering camp, Kerry spends her time in the garden, or making bricks for further extensions to the house, or studying for her degree. When Judith and David come into the homestead for the wet season, Judith spends most of her time making bricks. There are no idle hands on Bowthorn.

The station is a fauna and flora reserve and there are signs on the gates leading to the homestead which warn travellers about shooting the wildlife. 'Warlike attitudes are prohibited', one sign reads. These are Kerry's doing, but she does not confess to being an ardent conservationist. One gets the feeling that the signs are there to protect the animals to some degree and also to protect the serenity of Bowthorn and its sibling occupants. Kerry McGinnis in her cut and dried manner said she can't stand people who cry over kangaroos being shot, but at the same time she can't stand people who shoot a kangaroo just because it is there.

Lawn Hill

I left Bowthorn pleased with the knowledge that Russell Carrington of Planet Downs, near Gregory, was working on Lawn Hill with contract fencer Les Forshaw of Yeldham Station, also near Gregory. I knew Russell to be an easy bloke to get along with, as I had had a few beers with him on different occasions at Cloncurry and Gregory. They were camped at the road crossing on Elizabeth Creek, on the track between Bowthorn and Lawn Hill. The camp consisted of what looked to be an overworked caravan surrounded by coil upon coil of barbed and plain fencing wire, stacks of star picket posts and piles of bush timber strainer posts. At one end of the bank of Elizabeth Creek was a fireplace equipped with steel runners, on which stood blackened five gallon drums used for the cooking of the ubiquitous bush meal of corned beef and boiled potatoes. A trailer outside the caravan held a forty-four gallon drum filled with water which ran through a tap at its bottom into a battered enamel wash bowl. Two faded towels hung on wire hooks swung in the faint breeze. Russell and Les, it was plain to see, were camped in bachelor bliss.

There was no one at the camp, so Blair and I decided to drive the fence line until we found where they were working. As these things usually happen, we found them working at the last corner after having run the entire line of the holding paddock. They had just finished ramming a strainer post and were on their way back to the camp for lunch.

Les cooked corned beef curry and we sat around the small caravan table away from the swarming flies and talked away most of the afternoon. Les and Russell lamented the fact repeatedly that we did not bring any beer or rum. The truth of the matter was that our grog cache had run out at Cliffdale and, as there are no pubs in this part of the northwest, there wasn't much we could do about it. Doomadgee Aboriginal mission doesn't even sell cigarettes, let alone alcohol, in its fairly comprehensive store. Crashing into a bushmen's camp without the requisite bottle of rum is hailed in outback quarters as a faux pas and is unforgivable.

Late in the afternoon Les put a generous hunk of corned beef in one of the drums and it simmered away until we were ready to eat that night. Corned beef cooked in that manner over an open fire, with the potatoes and onions thrown in to boil, is always delicious. Corned beef cured and cooked in the

David Hughes of Koolatah, under the watchful eye of his young son Robert, butchering a bullock out in the paddock for the station meat supply. Such a kill is simply known as a 'bush kill'.

Nugget and Pam Finch and friends.

Winching a bull into the eight tonne Hino on Batavia Downs.

Dinny Sheahan puts his brand on another Kilclooney Brahman.

bush has a unique flavour, unlike its counterpart sold in city butcher shops which has a bland taste and is usually pumped with water to give it bulk. We sat around the table and talked until after midnight about the sort of things a couple of fencers living alone in the middle of nowhere might want to talk about—women, bad pubs and good pubs, cattle stations, women, and what a bastard of a job fencing was for a living.

Russell confided his secret method of washing clothes. This involved putting all your dirty clothes in a water-tight drum, adding detergent, and then driving around for a few days with the drum on the back of a vehicle.

'The bumpier the road the better, because this helps to shake out all the dirt. If you do it the right way they'll come out cleaner than if you put them in a washing machine,' he said seriously.

'Fair crack of the whip' and 'Ahh, go on' and 'Bullshit' were the type of replies shouted back at him from around the table. The next morning, though, as we prepared to leave for the Lawn Hill homestead, I filled a couple of water-tight drums with dirty clothes and added all the necessary ingredients. Four days later when I took them out at a Mt Isa laundromat they were as dirty as when they went in. Although I had embraced the principle of apparent ease which was the lynchpin of Russell's washing theory, there were, I said to Blair, considerable strides yet to be taken in this particular field of endeavour before the likes of General Electric and Westinghouse were threatened.

It was a seventy-kilometre drive from the camp to the grandiose Lawn Hill homestead complex. The countryside changes here to flat black soil plains, bordered on the western horizon by a line of cliffs and buttressed mountain ranges which flank the Northern Territory border. The homestead and sheds sit atop cliff-edged Lawn Hill; in the early days of the station's development in the nineteenth century it was a prime defensive site against Aboriginals. It has been said by observant house guests that Lawn Hill homestead boasts the only toilet in Australia where one can sit and look out across a sweeping plain to the Northern Territory border. Just the thought is enough to tingle the blood of an average man.

The pastoral holding of Lawn Hill consists of an area of some 6925 square kilometres, and it is one of the largest stations in the northwest. It runs an estimated 30 000 branded cattle and a roughly calculated herd of 10 000 wild, cleanskin cattle which have never been mustered. There are, in addition, an estimated 5000 brumby horses running free over the station.

The station boasts some of the finest freshwater holes and creeks in the northwest, not the least of which is Lawn Hill Creek which flows through one of Mother Nature's more generous gifts to mankind, Lawn Hill Gorge, a towering rock ravine dressed with palm trees, ferns, and fragile cress-like plants which cling to the smooth red surface of the towering rock wall. The almost spiritual silence of this most magnificent creation is broken only by the whistles, toots and warblings of birds. Indeed, over the years the gorge has become something of a haunt for serious ornithologists, and in 1981 noted north Queensland wildlife writers and artists Bill and Betty Hinton spent several weeks camped at the gorge, recording the birdlife for a book which was in the making. Ten thousand hectares of land around the gorge have been set aside as National Parkland and in the years to come the area

Coming in to land after a muster on Lawn Hill Station.

Senior Constable Alfred Wavell's grave at Lawn Hill. The piping rails to the left of the policeman's grave surround the final resting place of the outlaw Joe Flick.

will no doubt be visited by thousands of tourists. It is in a most remote region of Queensland and anyone making the trip should have a four-wheel-drive vehicle capable of negotiating the rock-studded tracks leading to Lawn Hill. It is hoped by the Lawn Hill manager and owner that the Queensland Government will supply adequate personnel to police the 10 000 hectare area to prevent its being turned into a junkyard by littering tourists. This has been the lot of so many other isolated north Queensland beauty spots.

A formidable workforce is employed on the station, which includes sixteen stockmen, a grader driver whose job it is to maintain the hundreds of kilometres of station tracks, a mechanic to maintain station vehicles and machinery, two cooks, a bookkeeper, two contract fencing teams, four professional bull catchers and a seven-man contract mustering team. A helicopter, piloted and owned by Phillip Kim, has become a standard mustering aid on the station. Kim was in the Korean army during the Viet Nam conflict and his Air Mobile Company was attached to the American army. He flew 100 hours of combat from 1967 to 1969 in UH-1H helicopters, which were better known by their tag name, 'Hughies'. Kim is now based at Bauhinia Downs near Borroloola in the Northern Territory, but he spends considerable time under hire at Lawn Hill. Station manager Terry McCosker claims the helicopter is especially useful in the 'outside' country where the wilder cattle run.

'Out there we wait for the chopper to get the cattle under some sort of control before bringing in the ground musterers. The wild cattle run like blazes through the timber, but the chopper is able to stay with them and keep the mob together. We let them run in a rough general direction towards where they want to go, and when they start to calm down a bit we bring in the men on horseback,' he said as we squatted beside a shed outside the Lawn Hill cattle yards.

The tuberculosis eradication programme occupies much of the mustering time on the station. As Terry McCosker pointed out: 'Every time you do two thousand it puts you two weeks behind in your mustering programme. We try and do them one thousand at a time. We muster the cattle, brand the calves and dip the mob and then let them out in holding paddocks for two days before mustering them again. Then they are needled and let out for another three days in the holding paddock before they are mustered again for the reading. After this they are turned out. The testing of the cattle takes a lot of time and if you weren't doing it you would be just mustering, dipping and branding. The TB programme is just a necessary evil, it has to be done,' McCosker said resignedly.

The station was bought by the Brazilian billionaire Sebastiao Maia in 1976. In the same year he also bought five properties totalling 20 000 hectares in the Julia Creek district of northwest Queensland, and 800 square kilometre Cargoon Station near Charters Towers. Store sized cattle are sent from Lawn Hill to be fattened at the Julia Creek properties. McCosker estimated that over 30 000 cattle, enough to pay for a station like Lawn Hill, have been sold since the billionaire's take-over.

In 1982 there were 1600 kilometres of fencing around twenty-two Lawn Hill paddocks. Most of the 'outside' areas, which include outstations such as Blue Hole, Elizabeth, Stockmans and Watsons, are largely unfenced.

However, they are equipped with yards so that cattle in those areas can at least be yarded and the basic husbandry practices carried out. A fencing improvement programme is under way and the idea is eventually to break these large unmanageable areas into fenced paddocks easier to control. This will make the overall goal of whittling down the wild cattle numbers and establishing an educated herd so much easier to achieve. But it doesn't mean that the task of ridding the station of the wild cattle and creating a manageable herd will become an overnight picnic. McCosker is quick to point out that it will be a mammoth undertaking and the results might not be tangible for many years. The cost of fencing is enormously high and, on a large station, the purpose and future benefits of a fencing programme involving hundreds of kilometres has to be carefully scrutinised. Total boundary fencing on stations such as this is out of the question, not only because of the material costs, but because of the sum it would cost to survey the boundary for a fence line. The surveying of the Lawn Hill boundary would probably exceed a million dollars. A fence surrounding a station such as this would be of such a length that it would be almost impossible to maintain.

As a young boy, Sebastiao Maia, the son of poor Brazilian ranchers from the small town of Passos, 800 kilometres north of Rio de Janeiro, dreamed of the day he would become rich, the same way other boys dream of becoming fire chiefs or engine drivers.

At Lawn Hill, sitting beneath a huge black and white photo portrait of himself, his steel gray hair brushed carefully, and his western-cut trousers and shirt perfectly creased, he told me he was the only member of his family to stay on in the ranching business. Now he runs over 60 000 cattle on ranches in the States of Sao Paulo, Gois and Mato Grosso. He owns two meatworks in Brazil, which have a combined annual throughput of 300 000 cattle, and four cold stores with a 10 000 tonne capacity. Somewhere mixed up in it all is a haulage company. There are, too, an additional 45 000 cattle on ranches in Uruguay. Last but not least is a multi-million dollar real estate and development concern in North America, based mainly around Las Vegas where the sixty-two-year-old playboy has lived for the past six years.

I interviewed the Brazilian in the living room of the Lawn Hill homestead while he drank coffee and smoked the occasional cigarette. Also in the room was Rui Maiera, the Brazilian's Australian general manager, who also doubles as translator when his Portuguese-speaking boss flies in for a visit.

In 1976, when it was aired in the media that Sebastiao Maia was amassing large chunks of grazing land in northern Queensland, cries of 'Shame' and 'Yankee go home' were heard from cattle industry quarters. No one in the industry was impressed with the news that yet another absentee landlord was being allowed to set up shop in the Sunshine State. Even now dark mutterings are heard from many corners when the Brazilian's name is mentioned. However, Mr Maia happened to drop a suggestion that he was thinking of building a meatworks at Julia Creek in the recession-hit north-western part of the State. The Queensland Premier, Mr Bjelke-Petersen, quick to embrace any injection of overseas capital, rolled out the red carpet for the Brazilian. The meatworks, it was said, would have a daily quota of 800 cattle, and would probably be built either in 1978 or 1979. Some six years have now passed and no meatworks has yet appeared to break the stark monotony of the Julia Creek downs country. The meatworks had been a tempting carrot to the westerners, and while it was in the offing there was some reluctance to criticise openly the Brazilian's land-buying orgy. Since the wool slump in the late 1960s the western towns had been suffering from decreased job opportunities and a general downturn in living standards. The beef slump in the 1970s further compounded things, and many sheepmen who had switched to cattle after the wool slump were caught in the vice. Towns like Richmond, Hughenden and Julia Creek, dependent on an economy generated by livestock production, fell into decline.

The proposal to build a meatworks which would generate employment and inject a mood of spirited optimism was naturally greeted with enthusiasm. The then Minister for Lands, Mr Ken Tomkins, was quoted in the Queensland edition of the *Australian* as saying: 'He [Maia] wants to be part of the action [that is, beef industry revival] and is backing his faith with big money.'

But Mr Maia's meatworks plan fizzled after a firm of Sydney-based feasibility consultants advised him not to go ahead with the project. According to Mr Maia, their report stated that unions would not tolerate a Brazilian-owned meatworks in the country and there would undoubtedly be industrial trouble. The consultants also advised that, because of Julia Creek's isolated position, any proposed meatworks would be expensive to build, and thirdly, they recommended that the proposed kill capacity and market potential could not be met by the existing cattle numbers in the State. The plan sank like a paper ship in a hurricane.

When Mr Maia had supervised the setting up of his cattle stations, he hired one of his countrymen to administer the Australian operation. The newcomer took to his job with undisguised glee. Not only did he think he was a real live cowboy; he even wore a six-gun as if to prove it. His eventual departure from Lawn Hill was directly related to his being a mite quick on the draw when his temper was aroused. This might be okay with a South American peon, but it didn't go down too well with your average Aussie battler. In the Lawn Hill area of the northwest he became known as Two Gun Tony (TGT).

Once when a charter pilot was flying TGT from Mt Isa to Lawn Hill, a storm settled on their flight path. The pilot, not wanting to fly into the storm, turned to TGT and told him he was going to fly back to Mt Isa to avoid the storm. TGT had other plans. A second later the pilot felt the muzzle of a pistol at his head, and TGT informed him that he *was* going to fly through the storm on to Lawn Hill. But the pilot gritted his teeth and turned the plane back to Mt Isa. TGT holstered his gun to await a very serious reception from airport officials.

On another occasion, cattle were being trucked from Lawn Hill when one of the drivers did something which annoyed TGT. He drew his six-gun and levelled it at the startled driver. The driver bunched his fist and knocked TGT to the ground. TGT apparently was very humiliated by this, as it happened in front of numerous staff subordinates. Somehow word got back to Sebastiao Maia that his Australian representative was not conducting himself in a fit and proper manner. In due course TGT the gun-slinger was relieved of his duties and drifted slowly away from the Lawn Hill horizon.

Maia knows how to enjoy his money and he is rumoured to spend vast amounts of it on beautiful women. He has married four times but admits happily that one marriage cannot be counted because it finished inside the church. In 1972 he married Miss Universe Maria Da Gloria, but this liaison, like all of his matrimonial adventures, was short-lived. A reporter from a Brazilian magazine once asked him what he thought was the most beautiful aspect of a thirty-year-old woman. Maia replied without a moment's hesitation that he had never had a woman as old as thirty. He now spends from four to six months a year at Lawn Hill and usually he brings at least one nubile nymphet to ensure that his stay in the outback is not too uncomfortable. The lithesome beauties who accompany him to Lawn Hill are usually a source of much interest at bush shindigs such as the Burketown Races, where young Gulf country bucks scan the ladies with rapt attentiveness. Maia's stays at Lawn Hill are viewed by his Australian staff as more of a rest and recreation period before he heads back to the Nevada gambling capital for another bout of terminally fast living.

I asked Maia what he wanted out of life, now that he was at an age when most men were thinking of buying a three-metre dinghy and spending the remainder of their lives fishing the local broadwater. He smiled softly and replied that he wanted nothing more than peace and tranquillity. I said, 'Mr Maia, what do you mean by peace and tranquillity?' 'Girls, girls and more girls,' replied the cheeky old reprobate. Clearly Mr Maia has no intention of spending his autumn years sitting by the fireplace with only a dozing Labrador for company. One of Maia's business associates once asked him: 'You have everything you asked God for?' The billionaire replied: 'No. I would never ask God for so much!'

Tragedy struck Lawn Hill late in October 1889 when one of Australia's lesser-known outlaws shot dead a senior police constable and an Aboriginal boy named Nym. The owner of the station at the time, Mr F. H. Hann, was also shot in the chest when the halfcaste Joe Flick beseiged the homestead. Today, the only physical reminders of this bloody encounter are the graves of Nym and Senior Constable Alfred Wavell and the unmarked grave of the outlaw. In 1979 a former Queensland Police Commissioner, the late Mr N. W. Bauer, wrote an account of Joe Flick's life in *Sphere*, a journal published by the Royal Geographical Society of Australasia. In the following account of Joe Flick's life, much of the credit should be reserved for Mr Bauer, who painstakingly researched this little known tragedy, and to the Society for allowing the information to be told on these pages.

Joe Flick, the son of a white man and an Aboriginal woman, was born at Burketown. He was raised as a white man but as he grew older he manifested the special bush skills unique to the Aboriginal race. As a young man he was a noted cattleman and horseman and was in demand around the local stations. Despite Flick's prowess as a bushman and the respect it earned him in some circles, the half-caste was subjected to much ridicule about his mixed blood. In the mustering camps on the stations he no doubt had to endure the taunts of being a 'creamy'. He would also have had to suffer the indignity of being described as a 'yeller feller' or a 'brindle'.

Early in his text Bauer asked the question: 'Did he [Flick] resent the

Nym's grave at Lawn Hill.

NYM

BLACK BOY
WHO WAS SHOT BY
JOE . FLICK.
28 OCTOBER 1889

A FAITHFUL BOY WAS
NYM

IN
REMEMBRANCE
—OF—
JENNY.
BLACK GIN.
DIED 14TH JANUARY 1894.

A GOOD GIN WAS JENNY.

Another grave on Lawn Hill Station.

white attitude towards his mother, of whom he was very fond, or did he resent the jibes concerning his breeding which came his way in the droving and mustering camps? Nobody knows just what went on in his mind.'

The events leading to the drama at Lawn Hill had their beginning early in December 1889 when Flick rode home from a droving trip to find his father thrashing his mother. Flick, in blind anger, attacked his father and gave him a savage hiding. About this time Flick was courting an Aboriginal girl who worked as a housemaid at the Brook Wayside Hotel on Beames Brook, south of Burketown. Suddenly the girl broke off the relationship. Flick believed that the owners of the hotel had persuaded her not to have anything more to do with him. Set on revenge, he waylaid the owners and savagely attacked them before they managed to fight him off. Flick was later arrested as a result of this assault and charged with attempted murder. He was placed in the Normanton lock-up but soon escaped into the bush.

Some time later Flick was sighted at Turn Off Lagoons, north of the Lawn Hill homestead, by an Aboriginal houseboy. Flick surprised the houseboy in the bush near the house and threatened him with 'pointing the bone' if the boy did not tell him where the police were. Flick also wanted the location of the police horses. It happened that at this time Senior Constable Wavell was at nearby Corinda Police Station suffering from fever and dysentery. On the night of 23 October he visited Mrs Anderson, who had been treating his illness at Turn Off Lagoons. Mrs Anderson told Wavell about Flick's visit and his threats to the houseboy.

That night, as Wavell and Mrs Anderson talked, a sound came from the vicinity of the back door. Mrs Anderson, thinking it was her husband returning, called out and opened the door. She saw a horseman galloping away into the darkness and the sound of a cooee came floating back through the night air. Mrs Anderson returned and told Wavell she was sure the horseman had been Joe Flick. Only a day or two before this, Wavell had received information that Flick had stolen a horse and committed a series of thefts in the Gregory area. Instructions had already come ordering him to search for the halfcaste escapee.

The following morning, 24 October, Wavell was personally thrown into the case when he discovered his troop horse Railway, and another horse he had bred himself, shot dead in the police barracks horse paddock. Wavell was enraged by the crime, and despite his poor health he borrowed some stock horses from the Andersons and set off in pursuit of the outlaw. Mrs Anderson begged Wavell to be careful, telling him she had had a dream which told her he was going to be killed. Mrs Anderson's warning must have had some impact on Wavell for, before he left, he wrote out his will and tidied up some personal papers and insurance certificates.

Accompanied by an Aboriginal tracker, Wavell arrived at Bannockburn at 3.30 am on 25 October. Here they found a Mr Symes who had been up all night after the house had been pelted by stones. Symes had fired a shot and heard someone hoot and gallop away. Early the next day Wavell and the tracker picked up fresh tracks which led them across the Nicholson River towards Lawn Hill Station. That same day Wavell met a Constable Gunn who had with him a police dray and horses. They exchanged horses and Wavell collected another tracker and followed Flick's trail until dark. Wavell's

One-armed Lawn Hill head stockman
Ron Maher.

Aspiring young Lawn Hill Station
jilleroo Tammy McCosker.

health was rapidly deteriorating, but he was doggedly determined to capture the outlaw.

At midday on 27 October they sighted Flick, who was alone with a loaded pack horse. The outlaw dropped the lead-rope on the pack horse and galloped off towards Lawn Hill, seven kilometres distant. Flick galloped up the incline of Lawn Hill. Near the homestead he turned in the saddle and saw Wavell and one of the trackers in hot pursuit. The outlaw fired a shot which felled the horse beneath the tracker.

Reaching the homestead, Flick leaped from his horse, ran to the kitchen-dining room and barricaded himself inside. Wavell and the two trackers surrounded the building and opened fire. Flick was an accurate shot and managed to keep the trio pinned down. Bauer has chosen to call a 'brave show of courage' the fact that Wavell walked towards the building calling on Flick to surrender. There was no sound inside. When Wavell was thirty metres from the building Flick appeared at a window and shot the Constable through the chest. Wavell was dead when he hit the ground. With the help of station employees, the two black trackers managed to keep Flick pinned down all through the afternoon. At about sundown the station owner, Mr F. H. Hann, a man named O'Shea and an Aboriginal boy named Nym arrived on the scene.

Flick was well known to Hann, as he had broken in horses on the station some time earlier. Hann had the reputation of being a fair man, and was well thought of by the Aboriginals. Hann thought he could talk Flick into surrendering. Calling on the men to cease fire, he walked towards the kitchen, quietly assuring Flick of fair treatment. Flick agreed to come out if Hann would go to the door. Hann did as he was told and as soon as he opened the door Flick opened fire. The bullet struck Hann in the chest, narrowly missing his heart. As he fell, Hann, who was also holding a rifle, fired a shot which missed the renegade. The men outside then fired at will into the kitchen, allowing Hann to crawl to safety.

That night, although a watch was kept on the building, Flick managed to escape down the cliff face at the rear of the house amid the confusion of a storm. At daybreak on 28 October the men charged the kitchen, only to find spent rifle cartridges, bloodstains and pieces of bloodsoaked rag. It was apparent Flick was wounded.

Hann had sufficiently recovered to lead a party, which included the Aboriginal boy Nym, in search of the desperado. They discovered blood marks and foot tracks which ran for some distance along Lawn Hill Creek. Less than a kilometre from the homestead, a shot rang out and Nym fell dead, shot through the heart. Then Flick unleashed a furious rate of fire, but the search party had taken cover at the first shot. Hann despatched a member of the party back to Burketown with news of the deaths, and his belief that Flick would head for a wild gorge further up the creek. This gorge, now known as Lawn Hill Gorge, would afford the outlaw a formidable hiding place, and Hann believed that should he be allowed to reach it he would be impossible to flush out. Hann ordered the grass along the creek to be set on fire and in a short time Flick was flushed from his hiding place. The search party opened fire on the running figure and the outlaw fell dead, hit by more than one bullet.

Today Flick's grave can be seen alongside that of Senior Constable Wavell. It is surrounded by steel pipe, but bears no headstone or epitaph. Wavell's tombstone bears the inscription: 'This monument was erected by the comrades (in conjunction with the Government of Queensland) of Alfred Wavell, a Senior Constable of the Queensland Police Force, who was shot dead whilst bravely performing his duty on the 27th October 1889. Aged 37.'

Nym's grave on the other side of the creek is alongside that of an Aboriginal woman. A crude epitaph written on the marble headstone reads: 'Nym, black boy who was shot by Joe Flick, 28th October 1889. A faithful boy was Nym.'

Burketown, Escott, Doomadgee Mission

Burketown in the western Gulf country might not be everyone's idea of a tropical honeymooners' paradise. A tawdry collection of government houses and corrugated iron structures, Burketown squats on a huge Gulf plain. Behind the town mud flats stretch back to the Gulf of Carpentaria. The mangroves lining the muddy waters of the Albert River are the only native greenery in the town. The visitor driving into Burketown is first struck by the enormity of the plain and then, in the distance, the silhouettes of the buildings and the glimmerings from the iron roofs. Over it all heatwaves swirl and dance and the dust from the willy-willies funnels into the velvet blue sky. For a second, just a split second, the visitor might think he has reached some lost civilisation in the Outer Limits. Nearly two and a half thousand kilometres from Brisbane and across the scantily populated horizons of the inland, Burketown in 1983 is still a frontier. With a voting voice that is nothing more than a barely audible squeak at election time, the 42 000 square kilometre shire pictures itself as a tiny David in perpetual battle with the government Goliath.

The shire boasts one of Australia's most independent and innovative shire clerks in the form of Alan Choveaux, who, armed with his slingshot, takes on the State and Federal bureaucrats.

After the numerous battles, scrapes and verbal brawls Choveaux has had with his friends who control the State and Federal coffers, he must be by now feeling a mite punch drunk. His sense of humour, though, has not flagged. One of his more memorable escapades involved writing to the Department of Foreign Affairs requesting foreign aid for poor, forgotten, Burke Shire. The staid, straightforward reply from the Department was that as Burke Shire was part of the Australian mainland it was not eligible for foreign aid. This would not have come as a great surprise to Mr Choveaux and his councillors, and one can imagine the chortlings the reply must have provoked at the council meeting.

Burke Shire is in cattle country. Some 20 000 cattle are sent to southern markets from the shire each year. Other industries include professional fishing, mainly for barramundi, and mineral exploration.

The shire, with the help of a public relations firm, has thrown itself into tourism promotion. The PR team, with a firm grasp on reality, has aimed the promotion at the more off-beat segment of the tourist market. Hilton- and Mayfair-lodging jetsetters might find the quarters at the town's Albert Hotel somewhat cramped, and have not been openly encouraged to roll their swags and head out to Big Sky Country.

A tourism pamphlet for the shire advises intrepid travellers to carry with them 'one toilet roll in the glovebox of your 4WD' (it is assumed that all tourists drive four-wheel-drives into Burke Shire); tourists should also carry one fire proof blanket 'for the purpose of sending smoke signals'; they should have two sets of 'hard wearing clothes'; and they should not be without one compass 'suitable for southern hemisphere'.

The following gear, the pamphlet advises, will prove utterly useless: 'Television, cheque forms or credit cards, rear vision mirrors and blue paint.'

'The explorer wishing to traverse outback Burke Shire a second time will be patient and long suffering (if he comes back—so will we). He will expect little and will not be disappointed and will gain nothing because there won't be much left of him after the first trip. And when you get there, not meaning "you" (just the mugs)—don't say you weren't warned.'

The pamphlet in its own crude way goes on to advise tourists that the shire offers little in the way of tourist comforts throughout the area. 'Those who arrive with 4WD vehicles and are self sufficient in camping and fishing gear usually fare best. Once off the main road conventional vehicles usually "chuck in the towel", particularly in the Wet.'

If your heart aches for the true acres of uncivilisation, the best recommendation is to head west from Burketown towards the Northern Territory border, 200 kilometres away. This is the dark, dreamtime land of gnarled eucalypts and mountain ranges that balance on the horizons like chipped and broken knife blades. This is the savage, primeval land that still, given the chance, will bake a foolish white man in a matter of hours. This is Australia's Congo—Joseph Conrad's Heart of Darkness.

Some twenty kilometres west of Burketown is the Escott Barramundi Lodge—a cattle station which has taken advantage of its 322 kilometres of waterway to create a haven for amateur fishermen. The emerald-green waters of the Nicholson River and the saline waters of the Gin Arm Creek have proved to be a bonanza in the past for fishermen nurturing that lifelong dream to catch a barramundi. But behind the tourist façade of Escott lies a living breathing cattle station which runs 6000 Brahman cattle over its 2600 square kilometre expanse.

For Len Stolk, the manager of Escott, the tasks of supervising the tourist operation with the help of his wife Lyn, and running the cattle business, do not go easily hand-in-hand. Fishermen from the southern capitals, excited by the prospect of being in the Gulf, see him as some sort of white Bwana—a taciturn Hemingway character filled with knowledge of bush lore. They enjoy the prospect of sitting up until the wee hours and drinking beer and whisky with him in the resort's comfortable bar. When I visited Escott in 1980 Stolk complained that this wasn't doing his health much good, as he usually had to be up at daylight to take charge of the cattle work. During my last visit in 1982 Stolk seemed to have adopted a more low-profile approach with the tourists, letting Lyn do most of the entertaining.

Escott was once called 'The Plains of Promise' by the explorer William

Travelling saddler Ted May on the road outside Burketown.

There have been more 'rough horses ridden' and 'wild bulls throwed' in the bars of the Hotel Boyd in Mt Isa than in any other pub in Australia.

Landsborough. Over the years this 'Promise' has included a commercial barramundi fishing exercise operated by the syndicate of owners, one of whom is Len Stolk. This was started in 1976, but folded in 1981 when a slight downturn in prices shook the market. The tourist operation, which was started in 1978, had never been taken very seriously by the syndicate, but in 1981 with the abandonment of the fishing venture it was decided to give tourism some consideration.

Now during each month of the dry season some 400 tourists stay at Escott. Former Prime Minister Malcolm Fraser stayed there in 1982 while he attended the celebrated Order of the Outback. This is an annual event honouring some organisation or individual who has contributed to the understanding and well-being of the outback. Past recipients of this award have been author Colleen McCulloch, cartoonist Eric Jolliffe, the Royal Flying Doctor Service and the Country Women's Association.

Stolk, a man not given to garrulousness, believes in the tourism potential of the entire Burke Shire. There are rivers like the Gregory and Nicholson, he explained, and all the kilometres of the deserted Gulf of Carpentaria coastline — a cornucopia of undeveloped tourist adventure.

West of Escott towards the Doomadgee Aboriginal Reserve and the Northern Territory border lies that quintessential, throbbing Heart of Darkness. The road, hilariously called Highway One, is nothing more than two deep wheel ruts filled with bull dust. For the people living at Doomadgee and on the remote cattle stations of Cliffdale, Westmoreland, and Bowthorn in Queensland and Wollogorang in the Northern Territory, this is their road.

Doomadgee lies some sixty miles west of Burketown and accommodates 1000 Aboriginals and about seventy Europeans. The mission is administered by the Members of the Brethren Assemblies.

I had written to the Aboriginal council which oversees the reserve, requesting permission to visit in July 1982. I explained that I would want to talk to 'old time' Aboriginal stockmen and to get a first hand look at the reserve's cattle operation. I did not receive a reply from the council and assumed either that my letter had been left in the bottom of the mail bag or that my visit was not welcomed. As Highway One passes the reserve, I decided to call in and chance my luck.

The relationship between on-site Aboriginal reserve administrators and the Press has become somewhat strained over the years. The administrators used to grant permission for reporters to visit, but the subsequent reports were not always favourable. Now they have become cautious about letting the gentlemen and ladies of the Press onto reserve land.

It was about 4.30 pm when we drove up to the administration complex at Doomadgee and spoke to the reserve manager Alan Hockey. For a split second after I told him what I wanted to do, a dark cloud passed over his face, and he told me to go back to the Nicholson River crossing, camp the night and come back the following morning. I considered this reception to be fair and just, considering that I had arrived unexpectedly, and drove back to the crossing and made camp. I did not know that only a few nights previously a story about Doomadgee had appeared on the ABC current affairs programme *Nationwide*. There is no television at Doomadgee but the message had been quickly relayed to the community that the programme had been less than complimentary. Had I known I might have packed up then and there and kept heading west.

However, the next morning when we returned Hockey was in high spirits. He had, he said, done some checking up on me over the two-way radio. 'I wanted to make sure I knew which side you were on,' he told me. This rattled me for a second as I wasn't aware that I was on any 'side'. In a matter of minutes a mud map was being drawn showing where I could find the station mustering camp. That was all I wanted.

We followed a grey strip of dirt which ran between the ti-trees in a northerly direction before arriving at the mustering camp forty kilometres away on Tarpot Creek. As it was still early afternoon, the ringers were away mustering and the only presence in the camp was that of a silent full-blooded Aboriginal named Pompey Jack, who was the camp cook. He greeted us without enthusiasm and quickly retired to the shade of a tree, where he sat cross-legged while smoking Log Cabin cigarettes. Blair and I attempted small talk for half an hour, but this proved fruitless, not only because of Pompey's conservation of speech, but also because of his dialect which we found almost impossible to understand. In the end we all retreated to our swags and slept away the hot part of the afternoon.

The camp itself was remarkable only for its austerity. The one visible refinement was a wobbly camp table which held an array of sauce bottles and the ubiquitous coffee, tea and sugar. Two tea boxes held the camp rations. The only other objects which suggested human habitation were some loosely rolled swags on the ground around a portable loading ramp, and Pompey's cooking fire surrounded on one side by blackened billies. It was a camp designed for rapid deployment—here today, gone tomorrow, with the minimum of fuss.

A few hundred metres to the west of the camp, hessian wings wound through the scrub and funnelled down into the gateway of a small portable yard. It was here each day that the small mobs of cattle were yarded after being run to ground in the timber.

The Doomadgee cattle country covers an area of 1813 square kilometres and runs from the mission complex through to the shores of the Gulf of Carpentaria. There are about 5000 cattle recorded on the books but, according to Aboriginal head stockman Stuart Foster, there would be 'a hell of a lot more if all the cleanskins were counted'. The country is nearly all thick ti-tree scrub; there are no hills, no landmarks, nothing to break the monotony of the stunted, drab ti-trees. The soul of this country has been baked in clay and preserved in a calloused palm through the silence of a thousand centuries.

In 1982 a helicopter was used on Doomadgee for the first time to muster cattle. It was successful, but shotguns had to be used to scare the wild cattle out of the scrub. The use of shotguns in the mustering of wild cattle has not gone unnoticed by some of Australia's beef importers. At a meeting of the Association of Central and Northern Graziers in Townsville in 1982, a delegate told a cattle committee meeting that Japanese officials had complained of too many shotgun pellets being found in imported Australian beef. The mental image of a Japanese family chipping their respective molars on lead-

A 'galah' occasion in Burketown.

A fisherman hoping for a barramundi strike on the Nicholson River.

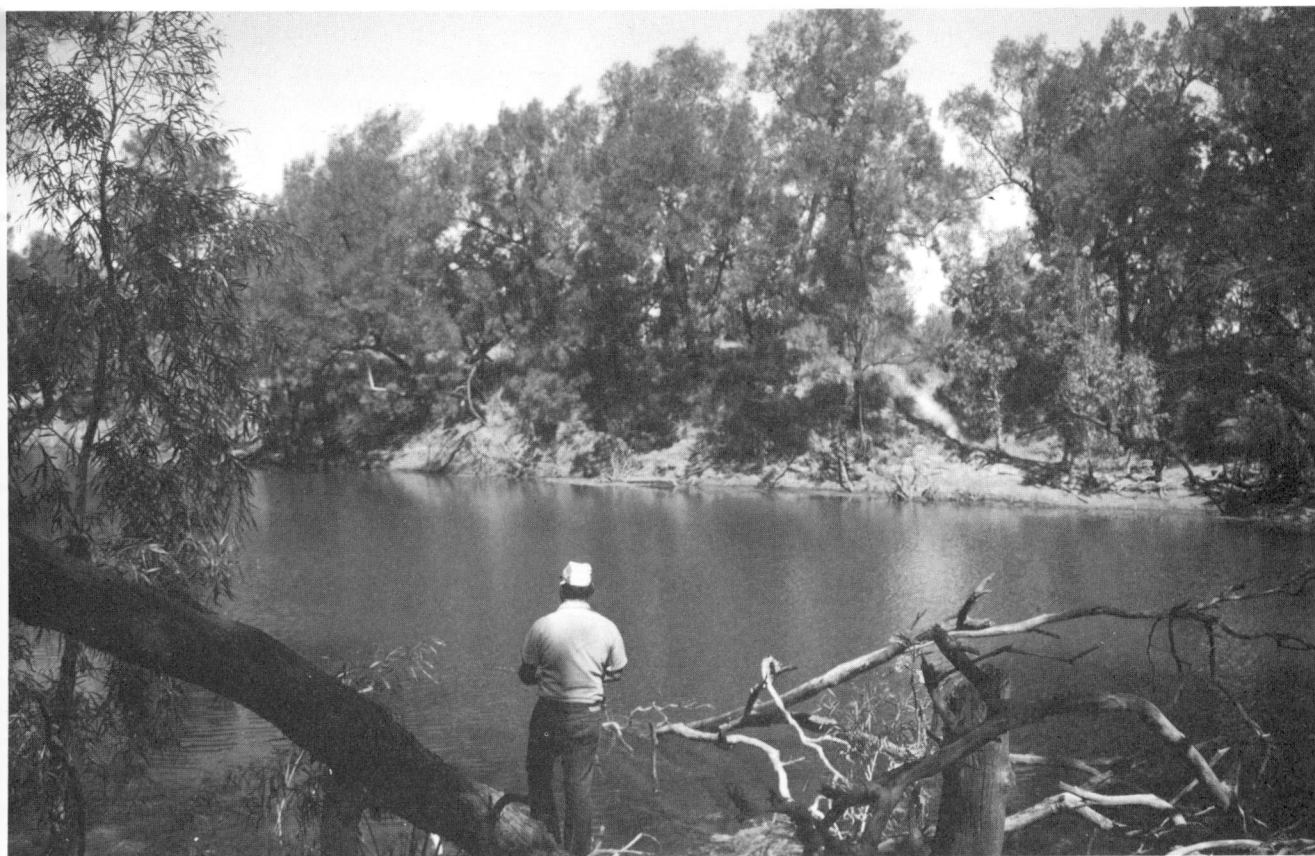

carrying Aussie meat brought forth many chuckles at the meeting. However, the underlying seriousness was obvious, as it was not long after the Roo in the Stew scandal, and the story was closed to the Press.

The United Graziers Association had already approached the CSIRO and various ammunition manufacturers to see if a dissolvable pellet could be made — something that could be fired into an animal but would dissolve by the time the meat was on the dinner table in a foreign country.

Meanwhile at Doomadgee and countless other cattle stations in the wilder parts of Australia, the traditional shotgun cartridge remains an accepted mustering tool.

Doomadgee Station is seen as a training area for apprentice Aboriginal stockmen. Young Doomadgee blacks interested in cattle and horses are encouraged to work on the station for two years before going to work on outside stations. Doomadgee-trained stockmen find employment all over the Gulf country and in the Northern Territory, and many of them become top men in their field.

An example is Stuart Foster, who returned to run the mustering camp at Doomadgee in 1981 after spending many years working on stations throughout the north. Foster has worked as horsebreaker and head stockman on some of the biggest stations in the Gulf, and now he has brought these extra skills home to Doomadgee. He is keen to stay on his 'homeground' for as long as possible and wants to put into practice things he learned on stations like Augustus Downs and Yelvertoft in Queensland, and Calvert Hills in the Northern Territory. Before returning to Doomadgee he rejected numerous offers from white station owners and managers to take control of their mustering camps. His ability is obvious at a time when good men are hard to find.

One of the new techniques introduced to the station since Foster's return is the use of the hessian wings. Now these wings are being used as an adjunct to the portable yards, which are shifted to a new mustering site every three or four days depending on the availability of cattle.

He is also responsible for the introduction of a tranquilliser which is injected into the tail of wild cattle after they have been thrown in the bush. The sedative, when it takes effect, allows the treated cattle to be walked calmly back to the yard with the coacher cattle.

Brumby horses are a problem at Doomadgee, as on most Gulf stations. During the mustering season the station horses, or 'plant' horses as they are called, have to be held in small wire yards at each of the mustering camps to prevent them from running off with the brumbies. Even if the plant horses are hobbled out at the camps with bells on, it can still take hours to find them in the mornings if their tracks become confused with those of a brumby mob. This is the land of no fences and once horses are out in the bush they have hundreds of square kilometres in which to roam.

During the worst months of the dry season most of the Doomadgee plant horses are put out in large paddocks where they can forage for feed. Sometimes these horses may be away for as long as a year or more, and when the time comes to muster them they are as wild as any bush brumby. When this happens they are spear trapped around waterholes. The waterhole is fenced with only one entrance made from a tier of sharpened, inwardly pointed saplings. The horses can walk through to get to the water but they cannot get out without hurting themselves on the pointed saplings. The same principle is also used in the trapping of wild cattle.

Doomadgee is also home to many 'old time' Aboriginal stockmen, many of whom can remember back to the days when the black stockman was treated no better than an animal on many of the northern stations.

Fifty-seven-year-old Stanley Doomadgee remembers an Aboriginal stockman who was shot on Wollogorang Station in the Northern Territory by a white stockman. The corpse was left draped over the homestead woodheap.

When he was a young boy Doomadgee worked on Calvert Hills Station not far over the border in the Northern Territory. The horses were hobbled out each night with bells on, and each morning before breakfast the Aboriginals in the mustering camp had to track them on foot and drive them back to the camp. 'Sometimes the horses go a long way looking for tucker during the night. Sometimes we walk five miles or more before breakfast,' he told me.

At Calvert Hills the blacks were never given knives or forks or plates with their meals. Food was either splashed into their cupped hands or ladled out onto paperbark.

'We were expected to eat like pigs,' he said.

Despite this sort of treatment Doomadgee revealed little bitterness, and even smiled when he told me that on the Queensland stations in the 1930s and 1940s knives and forks were issued with every meal. The meals, too, were served on tin plates. Working on the Queensland side, was, he said, a lot better than working on the Territory side.

His first job was on Escott Station when he was fourteen years old. These were days when the Aboriginals were under the Preservation and Protection Act. Their lives were controlled by 'protectors' who found them work and often determined their wages.

Under one of the guidelines of this Act an Aboriginal who wanted a job had to report to a local police officer, who was responsible for finding him a position of employment. Doomadgee remembered the wild cattle, the slogging seven-day weeks and the permanent isolation of the mustering camps — all this for thirty shillings a week. Out of this wage Doomadgee ended up with five shillings in his pocket. The remainder was held for him by the authorities.

The mustering season lasted for about seven months. This depended on when old Ma Nature decided to throw down the wet season and how long she intended it to last. Doomadgee said the length of the mustering season did not really matter to the blacks, as they had no real conception of money and knew only one thing — interminable work. They did get time off for local race meetings and rodeos but these were few and far between. When the mustering finished all the Aboriginals in the Burketown area had to report to the Burketown police. All during the wet season the blacks had to camp on the plain outside of the small township. Doomadgee estimated that at times there would have been as many as 600 Aboriginals camped out on the plain under whatever shelter they could manage to scavenge. The local police would deliver their rations of meat, flour, sugar, syrup and tea. During the months of the long downpours they lived, cooked, fought, laughed and made love under the dripping roofs of their pitiful humpies.

Gulf country jilleroo on Lorraine Station.

Doomadgee head stockman, Stuart Foster.

Escott Barramundi Lodge . . . a Gulf country cattle station with a difference.

Early morning at Doomadgee.

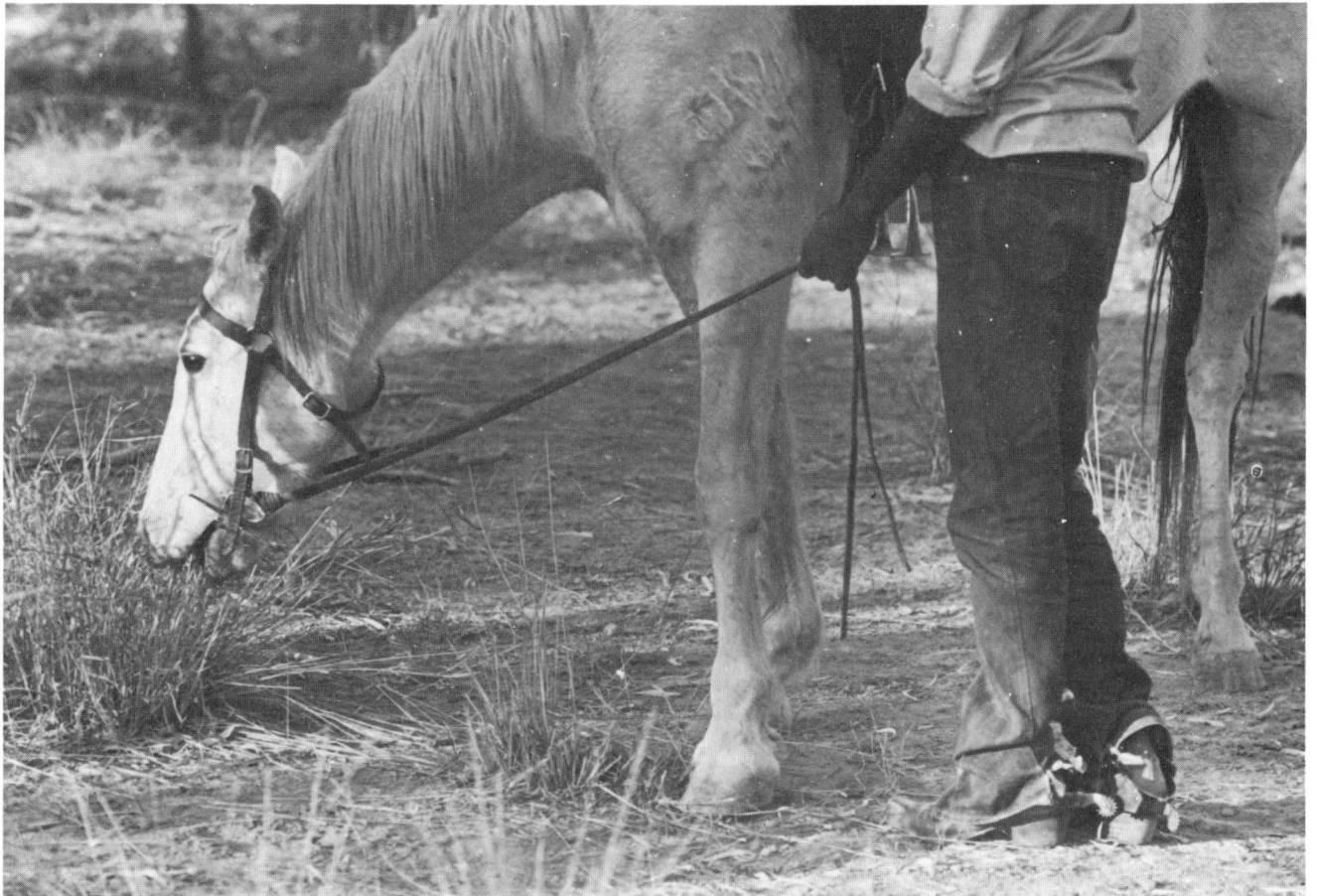

Doomadgee camp cook Pompey Jack in his 'kitchen' on a station mustering camp. Note the pile of branches on the left. These serve as a windbreak and make cooking under such conditions just a little more tolerable.

Old time Aboriginal stockman Stanley Doomadgee.

A horse paddock gate between Doomadgee Mission and Westmoreland Station. Graziers in areas such as this are common victims of vandals and uncaring motorists who not only leave gates open but sometimes drive right over them.

The author's four-wheel-drive Hilux pushing through bull dust on the track between Doomadgee and the Northern Territory Border.

After spending six years on Escott, Doomadgee took a job at Westmoreland Station on the Queensland side of the border. All the labour at the time on Westmoreland was black except for the white head stockman. Up to thirty men would operate from the one mustering camp. These camps were known as 'fly' camps, and all the necessary gear was carted from camp to camp by pack horses. (A fly camp means that only a tarpaulin or 'fly' is used for cover over the mess area. These camps can be erected hastily and are generally used when a camp is only going to be in an area for a few days.)

Doomadgee said that back in the 1930s and 1940s a white boss usually would not tell a black to his face that he was sacked. Instead he might tell the black to 'go longa walkabout'. This meant, translated: 'I don't want you anymore. Go.' If a black left a station of his own volition, the manager or owner could make sure that he never worked on a station again. Once the police responsible for that person were contacted and advised that he had 'run off', they could choose never to find him another job. The white station people, too, would spread the word among themselves that so-and-so had cleared out from such-and-such a place; they could make it almost impossible for him to find another job.

Bad treatment came Doomadgee's way on more than one occasion. He was thrashed with a greenhide whip at the Eight Mile Yards on Westmoreland Station, and when asked why, he replied: 'Maybe I only go too slow. Maybe I should run when I only walk.'

Stockwhips were often brought into play to punish blacks considered lazy or disobedient. Doomadgee said he could still remember the scalding pain caused by the horse hair 'cracker' on the end of a whip biting into his back. A common punishment for blacks who ran away from a station was to be dragged behind their capturer's horse. This practice was common in the Northern Territory as recently as the 1960s.

When he was about thirty years old Doomadgee went to work on Lawn Hill Station, but left when an inexperienced, white head stockman was put in charge of the mustering camp. The Doomadgee mission manager was annoyed with Doomadgee for leaving Lawn Hill and told him to report to the Normanton police where he would be punished for 'clearing out'. The policeman at Normanton turned out to be an understanding fellow, and he got Doomadgee a job cleaning the streets in Normanton. After doing this for a few weeks Doomadgee had had enough. He went and saw the policeman and told him: 'I'm not a man to rake up leaves, I'm a ringer.'

The policeman found Doomadgee a job as a stockman on Canobie Station in northwest Queensland. Canobie was owned by the Australian Estates and, according to Doomadgee, working there was 'paradise'. He was taught how to drive a car and was allowed to brand and ear mark stock. With all the vast years of experience behind him he had never been allowed to do these jobs by the whites on the big Gulf stations. But what counted most at Canobie was that there was no colour bar: 'We all ate at the same table.'

When Doomadgee was transferred by the company to Millungera Station he was head boy on Canobie and second in charge to the head stockman. He stayed at Millungera for several years. When the manager left, Doomadgee returned to Normanton and found himself a town job. He still lives in Normanton. Stanley Doomadgee is a ringer no more.

Cliffdale

Every three or four months Bill Olive of Cliffdale Station, between Doomadgee and the Northern Territory border, packs up the four-wheel-drive and heads into Burketown for a bender.

Bill is a character, one of those easy-going, devil-may-care graduates from the Stockwhip University who holds the reins of life in one hand and a bull strap in the other. Before taking over 1735 square kilometre Cliffdale, Bill had done everything from stock work to taxi driving to professional fishing. But always, deep down, he nurtured a love for the land and had his sights set on owning his own station. If there is a cattle station anywhere in Australia that can be described as pioneering, it is Cliffdale. In the bland terminology of today Cliffdale is referred to as a 'developing station'.

When Bill and a partner took over the station just before the beef slump in 1973 it was unfenced; a wild, virgin block of country overrun with wild cattle and brumby horses. It wasn't in any manner or form the sort of place Lord Vestey might buy as a fattening depot for his Northern Territory steers.

When the beef slump slammed the industry Bill and his partner were squeezed and squeezed in the jaws of the financial vice. Eventually Bill's partner dropped out of the partnership and Bill was left alone with a station that was losing money like an upturned barrel filled with five dollar notes.

Now, though, the worst is over and the station is quietly coming ahead. Financial backers were found who agreed to pour $20 000 a year into the station over a five-year period. This money goes into improvements and upkeep. There are few material luxuries on Cliffdale; almost every cent either invested in or made on the property is put into fencing, water development or the purchase of necessary equipment.

Working right alongside Bill is his companion, Lee. Together they draw only a living allowance from the station—enough to buy the basic food lines and their clothing. The myth of the wealthy grazier surely never had its birth on Cliffdale.

Together, they work seven days a week for as long as three or four months at a time. Then Bill usually straightens his back, has a look around, and finds some excuse for going into Burketown. He might spend three or four days blowing off steam in the pub while Lee stays with friends and sits out the bender. She doesn't hesitate to put her foot down when she thinks

Bill has had enough of the good life, and then it's back to Cliffdale for another three or four months of grinding, scalding hot work.

The three or four benders a year are Bill's only luxury, his only extravagance. In an age of sophisticated industrial relations, the thirty-five hour week and union demands, Bill Olive is an enigma. Like most of his counterparts he eats, sleeps, breathes and loves his cattle station. To it he becomes a slave, albeit a willing one.

The original plan of strategy was to have 1000 branded cattle in fenced paddocks by 1987. This plan is well ahead of schedule. By mid-1982 600 former cleanskin cattle had already been marked by the Cliffdale branding iron. Once the station has 1000 branded cattle it should be able to operate as an independent unit, and then Bill and Lee Olive can say that their station has been developed. But all the time the station is at the mercy of a fickle beef market; a market which doesn't hesitate to bare its fangs and slash its claws at the battlers.

One hundred thousand dollars was spent on the property in the twelve months of 1981 to 1982. Nearly all this money was spent on a tractor, a four-wheel-drive vehicle, fencing and a small homestead and out-buildings. Available investment finance is the obvious stumbling block on Cliffdale, and expensive improvements such as fencing can only be made at a snail's pace.

There were no branded cattle on Cliffdale when Bill and his first partner bought the station before the beef slump. Nearly all the cattle now branded had to be thrown in the bush. On an average mustering day ten cleanskin cattle might be walked back to the yard. But Bill and his team of Aboriginal stockmen from Doomadgee might ride for three or four days without even sighting a beast in the ti-tree scrub. Sighting cattle depends on which way the wind is blowing; like any wild animal these cattle will make themselves scarce when they get the scent of man. It's a slow business. Luckily Bill Olive is a patient man.

The stockmen who work on Cliffdale do not have an easy job. Not only do they need to be accomplished bushmen, but also they must be able to handle a horse at pace in thick timber and not be afraid to step off to a scrub bull when the going gets tough. Queen and Pitt street cowboys who nurture romantic notions about a rugged life in the outback would be well advised to steer clear of Cliffdale. This is *men only* country.

Cattle are thrown by the tail, and this can be done two ways. One way is for the horseman to gallop up behind the beast, grab the outstretched tail and then spur the horse past and at the same time swing the tail around to pull the beast off balance. Another way, and perhaps a more common method, is for the horseman to give chase until the bull starts to tire visibly. Then the stockman leaps from the saddle, sprints after the animal, grabs it well up the tail and swings it over to the ground. Of course big bulls are not all that easy to swing over, and usually, by the time someone actually has hold of his tail, a bull is not really in harmony with the world at large. His eyes are usually burning like bright red buttons and all he wants to do is kill, maim and mangle.

Even after a scrub bull has been thrown and herded in with a mob of coachers he is still potentially dangerous. He might walk along quietly with

A wild cleanskin bull feeding on Gulf country mangrove leaves warily watches the author as he moves in for a photograph.

No knickers, shirts or jeans, just saddle cloths on the line at Cliffdale Station.

the mob as though he were a nice old bloke who wouldn't harm a fly. But all the time his mean little bull's brain is hatching escape plans. The stockmen are lulled into a false sense of security by the bull's apparent change of manners.

The sun beats down and the ringer lolls in the saddle, puffing on his handmade cigarette and dreaming of the pretty little barmaid who smiled at him last time he was in Burketown. He's thinking how he's going to sweep her off her feet next time he's in town when all of a sudden . . . *whoooa*! He drags in the loose rein and bites the cigarette in half as out of the corner of his eye he catches a glimpse of the old scrub bull, head down, coming right for him. All carnal thoughts exit from his mind as he sinks his boots into his horse's ribs to escape the bull's blind charge. It's just another day on Cliffdale. No different from the rest.

Bill Olive is confident that eventually Cliffdale will carry 3000 branded cattle. They will be contained in paddocks by barbed wire fences and these paddocks will be improved and well watered. This is Bill Olive's dream.

Once the station is fenced and most of the cattle under control, Bill hopes he will be able to cut back on labour. One way he sees of doing this is by building trap yards at strategic points across the property. The plan is that every paddock will be equipped with at least one permanent water and at least one trap yard. Towards the end of the year, when the less permanent waterholes have dried up, the cattle will be forced to water at the permanent 'trapped' hole. Once they walk through the gate they are trapped and all that remains is for them to be drafted and for the rogues to be sent to the meatworks.

Trap yards are not successful in situations where there is a lot of water scattered over the area of a paddock. If all the traps are built around troughs and man-made dams, a considerable amount of control can be exercised. A trap can be built around one strategic water while access to the rest is stopped by a fence or, in the case of a windmill and trough, the water supply is simply shut off. This is done over a period of two or three weeks and gradually the cattle steer for the remaining 'trapped' watering point in the paddock. The obvious advantage is that fewer stockmen are needed to scour the country looking for cattle. It is a method of mustering which has to be adapted to suit conditions on individual properties.

Bill owned his own taxi business in Cloncurry before buying into Cliffdale, and for a time operated two cabs in and out of Cloncurry. The business was predictably called Bill's Taxi Service. It was quite a service. Nearly all his calls involved taking ringers to cattle stations, some of which were hundreds of kilometres from Cloncurry. Bill reckoned he also performed an important community service in that he operated as a sort of impromptu employment service. A station manager looking for men would contact Bill and tell him how many ringers he was looking for or if he wanted a cowboy or mechanic or some such, and Bill would find them and drive them out to the station. Some of these trips cost the passengers hundreds of dollars. It was a well known fact that Bill's Taxi Service would go anywhere. Sometimes Bill would be on the road for days on end taking men out to one station and then returning to Cloncurry to pick up another fare for a trip out to a station three or four hundred kilometres away in the opposite direction. On cold nights he would catch a bit of sleep by curling up on the cab's warm bonnet.

There was also a period when Bill and a mate would drive to the Gulf and spend a few weeks fishing for barramundi. Once they had a good load of fillets they would drive back and sell the fish either in Cloncurry or Mt Isa. Then they would go on a bender in a Cloncurry hotel for a few days, and when there was just enough money left to get them back to the Gulf they would leave.

When the beef slump hit just after Bill bought into Cliffdale, he turned to barramundi fishing as an economic alternative to cattle raising. But he admits he was a greenhorn when it came to professional fishing and he made just about every mistake possible.

One night early in his fishing career he was camped at the mouth of a creek on the Queensland side of the border when a big school of barramundi hit the net. Bill rummaged through his gear and discovered that he had failed to pack a torch. He used thirty boxes of matches to light the way while he wrestled the caught fish from the net. It took him ages, he said, and it wasn't until an old professional showed him how that he became proficient at twisting fish out of a net.

Another night he was checking the net, which was strung across a muddy mangrove channel, when the small dinghy lodged on a mudbank. Normally this would be no big deal, as it would only involve stepping out and heaving the boat back into deeper water. But while Bill had been checking along the net he had been keeping a wary eye on a four-metre crocodile resting on a mudbank. Unfortunately for Bill the crocodile was on the same mudbank on which the boat was stuck. This was a very dicky situation indeed, and Bill was not ignorant of the fact that a crocodile on a Gulf of Carpentaria mudbank in the middle of the night could be a mite peckish.

Now, Bill tried every possible method of budging the dinghy from the sticking mud without actually going over the side and pushing it. They all failed. If Bill had thought to throw his old .303 in the boat before leaving his camp, he could have blown that crocodile to Kingdom Come and then got out and moved the dinghy. But he had left the .303 back at the camp.

No one who knows Bill is likely to tell you that he expresses any great interest in religion. He has at times been heard talking to the Lord, but this has usually been when he has scraped his knuckles with the spanner when fixing the motorbike, or something like that. But out there on the boat that night it was as though Bill had been Born Again. He resurrected a few childhood prayers and offered them to the heavens. And then, with a torch in one hand, the beam of which was glued to one very interested crocodile, he jumped overboard and heaved the dinghy into deeper water. It was over in the blink of an eye and the croc didn't move.

Bill was running a net one night with legendary Aboriginal bushman Malcolm Hussan. All of a sudden Malcolm, who was holding the torch, gave a yell. There in the beam was a crocodile heading straight for the dinghy. Bill screamed at Malcolm to drop the torch so that the crocodile could see where it was going and avoid running into the tiny dinghy. But there was no way that Malcolm was going to let the croc out of his sight. The beam stayed levelled on the blunt snout and the red eyes. By this time it was only a couple of metres from the dinghy. Bill yelled again and Malcolm lowered the torch. The croc sank out of sight and swam below the boat.

Lee Olive with some Cliffdale wildlife souvenirs — saw-fish blade and crocodile paw.

Bill and Lee Olive and friends.

Bill Olive's pet wild pigs sharing a moment of togetherness. The pigs conducted many successful raids on the author's camp and managed to run off with delicacies such as a scrubbing brush and cakes of soap, not to mention assorted food stuffs.

A spear trap set up on a northwestern cattle station. When cattle are to be trapped the left side is blocked. Stock can then pass through the spears on the right side to get to water but they cannot get out.

The Cliffdale Station homestead complex.

Legendary Gulf country bushman Malcolm Hussen outside his home on Cliffdale Station.

*Malcolm Hussen's wet season hut hidden among sand hills behind a remote Gulf of
Carpentaria beach.*

Bull catcher Gary Gould in the swag on Westmoreland.

The story is told of another fisherman, who, when camped at the mouth of a creek one night, awoke to find that his dinghy had drifted across to the other side of the channel. No Gulf fisherman needs to be reminded of the munchies which patrol those waters; there are not only crocs but also sharks, and large groper are extremely common. This particular fisherman was not enamoured of the idea of swimming across to the dinghy. He pondered the problem for some time before inflating a truck tyre and, converting it to a raft, paddling madly across the black water to the dinghy.

Bill first met Lee when he was fishing with her husband John Culbert, a former rodeo professional. Culbert owned a boat called the Sea Marie and he and Lee and their young son Alan lived on board while they fished the Gulf waters. In 1977 Bill spent six months with them fishing the waters around Morning Inlet, Disaster Inlet and the mouth of the Leichhardt River. It wasn't long after Bill left the boat in that same year to strike out on his own that tragedy struck the Sea Marie.

John and Lee were fishing the Gin Arm west of Burketown; the tide was running out, the water was rough. Alan, little more than a toddler, was up on the deck when the boat pitched and he was thrown overboard. His father dived in immediately to save him, while Lee jumped into the tender, intending to save them both from the rushing current of water. But the outboard motor wouldn't start. By the time it sputtered into life there was no sign of John. She got to Alan and pulled him aboard and then went looking for John. Ten days later his body was found. He was the third person to have drowned off the Sea Marie. Some months later Bill and Lee met again and they have been together ever since. Now they share an existence on the land; an existence which Bill Olive in a moment of reflection described as 'true and pure. You can build something for yourself out here and be proud of it. If you can't feel like that you'd better not touch it'.

Bill Olive makes no bones about the fact that he is in love with the bush. 'I want to live here for the rest of my life. I want to die here. When I'm ninety years old my ambition is to chase a topless barmaid around the bar of the Burketown pub, and you can quote me on that in your book.'

Malcolm Hussan, the tall black man with the thinning dark hair and smooth, oily skin—a leftover from his Afghan forbears—is one of the northwest's most renowned bushmen, albeit one of its most mysterious ones. He is as at home in the wild northwest bush as the Kingfisher, the ti-tree and the wallaby. He knows it the way an ordinary man knows his own backyard.

Looking more like forty, he is said to be somewhere around fifty-six years old. He has done a lot of things, always in the bush, but remains a most arcane man.

He was born on the old Doomadgee mission site near Pt Parker on the Gulf and moved with the rest of his people to the present mission site when he was a young boy. When he was twelve he went to work with his father on Westmoreland Station and after this worked on Turn-Off Lagoons for Joe Salmon. He has spent his entire working life north of the Nicholson River, and in that time has become known as a recluse. He will disappear for months at a time, taking with him a .22 rifle, some spears and provisions, and will live off the land. He can do this just as ably in the rugged hill country around Lawn Hill Station as on the coast of the Gulf.

As Lee Olive said, Malcolm is not one to stay on a station if things don't suit him. The story is told of the time he went to a station and the manager put him on the books and told Malcolm he could take his gear down to where the 'boys' were camped. The next morning Malcolm was gone—no one was going to tell him where he could camp!

From 1960 to 1964 he worked as a professional crocodile shooter. His rifle was a .22 repeater and his transportation was a Honda 50cc motorcycle. When he ran out of petrol he would push the bike along with his billy can and swag tied to the frame until he ran into someone who could spare him some petrol. Sometimes he would push the bike for months on end before running into someone in that desperately lonely country. He still has that Honda 50 at Cliffdale and still rides it around the property.

Now, when he takes off every year for his few months of solitude, he rides out on the Honda. He either goes into the mountains or onto the coast north of Cliffdale, where he has built himself a bark hut which is nothing less than a work of art. Nestled in a hollow behind the coastal dunes, this hut has been seen by only a tiny handful of outsiders, and it remains to this day a most secret home for this secret man.

At Cliffdale, Bill and Lee can tell when Malcolm is thinking of going bush. He becomes moody and crotchety and won't talk to anyone. After a week or so he will come and tell them he is going, and that will be the last they see of him for several months. During these periods Malcolm rarely sees or talks to another human being. Professional fishermen talk of sometimes sighting him walking naked along a mud flat with his spears in search of fish or crabs.

He is an excellent cattleman, horseman and tracker and still throws big cows and bulls out in the bush on Cliffdale. Few men, it is said, can stay with him in the timber when turning a mob of runaway cattle.

He has a soft spot for children and young animals, and once related a story to Lee about an incident which happened in the mountains when he was out hunting for meat. Lee said: 'He had run out of meat and was out looking for something to shoot. Darkness caught him a fair step from his camp, and while he was walking back he heard a porcupine coming along the track in the opposite direction. He stepped off the track and hid himself and let the porcupine go by. It walked past him and then moved from the track and started to dig. As the night was getting dark and the track was rough, he decided to keep going and come back the following evening. The porcupine showed up at the same time the following evening and started to dig in the same spot. Soon she had uncovered her baby, and then lay down so the little one could drink. Malcolm could not kill her and leave the baby one to die, so he watched for some time and then left them undisturbed.'

When he is living on the coast he collects salt from the rocks for his cooking. Most of his meat is boiled and any fish or birds are cooked in ti-tree bark under hot ashes. His main diet on the coast is fish, water lily bulbs and honey, while in the dry mountain country he lives on walleroo, wallabies, birds, wild turnips and yams. He also knows which berries are edible. When he goes bush he takes some coffee and Milo, sugar, a little flour, some bullets for his rifle, and his fishing lines and pocket knife.

In 1982 Malcolm discovered cigarette lighters and according to Lee he thinks they are an ingenious invention. 'Whenever he gets a dingo scalp we cash it for him and buy him something he wants. Last time we had to get fifteen dollars worth of Bic lighters.'

In his estimated fifty-six years Malcolm has only ever been to three towns—Burketown, Camooweal and Cloncurry. He has only visited each of them once.

Note: Malcolm Hussan died in the Mt Isa Hospital in 1985 from cancer. The man who was one with the bush died in pain between white sheets in a city hospital bed. The bush eluded him at the last moment. He wouldn't have wanted it that way. Malcolm's wet season hut was discovered by vandals during that same year. They burned it to the ground.

Westmoreland

Westmoreland Station has fascinated me ever since I was a young boy. It lies just a few kilometres east of the Northern Territory border and only a short distance south of the Gulf of Carpentaria. When I was young, a map of that part of Queensland was better to me than a *Boys' Own Adventure* annual: this was the dark, mysterious land — the Back Country.

The station is owned by a syndicate of three — Donald Jorgensen, Alan Gould and Alan's son Anthony 'Jack' Gould, who is the manager-in-residence. Westmoreland boundaries the stations of Lawn Hill, Cliffdale, Wollogorang, Wentworth and Troutbeck on the coast, and the Northern Territory border.

The road west from Cliffdale to Westmoreland does not improve — the dust and deep ruts continue to challenge even the sturdiest of vehicles. There is a pleasant change in the countryside, from ti-tree scrub to taller timber, rocky outcrops and distant mountain ranges. This is a picturesque drive alive with colour and stark beauty — red sheets of rock against the blue sky; yellow spinifex leaning from the outcrops like sheaves of dried straw; and the slender white snappy gums standing out like sheets on a line among the mauves, reds and yellows of the wild flowers.

The station was deserted when Blair and I drove in, and for a time I wondered if we had arrived at the right place. Years ago I had drawn a mental picture of Westmoreland which showed the station complex to be alive with tropical trees; there was a rambling old homestead and numerous sheds and out-buildings which housed the stockmen and station machinery. It was a busy scene, alive with all the activity common to a large station. Instead I was confronted with silence and a small highset prefabricated homestead surrounded by a neat garden. Away to the right was a corrugated iron machinery shed and alongside of it was a fabulous old homestead built from stone slabs. In between the two were a shower complex and quarters while down near a set of stockyards some three hundred metres distant was another small machinery shed. Still nursing some small doubt as to where I was, I walked into one of the sheds and rummaged along the bench until I found a carton of machinery parts with a label on it. It was addressed to A. Gould, Westmoreland Station, Burketown. I was at the right place!

I took the liberty of having a shower in the outdoor shower block and about one hour later a red Hilux came up the track with Francine Gould at

Bull catching on Westmoreland.

More money for the Westmoreland bank account.

Fran Gould splitting fence posts on Westmoreland Station.

Cleaning out the bull catching vehicle's radiator on Westmoreland.

the wheel. She was accompanied by Diane, who is married to Jack's brother Gary. They had returned from dropping a tractor out to a place called Valley Yards where Jack and Gary were setting up a bull catching camp with Aboriginal stockman Rex Shadforth and his wife Maggie Charlie.

Fran Gould, twenty-nine, a petite Sydney-born redhead, worked in an office for several years before she answered an advertisement in the Sydney Telegraph for a jilleroo on Wollogorang Station. Soon after she arrived at Wollogorang there was a gymkhana, and who should roll up but bachelor Jack Gould from neighbouring Westmoreland. The two got to talking, but when the gymkhana was over Jack went back to his single man disaster meals and Fran worked away on Wollogorang. Fate, though, was being generous. Several weeks later there was a race meeting in Burketown, and Jack and Fran once again got together for a confabulation. Jack told Fran he was heading down to Adelaide for a few weeks to help with the shearing on his father's property. Fran was invited along, and she went and worked in the shed as a rouseabout. After returning they lived together at Westmoreland, and in 1980 Jack got around to popping the Big Question. Soon after he and Fran were married.

Fran has only one regret about leaving Sydney—she misses the beach. Her closest beach at Westmoreland is not far away on Wentworth Station, and the only sunbather you are likely to encounter there is the odd saltwater croc. The water on a clear, hot day is invitingly blue but swimming there is akin to playing Russian roulette with a .357 magnum.

Social life at Westmoreland is almost non-existent. But Fran and Jack make two or three trips a year to Mt Isa, and on these, journeys they lash out, eating at a different restaurant every night and generally painting the town as brilliant a shade of red as they can. Their social life otherwise is unpredictable. Because of the distances involved and the demanding work schedule, they cannot always get to the annual Burketown race meeting, which is a must on the local social calendar. Pictures are shown every Saturday night at the Burketown State School, but it is not worth the four hour, 190 kilometre drive over the woeful road to see them. A mineral exploration crew camped on Westmoreland has invited the Goulds over to their camp on movie nights, but usually Jack and Gary are tired out from work and no one wants to make the effort to go. The sad irony is that during the wet season when they do have the time to socialise, they are prisoners on their own stations and cannot go anywhere because of the wet conditions.

Even when the men come in from the mustering camp there is still no time for relaxation. There are the endless mechanical repairs to make and the preparation of gear for the next round of mustering. It is the solid, grinding, monotony of work, work, work.

Christmas 1981 was a real treat for the Goulds as they were able to celebrate both Christmas and New Year with their Cliffdale neighbours Bill and Lee Olive. Usually by Christmas the roads are cut and they cannot go anywhere, but 1981 was a poor wet and most of the roads were open. 'It was really good being able to share Christmas with someone,' Fran said. 'Really, really good.'

But she said that Christmas in the bush never feels like a real Christmas— the kind a Sydney girl might be able to look back on: the streamers and tinsel in the shops, the red-robed rotund Santa Clauses jingling little brass bells on street corners and the looks on the children's faces as they stroll through the toy departments. At Westmoreland life goes on, the heat becomes more humid and Christmas Day is only as joyous as the human element can make it.

The Goulds have a weekly mail service from Burketown. Two years ago this service ran fortnightly and was unreliable. One year the Goulds' Christmas cards did not arrive until April when the roads were opened after the wet. Now with a reliable service they are able to get some fresh fruit and vegetables every week. Their only communication link with the outside world is a two-way radio connected to the Royal Flying Doctor Service in Mt Isa. In an emergency situation the flying doctor can be at the station within ninety minutes and at best a patient can be in a Mt Isa hospital bed within four hours.

There has not been a serious accident on Westmoreland since the Goulds have been there. In 1981, though, Rex Shadforth's scrotum was torn open when he was horned by a scrub bull out in the bush. By the time he was driven back to the station both his testicles were plainly visible beneath the torn skin of the scrotum. Fran called the flying doctor immediately and told him what had happened, but the doctor calmly told her it wasn't serious and outlined a treatment which she was to carry out. Fran went back, took another look at Rex's injury and got back on the radio again to the doctor. Once again he told her not to worry and to carry out the treatment. This she did, and in no time at all Rex was up and about. Three weeks later he even skited to a barmaid in Burketown that 'it didn't stop me and Maggie one little bit'.

Fran's only contact with other women is with Dianne and naturally enough the two have become good friends. She speaks to Lee Olive and Kerry McGinnis on the radio every now and again, and although she sees Lee two or three times a year she has never met Kerry. On her rare trips to Burketown with Jack to pick up ringers or when just passing through to Mt Isa, she might, she said, meet a woman she has spoken to on the radio.

She does not bother about keeping up with the latest fashions because, as she said: 'I have absolutely no use for good clothes up here.'

The continual demands of outside work, much of it very physical, make the acquiring of a fashion wardrobe about as logical for Fran as a desert tribesman buying a Cartier wrist watch. And, she said, with the heat and dust and day to day work it was inevitable she neglected her appearance to some degree. Even when making the trips to Mt Isa, where there is a chance to dress up for a night out, there are still problems. The road is so dusty that by the time they arrive at Mt Isa the bull dust has usually seeped into all the suitcases. Clothes have to be especially sealed in plastic bags to protect them from the dust, and if there is one small split in a bag, it will find its way through.

Because of her commitments around the house looking after the vegetable garden and tending the poultry, Fran does not get out into the mustering camp very often. As a result she may not see Jack for days or even weeks. This depends on how far the camp is from the homestead and how smoothly everything is running. She admits to being frightened of horses and recalled

Di Gould supervising correspondence lessons on Westmoreland.

Graffiti in the Kajabbi pub in the Queensland Gulf Country.

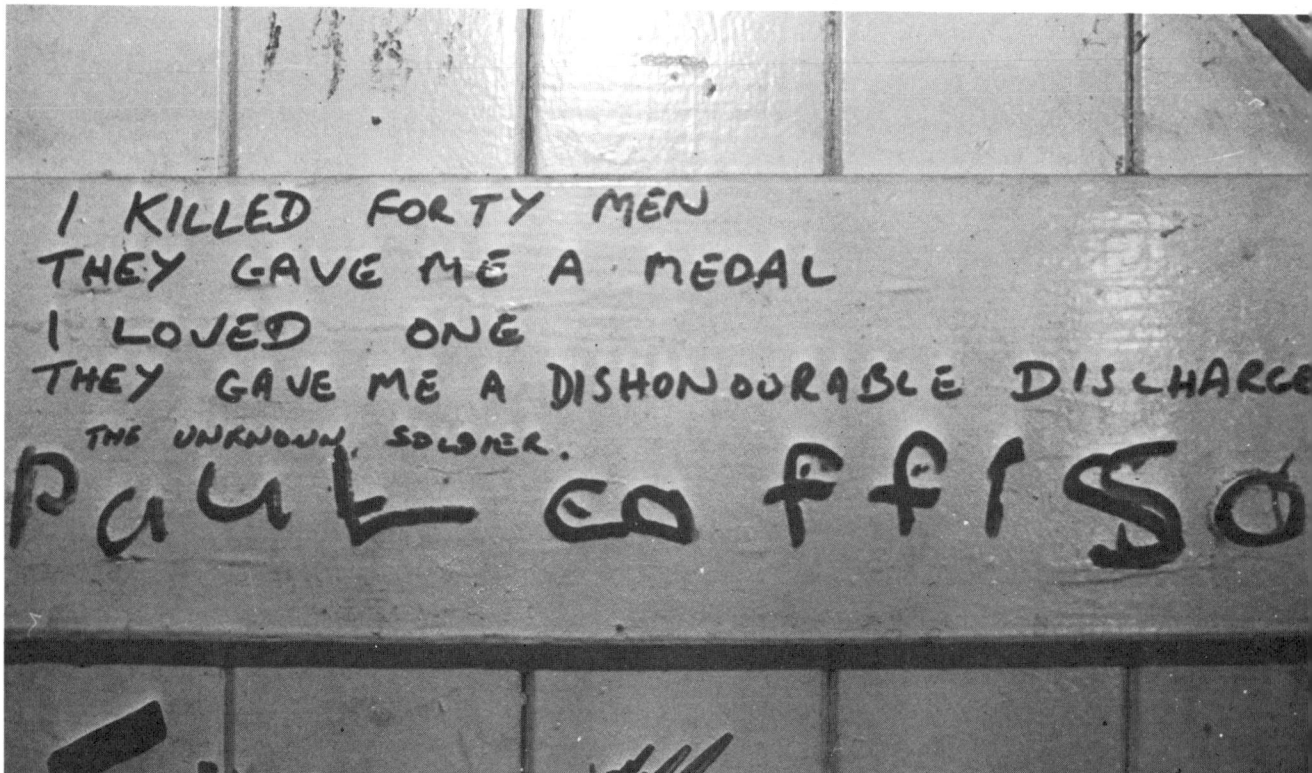

the time Jack put her on a young horse which had been especially broken in for her.

'I took him for a run around the pegs and then I dropped a rein. The horse bolted for the hills and when I saw some rocks coming up I dived off. Someone caught the horse and they led him back to the yards and I hopped on another two times and he threw me both times. I think that was the last time I got on a horse,' she said with a laugh.

Since the Gould family bought Westmoreland twenty years ago considerable improvements have been made in the way of fencing, cattle yards and trap yards. Three-quarters of the property is still open, unfenced country, but the six trap yards which have been built are considered a great mustering aid by Jack Gould. Each yard measures one and a half miles around and is fairly large by most standards. Cattle are tailed around the yard for four days to get them used to men on horseback before being driven back to the nearest set of stock yards for branding.

The mustering season usually gets under way in May or as soon as possible after the wet. The pressure is on towards the end of each year as meatworks close and cattle sales finish. Fat cattle mustered late in the season often have to be held over until the following year when they can be transported out. Inevitably some get away back to the open bush when fence lines and creek crossings are washed away by the wet season floods.

Jack Gould believes that the most important management principle on a station like Westmoreland is fencing. Ideally he would like to see the station fenced into paddocks about fifty kilometres around.

He used a helicopter to help with the mustering for the first time in 1981, but the exercise left him fairly sceptical and he doubts if he will again bring in a chopper. The chopper was used for a day and a half to muster a paddock measuring fifty kilometres around the fence. The chopper mustered a total of 650 cattle and cost Jack $1900 for the time it was in the air. When Jack mustered the same paddock in 1982 with five stockmen he collected 750 cattle and made a total labour payout of $1000. So it is going to be pretty difficult to get Jack Gould to carry out another chopper muster.

It is interesting to note that all the stock watering places on Westmoreland are surface waters. This means they are either natural waterholes or man-made dams. When cattle are sent away on agistment from the station they will refuse to drink from troughs or bore drains and have to be held on these sort of watering points until they become used to them and then thirsty enough to drink.

The station carries a herd of 5000 cattle but Jack Gould estimates that there could also be as many as 3000 wild cattle on the station. A major effort is currently under way to capture as many meatworks size scrub bulls as possible. These bulls are knocked down by an old Nissan Patrol equipped with a tyre-padded bull bar. Like the bull catching at Batavia Downs, this is not without its share of excitement. Most of Westmoreland is lightly to heavily timbered and squeezing a big, fat Nissan Patrol through some of the gaps between the trees at high speed is an exhilarating experience. Once the bull is sighted, the chase is on, and when he begins to tire he is bumped with the tyre-padded bull bar until he falls. When he goes down the vehicle is run forward so that the animal is held down by the protruding bull bar while its back legs are tied. A three-man team, which includes Jack Gould as the driver of the vehicle, Gary Gould and Rex Shadforth, usually manages to knock down at least six bulls a day. Some days they get a lot more. The bulls are trucked to Cloncurry at a cost of $30 a head. This trip takes fourteen hours and one-third of the journey, from Westmoreland to Burketown, takes nine hours. The actual labour costs involved with running down each bull amount to about $20. After paying additional sale costs it becomes clear that the profit margin involved with catching bulls on Westmoreland is there, but only by the skin of its teeth.

Westmoreland was declared tuberculosis free in 1978, but is now listed as a 'suspect' property because some of the neighbouring properties are infected. This happens because there are no boundary fences separating these properties and cattle can wander onto adjoining stations at will. The cost of surveying a fence line around a large area station could be as high as one million dollars and that's before a post is put into the ground. Needless to say few large area stations are equipped with reasonable boundary fencing.

Disease eradication is one of the most significant operating cost factors for many northern cattlemen today. The tuberculosis and brucellosis eradication scheme involves a high labour demand because of the extra mustering which must take place so that cattle can be treated and inspected. It also means much handling of cattle, and this, in the hot, dry months at the end of the year, puts animals under considerable stress. It means that calves often die and female stock have less chance of conceiving because their body cycles react to the harsh demands being made on their systems. Cattlemen agree that disease eradication is a necessary evil. No matter how much they complain and curse the Department of Primary Industries they know in the back of their minds that disease has to be stamped out for the overall good of the industry.

Jack Gould was thrown into the deep end of cattle station life in 1973 after leaving his father's 2430 hectare sheep and cattle property in South Australia. Many people might think the change a dramatic one in terms of management principles and bush skills, the major difference being that on one property you are rarely out of sight of a fenceline, while on the other you're lucky if you see a fence. Jack Gould, though, does not admit to any great traumas involved with the changeover.

During the wet of 1973, which was the year he arrived at Westmoreland, he was recued by helicopter from raging flood waters. He was camped with three ringers, Tommy Dukes, Alan Petersen and Les Rabbit, out at a cattle yard on the station when 875 millimetres of rain fell in two days. The water rose rapidly and, as there was no high ground in the area, the three were forced to stack forty-four gallon drums on top of a high trailer and sit on the drums. But the water rose and during the dark night they continually had to fill the drums to stop them from floating away beneath them. Jack recalled the blackness of the night. There was no moon and they could hear the floodwater sweeping away beneath them. Towards the early part of the morning the water began to rise rapidly and when the sun came up it was only ten centimetres from the top of the highest drum. Just as the trio thought they would have to swim for it they heard a familiar 'chop-chop' noise — the rescue helicopter had arrived.

Three weeks later Jack was able to ride a horse back to the camp only to find that all the vehicles, including a tractor, a Land Rover and a Landcruiser, had been under water. All the injectors in the tractor had to be washed out with petrol. The Landcruiser motor seized two months later but the Land Rover is still going strong. Jack also remembered with a chuckle that he had put all their riding boots on the seat of the tractor to keep them out of the water. After the water had subsided they found that each one of them had lost one boot and they were left with four odd-sized riding boots.

Back at the homestead Jack walked a radius of two kilometres from the house and counted sixty dead cattle. How many more there were scattered across the station he does not know. But they only branded 100 calves the following year. Normally 400 calves are branded during a season.

The story, or rather the saga, of the current Westmoreland homestead is one worth repeating. The house in its prefabricated state and a tractor were railed from Adelaide to Alice Springs in November 1972. Jack and his brother Philip met the train, off-loaded the house parts onto a 9·75 metre trailer, which was enclosed with a stock crate, linked the tractor and then proceeded to drive to Westmoreland.

The journey from Alice Springs to Camooweal took sixty hours. The tractor, a Chamberlain 236, had a top speed of 30 kilometres per hour on the open highway. The two brothers used to camp under the trailer during the day and drive at night to escape the heat. They picked up hitchhikers, they sported with truckies, and they stopped at every pub along the way. It was, according to Jack, a great trip and one he'd do again any day. But after getting sixty kilometres past Camooweal, the Chamberlain failed to pull the load over the range. There was no alternative but to go back to Camooweal and have the house trucked to Burketown. Jack then had to pick it up there and continue the journey.

Romanticism aside, Jack Gould, like nearly every cattleman who lives in the isolated outback, is for one reason or another in love with his land. Despite its floods, its droughts, its built-in costs associated with distance and its ability to wreck a man no matter how good a cattleman he is, Jack Gould wants to live there until he dies, or 'as long as the Lands Department don't kick me off first'.

Wrotham Park

Wrotham Park Station, all 9983 square kilometres of it, starts its huge run on the western slopes of the Great Dividing Range west of Cairns and sprawls in a north-westerly direction towards the Gulf of Carpentaria for 193 kilometres. The station is over 161 kilometres long and 64 kilometres wide. Out of its total approximate boundary length of 644 kilometres, only five kilometres are fenced. The Park, in anybody's language, is a Big Spread.

From the western slopes of the Dividing Range the station follows the Mitchell River down to the Palmer River junction where the out-station of Drumduff is situated. Wrotham Park and its out-stations of Gamboola, Highbury and Drumduff carry in excess of 40 000 cattle. Each year at least 6000 fat cattle are turned off the station. The owners, Australian Agricultural Company Limited, have extensive grazing and agricultural interests in Queensland, the Northern Territory, Western Australia and New South Wales. The company, which has been in operation since 1824, is one of the oldest pastoral companies in Australia and is also the owner of the 12 251 square kilometre Brunette Downs in the Northern Territory.

Wrotham Park was taken up in 1873 by A. C. Grant, who set out from Havilah in the Bowen district with 300 cattle to take up the land. Grant's adventure was motivated more by entrepreneurial ambitions than by pioneering zeal. One of his main aims was to establish his presence in the area and corner the lucrative butchering trade on the Palmer River gold fields.

A written history of the station undertaken by Nell Arnold, wife of the incumbent manager Gordon Arnold, tells us that Grant sold his 300 cattle to the meat-hungry miners at the exorbitant sum of twelve pounds a head. Food shortages were common on the hardscrabble gold fields. In 1874 flour was selling for four shillings a pound, while the stringy meat from an old working bullock was bringing two shillings a pound.

Grant, realising there certainly was gold in them thar hills, returned south posthaste to enter into a partnership with the owners of Havilah for the supply of more cattle. The idea was that Grant would buy cattle at Havilah and walk them to Wrotham Park, where they would be fattened before being sold to the miners.

His second trip north with cattle was not entirely without incident. At Mt

Surprise heavy rain began to fall and to Grant it looked like the beginning of the wet season. With three rivers, the Lynd, the Tait and the Walsh, to cross, the party lost no time.

They crossed the swollen Lynd without loss of stock and pushed on through belly-deep mud to the Tait. Pulling into camp that night, Grant was surprised to see a tilted dray beside a fire around which five women sat dejectedly. Their horses had strayed and they were trapped between the two rivers. The man who had been accompanying them on the journey had deserted when the trouble struck. Grant, chivalrous to the core, caught the ladies' horses, righted their dray and sent them on their way. The women, we are told, were on their way from the Charters Towers gold fields to the more lucrative pickings of the Palmer. Like Grant, they knew there was more than one way to get rich in a gold strike, and none of them involved swinging a pick or sifting gravel.

After swimming the Tait and Walsh Rivers, Grant moved his cattle slowly across the black soil towards the Mitchell. With the early rain the country was in splendid heart with an abundance of sweet herbages and fresh green grasses. It was a slow trip as the hungry cattle grazed on the new feed, but on Christmas Day 1874 Grant and his drovers reached their destination.

Constant fever, scarcity of rations and never-ending conflict with Aboriginal tribes were the lot of the early Wrotham Park settler. In 1878 Grant sold all his interests in the property and spent two years travelling about Europe, after which he wrote a book titled *Bush Life In Queensland*. Eventually he settled at a most unlikely spot for a north Queensland bushman—Long Beach, California, where he lived until his death in 1930 at the age of eighty-nine.

Since those hazarous early days much water has rolled down the Mitchell River; water which at times has claimed lives and swept away cattle and horses in their hundreds. The Mitchell River in flood is an awesome sight, a hellstream of swirling brown water that can pluck away a homestead with the same ease with which a storm-filled gutter might sweep away a child's paper boat. In 1911 the Highbury homestead was washed away in the river's frenzied rush to the Gulf waters. In the 1974 floods 3000 cattle were drowned on Wrotham Park after 1295 square kilometres of country were innundated.

In the past twenty years the station has prospered under the innovative management of Gordon Arnold. One of the major developments taking place during Arnold's reign over the station is the clearing of vast areas of country which have been sown to the legume Townsville Stylo. Formerly useless country has been turned into highly productive grazing land, but because of economic constraints imposed on the industry in recent years, follow-up maintenance in the form of ground fertilising and sucker removal has not been carried out. This has meant a corresponding drop in plant production, but nevertheless the hardy legume continues to grow after each wet season and Wrotham Park bullocks continue to thrive on it.

There are around fifty people employed on the station, performing a variety of tasks from stock work to domestic work. Four head stockmen are employed to run each of the four mustering camps which operate all through the dry season. In all, thirty-two stockmen are employed and included in this number are jackeroos and jilleroos who are being trained in the industry.

Gordon Arnold is obviously proud of the step taken by the company in 1980 to employ its first jilleroo, and he admits he has been pleased with the performance put up by the girls in the rough and tumble of mustering camp life. However, Arnold does not think that a jilleroo will ever be promoted to head stockman rank. This might mean that a jilleroo who wants to carve a career in the company can never hope to achieve management status. The usual stepping stones to manager level are: head stockman, overseer and then manager. If the usual steps are denied her, it is doubtful if any girl will see the day when she is managing an AA station. After all, there are still plenty of men around who say the bush is no place for a woman. The women who want to spend their lives on the land, however, would probably like the benefits offered by equal opportunity.

Gordon and Nell Arnold have six children, four of whom are employed on the station. David doubles as the overseer and chopper pilot, Geoffrey is head stockman at Gamboola, Tom is a jackeroo on Gamboola and Fiona helps with the housework and cooking at the main station homestead.

Gordon Arnold himself is the classic case of the jackeroo made good. After finishing school and studying Veterinary Science for a year, he opted for a career on the land and went jackerooing on Enniskillen Station near Blackall in central-western Queensland. Eventually, after working on a variety of stations, he took on the position of head stockman on Brighton Downs Station near Middleton in Far Western Queensland. Brighton Downs was owned by the Australian Agricultural Company. After six months he was transferred to the Kimberleys where he took over the management of Ivanhoe Station. After eight years at Ivanhoe he was transferred to Wrotham Park to what is one of the most pretigious management positions the company has to offer.

Helicopters have been used on Wrotham Park since 1973 and in Gordon Arnold's opinion they are there to stay. A good pilot who knows the country can, he said, save a lot of time and money. A not so good pilot, on the other hand, can cost a lot of money and lose a lot of time. The point is made by many station people that the difference between a good and a bad helicopter mustering pilot is that a good one can predict what the cattle are going to do and will react correctly to the varying situations. The pilots who best cope with this are the ones who have worked on the ground as stockmen. A city-trained pilot who doesn't know the difference between a Braford and a Brahman is as handy as the proverbial back pocket in a jock strap.

Labour is a problem on Wrotham Park, like anywhere else. Gordon Arnold maintains that labour is plentiful but that it is young and inexperienced. There are not, he said, as many men following the business through as there were fifteen or twenty years ago. He concedes that this could be the fault of the industry, in that too few stations supply married accommodation.

For a station its size, and for the number of employees it supports, Wrotham Park has an excellent safety record. The only recent serious accident occurred in 1980 when an eighteen-year-old jilleroo suffered a head injury after a horse fell with her while chasing a beast. The damage to the brain was irreparable and now the girl is dependent on a four point walking

Peninsula identities Maurice (left) and Barry Shepard.

Knockabout Peninsula identity and now a Hughenden district grazier Boof McDowell having a beer in a Mt Garnet pub with his wife.

stick for mobility. This sort of accident is not common on stations, but it and other serious mishaps like it are always on the cards when a rider is taking a horse at speed over rough ground.

Having a good safety record on a station is more often than not the result of good sense on behalf of the manager and his head stockmen. In the Royal Flying Doctor handbook which is distributed to all stations dependent on the network, considerable space is given to unnecessary station injuries. The booklet warns: 'Conducting rodeos should be left to bodies officially responsible for organising the sport. Private rodeos on stations should be discouraged as they lead to unnecessary injury.'

The booklet tells the story of one doctor who noticed he was having an inordinately high number of calls to one particular station on his network. A neighbouring station, comparable in most respects, had not made one call over a horse accident in years. When the doctor enquired from the manager of the neighbouring station why it was he had no horse-related accidents, he got the following answers.

First, the manager did not employ 'Queen Street ringers'. Secondly, every man was given a riding test on a quiet horse before he was delegated to a particular job. Thirdly, any head stockman found putting greenhorns on rough horses was sacked on the spot. Fourthly, rough horses were not kept on the station.

Further enquiry revealed that no such precautions were taken on the neighbouring station. In fact, the booklet noted, nothing overjoyed the head stockman more than to see a new chum climb onto the back of the most treacherous, ill-mannered knave in the yard and be sent flying through the air in the most undignified pose.

There are 800 horses on Wrotham Park and each mustering camp works thirty to forty horses. This works out to three to four horses per man for the season. In the early part of the mustering season, when the ground is still too wet for trucks to carry the camp gear out to the mustering camps, pack horses are used.

Nell Arnold wrote in the station's centenary booklet:

> It is a grand sight to see the plant leave for its first camp of the mustering season and hope runs high in the hearts of the station children that one of the fresh pack horses might cause some excitement by tossing off the pack. This invariably happens much to the delight of the children but not to the frayed tempers of the ringers who not only have to repack the horse, but first collect a wide variety of goods scattered over a large area of country.

When I was eighteen I was jackerooing on Toolebuc Station near Middleton, which coincidentally was owned by the Australian Agricultural Company at the time. There came the time for the Middleton horse sports, which was a big event in the district, and Toolebuc was to supply a string of horses for people to ride at the sports. An old ringer, Billy Wellesmore, and I were given the job of walking the horses the eighty-odd kilometres into Middleton. As it was a good two-day trip, we needed a pack horse to cart some tucker and our gear for the sports. There was no pack horse as such on the station, so we opted for the quietest horse, which happened to be the station night horse—a genuine rogue like most night horses are. We were about twenty kilometres out from the station on a blistering hot plain when the night horse decided he'd had enough and bolted away towards a gidyea scrub. The pack rolled under his belly and he really turned it on as Bill and I, in hot pursuit, dismally watched our gear being spread across the plain.

Eventually we caught him in the scrub, but the damage had been done. Bill lost a brand new pair of R. M. Williams riding boots he'd bought especially for the sports, and his shaving kit. Our meat and tea were lost somewhere in the scrub. We gave the old night horse a bit of a lesson in manners and then repacked him and he walked the rest of the way to Middleton like a veteran.

The story is told, too, of a couple of ringers in the Forsayth district in the lower Gulf country who were bringing their camp gear out of the Newcastle Range on a pack horse. They were riding through some thick scrub country when all of a sudden the pack horse took off with flames leaping out of the pack saddle. The ringers, after a mad gallop through the timber, caught the horse and put out the fire before too much damage was done. What had happened was that a packet of wax matches in the pack had rubbed alight. So there is no need to ask why the station children at Wrotham Park hang around when the plant is heading out with fresh pack horses.

Rising costs and remoteness are the major problems facing Wrotham Park, and nearly all of the Gulf and Peninsula Stations. Fuel prices have doubled in four years, whereas cattle prices have been in a trough. The tuberculosis eradication programme currently under way on Wrotham Park represents serious cost considerations. Even though the incidence of tuberculosis is low — one in four thousand — the cattle still have to be tested. This involves the repetitive mustering and yarding and the associated problems of mis-mothering and general stock trauma, particularly in the hotter months of the year. A small amount of compensation is paid by the State Government for disease suspect cattle which are destroyed. No compensation in any form is handed down for the massive amounts of time and the enormous costs involved in handling cattle for the eradication programme. Gordon Arnold has estimated that by 1984 (when he hopes Wrotham Park will be classified as disease free) at least $500 000 will have been spent on disease eradication. The figure could go as high as one million dollars, he said. Any untested cattle left after 1984, especially wild cattle, will probably be shot.

One of the problems facing Gordon Arnold in terms of eventual disease eradication is the Staaten River National Park, part of which joins a southern boundary of Wrotham Park. There are hundreds and perhaps thousands of wild cattle in the National Park and no attempt has been made by government agencies to clean them out. Disease-infected cattle from the National Park are free to cross over into Wrotham Park at any time and this places the entire eradication programme in jeopardy. The State Department of Primary Industries, which is zealously monitoring the success of the tuberculosis and brucellosis eradication programme, is strangely lax when it comes to controlling wild cattle in National Parks. Most Peninsula cattlemen admit that they are looking a Catch-22 situation right in the eye when they have to spend vast amounts of money on disease control while feral cattle are walking around as free as the wind on neighbouring National Parks and reserves.

A hopeful young rider parts company with his mount at the 1982 Laura rodeo. The bulls used in the bull ride event were all cleanskins and had been mustered out of the Cape York scrub only a day or two before the rodeo.

Time to say good-bye at the 1982 Laura rodeo.

Rubber vine is also a problem on Wrotham Park, and it has already choked out some of the best river country. This exotic vine is one of the gravest plant pests facing the north Queensland cattle industry, particularly in the wetter areas. The vine gets a rapid hold and quickly chokes out good grazing country. It grows into an inpenetrable jungle that a man cannot even walk through, let alone ride a horse through.

On parts of Wrotham Park where the vine has established itself along the banks of the Mitchell, Walsh and Palmer Rivers a bulldozer has had to be used to grade paths through the jungle so that stock can get to water. Chemical control is sometimes effective, but on large areas it is absolutely cost prohibitive. Very little has been done by Government-sponsored research organisations in trying to find an effective biological control agent for this pest.

On a station like Wrotham Park it is inevitable that there will be a few characters around: someone like Wangie Jones, who can be credited with being something of a motion picture pioneer in north Queensland. Snaggly toothed Wangie (pronounced Whang-ee), who stands about 170 centimetres tall and weighs in at 51 kilograms, with a mechanic's box of Sidchrome sockets in his right hand, ran the Normanton picture show back in 1941. And what a wild and woolly turn-out it must have been. Every Saturday night the Normanton audience would come to see such classics as *Gone With The Wind*, *Kentucky* and *Lassie Come Home* cranked out on Wangie's Raycophone projector.

Power was supplied from a spiteful second-hand generator which was in the habit of breaking down just as the hero was about to rescue his leading lady from the clutches of the evil villains. Amid the catcalls, whistles and boos, Wangie would bend to the task with spanner in hand and in no time at all the story would once again begin to unfold in black and white on the moth-eaten screen. A one-man orchestra had nothing on Wangie. He sold the tickets for the show, sold peanuts at interval, ran the projector, cleaned the picture hall and quietened down the more rowdy members of the audience. Every Saturday night, the School of Arts where the pictures were held was packed, and on a typical night Wangie would take thirteen pounds, which was a healthy sideline to his garage. The favourite fare of the audience, though, was not love stories and bitter-sweet romances, but tough, gutsy films of the Western genre. The more blood in 'em, the more the audience liked 'em, Wangie reckoned.

Wangie was born in 1918, in the Gulf township of Croydon where his father had a cattle property and butcher shops. He left school at the age of fourteen to help with the family business, but not long after his father died and the business ran into trouble. The banks, Wangie said with a wry smile, kindly moved in and sold the business, after which he was left virtually nothing. He had always been interested in mechanics and so he enrolled in a correspondence course in the subject from a Sydney Technical College. In 1940, qualified and confident, he moved to Normanton where he started his own garage and the picture show business.

In 1946 romance reared its head in Wangie's life and he was married. The following year he and his wife moved to Julia Creek, where he bought a cafe and dance hall. Julia Creek in those days was a more prosperous centre than it is now, and numerous wedding receptions and dances were held in Wangie's dance emporium.

Things didn't work out on the marital side, and in the same year, Wangie said, his wife 'blew through'. He hasn't seen her since. Not long after, he sold his business in Julia Creek and moved to Brisbane where he worked as a mechanic for five years.

In the end the city life was too much for Wangie and he packed up and returned to the Gulf, where he worked as a mechanic on a number of stations. 1974 found him on Dunbar Station, where he spent three weeks of the famous January floods in water 'up to his waist'. There were snakes, pigs and cattle being washed down in the floodwaters and it was only a miracle that no human life was lost.

'There were plenty of crocs around too, you had to keep an eye out. We used to tell anyone wading through the houseyard to leave the gate open so the crocs could get in and we could catch them when the water went down,' he said with a grin. Fortunately no one from the station had been camped out in the bush when the flood started. If they had, they would have been washed away for sure. It was just a sea of water, Wangie said.

Wangie arrived at Wrotham Park in 1981, and reckons it's a pretty good life. It's quiet, and after all, there's not too many things to spend your money on.

'A bloke can save a quid here,' he reckoned.

Wangie Jones is not your average suburban-type mechanic. A typical morning at Wrotham might see him taking apart one of the station lawn-mowers. Around lunch time he might drop the slave cylinder out of a Landcruiser and in the afternoon he might start work on the hydraulics of a prime mover.

'That's what I like about it,' Wangie exclaimed. 'We work on everything from washing machines to road trains. Now you can't do much better than that, can you?'

Wangie goes to Cairns twice a year for a blow-out and looks up his old mates, and he travels to Brisbane once a year to visit his son. He's due to retire in 1983, but Wangie wants to stay on at Wrotham Park.

'What would I do if I retired?' he asked. 'Not much.'

Sitting on a forty-four gallon drum outside one of the station workshops, I asked Wangie what it was he liked about the Gulf.

'It's the people, the people that make it, and I was born here. I know it so well and it's better living up here than in the cities. When you're in the city you can't even have a yarn with a bloke in a pub. If you do they think you're either going to put the bite on them or rob them. It's just not the same as the bush, not the same at all.'

Merluna

After leaving Wrotham Park I took a shortcut to Laura. I crossed the Mitchell River at Mt Mulgrave Station and passed through the properties of Fairlight and Fairview before coming out on the main Peninsula track to Laura. And then it was the long dreary haul up to Merluna with no more respite from the olive drab bush than the store at Musgrave Station and the bar of the Coen pub where I intended to lay over for (quite) a few beers.

Driving up the Peninsula is about as much fun as riding a pogo stick to hell. This was only my second trip up the Peninsula but already I was inured to the tedium of the slow driving demanded by the deep bull dust and the rippling corrugations. The red slash of the road carved through the bush and disappeared as a minute cleft among the greenery of the distant horizon. If you're in a hurry on this track you lose. Try and push it too hard and it will knock you down and sink the silver slipper in while your head is in the dust.

I crossed the Archer River north of Coen, pulled over and had a swim and washed some clothes. A few hours later I pulled up to the Merluna homestead and parked beside the house with a feeling of uncertainty about the reception which might be accorded by station part-owner Clive Quartermaine.

Only weeks before we had had a disagreement over the telephone about a story I had written on the station for the *Queensland Country Life* newspaper. We had come to an amicable parting on the telephone, and when I asked him if I could visit Merluna and see his team of bull catchers in action, he told me I would be welcome. As I stood at the car outside the house arranging gear, Clive came through the gate, right hand extended, with a wide grin across his face. A few minutes later while we were having coffee out in the garden he mentioned the telephone conversation and said: 'It's all in the past. Let's forget it.' That was okay by me.

The bull catching team was operating on Batavia Downs, an out-station of 6500 square kilometre Merluna. After lunch Clive drew a mud map showing a short cut to Batavia via a place called Picaninny Plain, which was the scene of a second mustering camp on the station.

Graham Jones, the mustering contractor operating from Picaninny Plain, was standing outside a ramshackle set of small cattle yards as I drew up to their camp. Inside, about two hundred Brahman cattle, a lot of them clean-skins, milled about. Introductions over, Graham explained how, as I was driving towards the camp, a bull had nearly got him down in the yard. 'I only just made it through the rails,' he said with a gap-toothed grin.

I glanced over and saw the bull in question eyeing us from the centre of the mob. The bull shook its head and snorted violently, letting the black tips of its horns carve through the air like a street fighter's stilletto.

One of Graham's ringers was inside the yard, repairing a dividing fence the bull had smashed in its charge only minutes before. The ringer was swearing loudly as he tried to wire new rails into position and watch the snorting bull at the same time.

'He won't hurt ya,' Graham called out.

'Like fucken 'ell!' the ringer shouted back.

I arrived at Batavia about an hour before dark and met Jeff Hawkins, the bull catching contractor, his wife Eileen, and the three bull runners who work for Hawkins under a percentage arrangement.

Hawkins outwardly appeared as though he was going to enjoy having an outsider along for a spot of bull catching. This was reassuring, as I had thought I might be viewed as a nuisance by the tightly-run team and could picture them saying: 'Some silly reporter bastard wants to come out with us. Well, we may as well jack it up 'im and get rid of 'im.'

That night I camped on a creek not far from the Batavia homestead, cooked some fillet steak Eileen had given me and rolled out my swag before the moon was up. Tomorrow, I thought, I'd better be ready to hit the pins at sparrow's.

The first creamy light of the sunrise played into the forest. The three motor bike riders, Peter Aitken, 30, Wayne Miller, 19, and Mick Cole, 18, fanned out in front of the Suzuki four-wheel-drive. Dressed in heavy protective gear and with the wide leather tying straps slung over their shoulders, they looked more like the bad guys from a Mad Max movie than Cape York Cowboys.

Hawkins sat at the wheel of the Suzuki, a scrawny Log Cabin cigarette poked from one corner of his mouth. The butt of a .357 magnum pistol hung from a leather holster at his hip. Hawkins explained the gun's role as being there to 'blow away a bull' if one happened to get someone down on the ground. Considering the nature of the work there was a fair chance that before the season was out Hawkins would have to 'blow away a bull'.

Behind us in the weldmesh crate were the five scarred and ugly 'hanging' dogs. Back on the track Eileen waited beside the eight tonne Hino for Jeff to drive back and direct her to a downed bull.

Then something lashed my neck. It was the Suzuki launching off at full throttle over a melon hole.

'Grab the goggles,' Hawkins yelled. 'And hang on.'

I slipped the heavy duty plastic goggles over my eyes and braced myself against the dashboard of the bouncing Suzuki. Up ahead the mob of cleanskin cattle spread out through the timber. The three bike riders in the mad confusion of the initial rush had managed to spread themselves out evenly between the cattle and a wall of fast approaching jungle.

Hawkins had the pedal down on the Suzuki, and we squeezed between box trees and bloodwoods at speeds of up to 80 kilometres per hour. Saplings were snapped by the heavy bull bar on the front of the vehicle.

Smaller dry branches rained into the open Suzuki and larger, more lethal, branches speared into the weldmesh screen which took the place of the conventional windscreen.

Hawkins yelled at me again: 'Don't look up when we knock a tree, you'll cop a stick through the goggles.' I tried to lower my head each time, but the urge to see what the timber was doing was irrestible.

My pulse rate began to normalise and I remembered what I was there for. Photos, get some damn photos. I unzipped the camera bag at my feet and took out one of the Minoltas and checked the exposure setting, knowing that when the time came I would only have time to focus and shoot. Even focusing at this speed through the bush on a moving target was going to be difficult enough.

I glanced at Hawkins. Grim faced, both hands on the wheel, spinning, slowing, making instant decisions on which way to go. Find the fastest route to the bull, don't get trapped by a barrier of trees, and don't roll the vehicle. Roll the vehicle and the operation goes bust. But speed, maximum speed all the time, make the right decisions and don't prang up. The dogs in the back were creating a cacophony of yowls, growls, barks and yaps which drowned out the sound even of the high revving motor.

I could feel my heart miss a beat each time the trunk of a huge tree seemed to be on an unavoidable collision course with the Suzuki. Each time I had to fight the temptation to sing out: 'Watch the tree!' And each time Hawkins slewed past leaving a gap between vehicle and tree that would not have taken a cigarette paper.

A large red bull broke from the fleeing mob and Hawkins spun the Suzuki in pursuit. The three bike riders were on the other side of the beast, keeping him moving, wearing him down. A look of lugubrious dread came into the animal's eyes as we drew parallel at a distance of about three metres.

Hawkins edged the Suzuki in closer. I shifted my legs uncomfortably, thinking of the tear in the front passenger side where a bull's horn had ripped through the metal on one of these chases.

Hawkins jerked a lever at his side. A gate on the dog crate flew open and the five mobsters in the back leapt from the opening. In the same instance Hawkins cut the motor and jumped from the rolling vehicle. Three of the dogs already had hold of the bull's ears and nose and the other two hung from its brisket like spotted cancers. Hawkins grabbed the tail of the animal and with a heave swung it over onto the ground.

As the bull hit the ground one of the bikers grabbed its tail and pulled it through the animal's hind legs and over its flank, holding it down as Hawkins wrapped a tying strap around its hind hocks. The battle, the chase was over. The team stood around and discussed the size of the bull and debated what he might bring at the Cairns export abbatoir 800 kilometres away. Hawkins, with a satisfied smile on his face, rolled a smoke and then hopped in the Suzuki and drove back to where Eileen waited.

Ten minutes later the Hino bulldozed its way through the timber to where the bull lay. A drop ramp was lowered and a saddle girth hooked to a winch cable was looped around the bull's horns. The button went down and slowly the scarred Cape country monarch was hauled up the ramp. The animal's tail flicked in agitation.

'See, he's happy, he's wagging his tail,' Hawkins said with a triumphant grin.

But there was no time for self-congratulation. As soon as the bull was in the truck the tying strap was removed and the search was under way again.

On every chase the scenario was the same. The quiet, fanlike search through the bush, heads turning looking for that colour, that movement which would betray the presence of a herd of wild cattle. Later in the day we did a sweep along a lightly timbered plain which ran parallel to a creek for about two miles. Topping a slight rise, we saw spread out below a herd of forty cleanskins. The wind was in our favour and as the cattle grazed two of the bike riders idled quietly around to one side. When they were in position Hawkins slammed the accelerator and the feeding cattle lifted their heads at the shrill pitch of the motor. Five seconds later they were thundering towards the cover of the creek.

Hawkins attacked the cattle at high speed, getting the best possible pace out of the almost treeless countryside. But there were deep melon holes and breakaway gullies hidden in the long grass. The leaders of the galloping cattle were now only ninety metres from the jungle at the side of the creek. Hawkins pressed his boot down on the pedal and the vehicle surged forward. Suddenly we were in the air and out of control after running into a hidden melon hole. The vehicle hit the ground and bounced before sliding away to the left towards the steep bank of a breakaway. Hawkins spun the wheel violently and his left boot went down on the brake. The vehicle slid to a stop at the lip of the gully. Looking down from my seat I could see one of the bike riders, his hands covering his head, looking up at us with undisguised fright. Clearly, he thought the Suzuki was going to come tumbling down on top of him. Mick Cole had ridden straight over the bank of the gully, which was nearly four metres deep, and somehow had escaped injuring either himself or the bike.

The greatest danger to the bike riders are the melon holes and the stumps. Hundreds of square kilometres of the country in which they operate has been burned for the purpose of exposing these obstacles, but in areas where the grass won't burn they have to make their own adjustments. Long pursuits through heavily grassed country are not taken with relish. The dangers are too real, and to hurtle blindly through the undergrowth is a surefire way to court disaster. The team, even though it is professional and with a distinct liking for an almost perpetual adrenalin buzz, likes to have the odds stacked just slightly in its favour.

The three bikers work for a percentage of the take and they are go, go, go all the time. More bulls, more money. No bulls, no money. It is as simple as that. And they are young men, too, stricken with the romance and exhilaration of running down wild bulls in Cape York Peninsula.

Hawkins, from the vantage point of his forty-odd years, quipped that the bikers were 'in their glory out there', and added that when they go back to their home towns when the season is over they will be the local heroes. The girls, he said, will really go for them.

Becoming one of Hawkins' bull catchers is no small feat. An individual selected for the job has to possess special personality traits and skills. A bike rider must have three attributes. First, he must be able to ride a motor bike upside down in rough country. Secondly, he has to have some cattle knowledge. A city boy might be able to make a 500 cc competition bike do the rhumba. But without a knowledge of cattle and the way they are likely to behave, he might very quickly rhumba his way on to a set of extremely hostile horns. Thirdly, he must be able to get on with the rest of the team and he must work as a part of that team. Heroes, loners and loud mouths are out as far as Hawkins is concerned.

The concept of team work was designed to incorporate the modern business trends of motivation and safety. The fact that they are living together in a very isolated area for seven months of the year makes it imperative there are no personality rifts. During that seven month period they work seven days a week from daylight to dark. If you like having a girlfriend, going to the movies and generally hanging out for a good time, don't go bull catching in Cape York.

The bikers, as part of the bargain, get a top machine to ride. Assuming that each of them loves the growling sound of a good bike and appreciates the laws of physics as applied to motorised two-wheel travelling, then they must be in seventh heaven with the Suzuki 500s. These are a four-stroke machine designed for fast acceleration and low gear work. In the job of bull catching there are two speeds—the slow search and the fast chase. The top speed of the bikes is nothing to write home about, but they do have rapid acceleration which gets the men to the bulls in quick time. The four-strokes have a low maintenance factor and can run at a low idle all day without overheating.

The Suzuki four-wheel-drive was chosen because of its lightness and wheelbase size. Its size allows it to squeeze through the narrow gaps between the trees and generally cover country that would stop a larger vehicle. The only modifications carried out to the Suzuki have been the attachment of roll bars, heavy bull bar, and side bars. There is a steel protection sheet over the fuel tank and the radiator has a reinforced front. A lot of the bulls charge the Suzuki head-on, and early in 1982 one shoved its horn right through the radiator.

Predictably enough there have been one or two mishaps. In 1982 Hawkins hit a melon hole at high speed and came out of it with all four wheels in the air. The only thing that stopped the low-flying Suzuki was a rather large bloodwood tree. Hawkins managed to walk away but the chassis of the vehicle bent on impact. The Suzuki was towed back to the homestead and chained to a large mango tree, and the chassis was pulled straight by a tractor. The steering wheel still sticks out of the column about half an inch, but, 'What the hell,' Hawkins reckoned. 'It still catches bulls.'

How, then, does Hawkins, who has worked at executive level for mining companies at Collinsville, Greenvale, Peak Downs and Goonyella in Queensland, arrive at throwing bulls for a living in the forgotten end of Cape York Peninsula?

He was born and spent his childhood at Tangorin, a whistle-stop, no-horse burgh in northwestern Queensland where his parents ran the post office. Hawkins' love for the bush was fired out there on the rolling Mitchell grass downs country.

In 1980 he quit the mining industry and with a partner bought 33 000 hectare Texas Station at Jericho in Central Queensland. The block was overrun with wild cattle and Hawkins, a neophyte at the time when it came to handling feral cattle, decided he was going to turn the scrubbers into dollars. The cattle were worth money and at the time the partnership had run into a cash flow problem. Even though the industry had stabilised somewhat after the big beef recession of the 1970s, it was still not sufficiently buoyant to float an ambitious cattleman who had poured his life savings into the land. Using choppers, bikes, horses and trap yards, Hawkins set out to capture the scrubbers. He had caught 400 before the depressed state of the industry made further mustering uneconomical. The cash flow crisis worsened and Hawkins realised he would have to find some other employment. He had vowed never to return to mining or to work for someone else. He searched the sum of his experience and came up with bull catching. 'I'd realised at Texas that there was a great need in the cattle industry for a specialised mustering outfit. I decided to fill that gap and be bloody good at it. That way when people hear about you they only hear the best,' Hawkins said.

He borrowed $35 000 and bought his plant, which included the bikes, the Hino truck, the Suzuki and assorted other gear. Hawkins then set off for Merluna at the invitation of Clive Quartermaine who, like nearly all other Peninsula cattlemen, was and still is trying to clear his property of wild cattle. A tuberculosis and brucellosis disease eradication programme being conducted by the Queensland Department of Primary Industries might well have its deadline in the mid-1980s. It is possible that when this deadline occurs, graziers with unmanageable wild cattle will have to shoot them. There is also the possibility that America, as it draws towards a brucellosis and tuberculosis free cattle industry, will cancel all beef orders from all areas with the disease. Quartermaine and others like him are thus making serious efforts to clear their land of feral cattle.

Contractors working for him prior to Hawkins' arrival had tried everything from planes to horses in efforts to yard the scrubber cattle. What Hawkins did was to combine the best components of all the previously tried methods. He wanted bikes for their versatility and speed, and dogs to run the beast to ground and to keep its head occupied while someone swung from its tail. The Suzuki was primarily for transporting the dogs and for getting them to the bull fresh and full of fight. The dogs are the lynchpin of the operation and Hawkins admits that without them he would probably go bust. He has about thirty dogs on the payroll and they get all the entitlements of a good employee—days off, good tucker and generous sick leave.

They are a blend of traditional hunting dogs including Bloodhound, Bull Terrier, Rhodesian Ridgeback and Australian Cattle Dog. There is even a bit of dingo somewhere in the lineage.

Hawkins looks for speed, stamina and weight in a dog, and it has to 'hang'. This means that it has to grab onto the ear or nose and stay there even while the bull is charging through the undergrowth. Hanging dogs have two outstanding characteristics: they are almost always horrifically ugly, and they exhibit an extreme lack of propriety in the face of personal danger.

There is another ace in Hawkins' cattle-catching arsenal. Some of the country on Batavia, particularly some of the swamp and creek country, is too rough for the vehicles to chase the cattle effectively. In these areas camou-

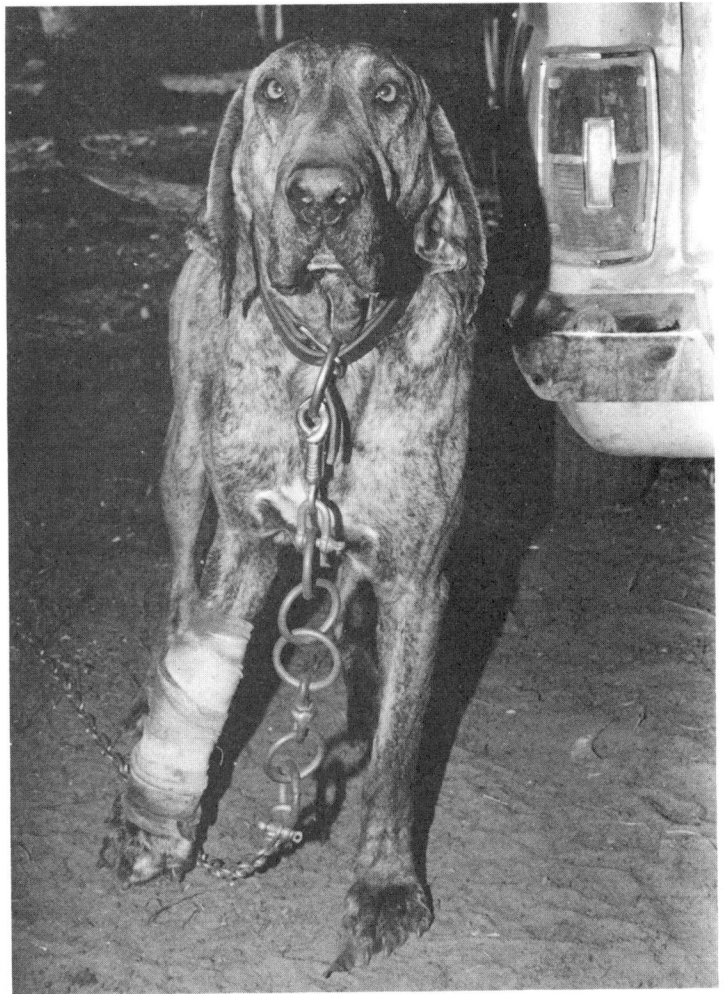

A part Bloodhound 'hanging' dog convalescing after a bull jammed him against the side of the Suzuki.

Buckling up the leggings, Koolatah Station.

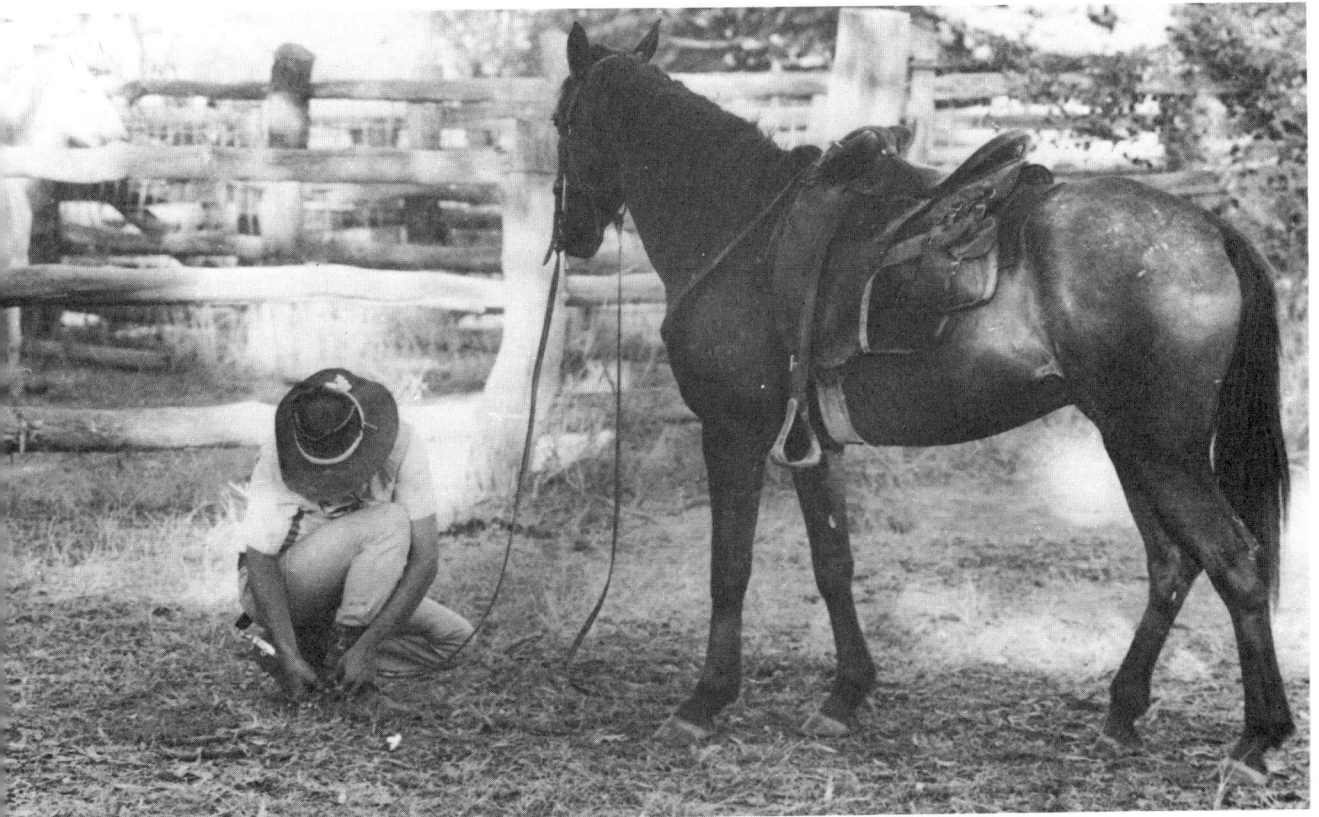

flaged trap yards are used. These are portable steel yards which can be fitted together in a few hours by two men. The yard is set up in a suitable location and then its framework is covered with branches and long hessian wings are run out from the receiving gate. Once the cattle have been steered towards the wings they will run between them until they pass through the hidden gate and hit the leaf-covered wall at the rear of the yards. Meatworks sized bulls are transported out of this rough country by a four-wheel-drive Blitz truck. But anything can go wrong. If there is a gap in the hessian, the cattle will rush through it, and if they detect any human scent they will turn in their tracks and gallop back to freedom.

Setting up a trap yard is not just a case of placing the yard where you think the cattle might run. Hawkins gives the cattle one or two 'dry runs' and works out their course of escape before deciding on where to build the yard.

Trapping wild cattle is the same as trapping any wild animal. It is important to know the country, to know your quarry and to exercise considerable cunning. The smallest detail ignored could jeopardise the success of the operation.

As soon as the cattle are between the wings, the vehicles move up from behind and put pressure on the herd. With the danger so close behind they have no alternative but to run forward into the mouth of the trap. If they should decide to turn, though, there is very little likelihood that the machines would be able to stop them.

Someone has to be hidden at the entrance gate to the yard to slam it shut before the bewildered cattle can take stock of their situation and escape. This job is usually given to Eileen and, because of the risk involved of the wary scrubbers picking up the scent of anyone on the ground, she usually hides in a tree. When the last of the cattle has gone through the gate she leaps from the tree and closes the yard.

Once, the only tree near the gate had its lowest branch some six metres from the ground. Eileen was helped up into the tree and a rope was tied to the branch so she could swing down. Feeling like Jane of the Jungle, Eileen waited patiently in the tree for the cattle to come. When the last beast passed into the yard she swung down towards the gate, but at that same moment a suspicious bull turned back from the mob and stood in the gateway. And there was Eileen dangling miserably from the rope, her feet only a few centimetres above the head of the mystified bull. The seconds passed but eventually the vehicles arrived and Eileen was rescued from her precarious solitude.

Despite the success Hawkins is having with his bull-catching operation there is no shortage of critics. Peninsula old timers laugh at 'that mad bastard trying to catch all them mongrel cattle on motor bikes'. Hawkins in turn accuses some of the crusty old-timers and some of the younger men of still having a romantic notion about a man and horse riding the range. In many cases, he said, they have failed to turn the new technology to their own advantage.

'I've got nothing against horses. They can do a job well. But in our case they would be too slow and bikes can do the job so much faster,' Hawkins argues.

He described the Batavia operation as 'catching hard-to-get cattle in wild country'. The best way to get these cattle is with bikes and dogs.

Only twenty to twenty-five per cent of the cattle sighted on Batavia are branded. The rest are cleanskins. The blame for this should not be left with the owners entirely. Hawkins lays most of the blame on slapdash contract mustering outfits that either miss cattle in the bush or simply leave the wilder cattle behind. Self-esteem comes into the picture at the end of the contract when they can't bring themselves to tell the owner or manager that they missed cattle. After all, 'good men' don't miss cattle.

Hawkins produced a rum bottle on our last night at Batavia and we sat around the dinner table and talked about things in general. I asked him: 'Do you have some sort of romantic notion about chasing wild bulls for a living in Cape York? Or is it just a plain old boring job?'

Hawkins looked away with a half-grin tugging at the corners of his mouth. The answer was written all across his face. Eileen laughed and punched him lightly on the shoulder. 'Oh, he loves it, he just loves every minute of it out there.' She threw her arms around him and for a split second, Hawkins, the tough bull catcher, the guy who, if you gave him a broken bottle and a dark alley, could make King Kong beg for mercy, looked bashful.

Hawkins extracted himself from the embrace and commented somewhat sombrely that he responded to the freedom of the bush. 'It's better than working in the cities and it's a chancey game, a bloody dangerous occupation at times.' He stared thoughtfully at the ceiling for a few moments and added: 'I get a kick out of the adrenalin charge. When I'm by myself in that Suzuki I just go berko and drive like crazy.' He looked at me with a smile and explained: 'While I've had you in with me I've been taking it pretty easy. I get a bit responsible when I've got someone in with me.'

I looked at him to see if he was serious. He was.

For Clive Quartermaine, owning a fifty per cent share of Merluna is the climax of a lifelong dream. His is an unlikely background for the management of a large Cape York cattle station. His business background at first glance would appear to lend itself more to the marketing of soap and detergents than the operation of wild Merluna.

He retired from business life initially as a senior marketing executive with the Shell Company. Soon after he took on the job of marketing manager for the rubber manufacturer, Bandag Manufacturers, owned by his Merluna partner Gordon MacNicol.

Quartermaine had always dreamed of the day he would raise beef cattle, and after three years with Bandag he quit and bought Welcome Station near Laura. He confesses that at the time he could have moved to the Gold Coast and bought a Mercedes. 'But I wouldn't have lived long, as I was about eighteen stone at the time,' he laughed. Now several stone lighter and a picture of middle-aged vitality, Quartermaine knows he made the right choice.

He bought Welcome Station at the worse possible time—1973—just before the beef collapse. It was a tough period and the family belts were drawn into the last hole. He looks back now with pride at the way his wife and two sons toughed out the recession. 'No one broke. We stuck it out and I think it did us a lot of good,' he said.

In 1979 he moved to Merluna after selling Welcome Station to his eldest son Cameron. Merluna had previously been owned by an American concern and had been allowed to deteriorate. In Quartermaine's own words the vehicles were buggered, the paddocks were buggered, and the cattle had been let go. 'We had to spend tens of thousands of dollars upgrading equipment. It was just a mess,' he said.

But Quartermaine is quick to point out that the blame for the state of the property should not be left with the Americans. Instead he blames the managers who were in charge. The Americans poured a lot of money into the place and bought some top-line Brahman bulls. But they were given the wrong advice and this was their undoing. The money they spent on the Brahman bulls went straight down the plughole. As soon as the bulls were released into the bush they were either killed by the wild cleanskin bulls or they went wild themselves. In any case not one of them ever saw a stock yard again. Quartermaine believes firmly that it is foolish to bring expensive, high quality cattle onto a Peninsula station until the wild cattle have been removed.

The main Merluna yards are over 700 kilometres from the nearest meatworks at Cairns. 'When you're this isolated the only way to get ahead is to be in control of your own destiny. If you can't do that then you are at the mercy of outsiders who don't know and who don't care much for this country.' And as if to emphasise the point: 'We're still waiting for a fleet of semi-trailers we booked two years ago to pick up some cattle. Where would you be if you had to rely on that sort of incompetence all the time?'

It is this sort of incompetence, and a desire to control their own destiny, that prompted the Merluna owners to buy their own prime mover and double decker trailer. The Mack Superliner is almost continually occupied through the dry season carting cattle from Merluna to the Cairns meatworks. It's expensive, but no one ever said the price of controlling destiny came cheap.

Like Hawkins, Clive Quartermaine is prepared to break with tradition to get the results that he wants. His tentative plans are to sell Batavia and fence the remainder of the station into 5000 hectare paddocks. This, he believes, would give the property a more manageable size and greatly assist in the education of the cattle.

But, once again, if it was left to the old timers there wouldn't be any fences in Cape York apart from the odd horse paddock and holding yard fencelines. They say that the only way to run cattle in the Cape is on a free range system. Cattle have to be able to spread out to find the good feed in a bad season. If they are locked in by fences they will starve. But Clive Quartermaine believes it can be done and he intends doing it.

Fencing, he believes, would enable controlled mating which would result in a higher conception rate. He estimates that the conception rate in the Peninsula using the free range system would only be twenty per cent. Husbandry practices such as weaning and supplementary feeding, which are almost unheard of on the large Cape stations, could be implemented.

'There's a lot you can do, but it all takes time and it all takes money.'

Dunbar

I first visited Dunbar Station in 1978 when I was one of a party of six who canoed the Mitchell River from its upper reaches down to the Aboriginal settlement of Kowanyama. We had been on the river for fourteen days by the time we reached the Dunbar-Koolatah river crossing. Our staple diet during that time had been fish, wild duck and wallaby, and we were in the mood for steak and mashed spuds.

I was an old school friend of David Hughes of Koolatah, and had promised my five companions that when we got to the crossing we would walk the nine kilometres to the homestead and see what we could sort out in the way of the aforementioned comestibles.

We walked all the way up the hot, unshaded track to the homestead, only to find the station deserted except for a one-armed cook who gave us a drink of water and sent us on our way. The Hughes family, he told us, were on the road with cattle and wouldn't be back for a few days. So that ended that. We were all wearing canvas jungle boots which are ideal for canoeing but hopeless for walking long distances. By the time we made it back to the river we were all nursing blisters the size of saucers, and no one bothered to thank me for the exercise I had so thoughtfully provided.

We made a drink of tea and discussed our prospects of reaching a prearranged rendezvous at our finishing point on the South Mitchell River on time. Our finishing time had to coincide with the arrival of two Cairns-based fishing inspectors who had agreed to drive us back to the east coast. Three of the party decided then and there to fly out from Dunbar rather than risk running behind schedule and missing the fishing inspectors. Three of us decided to press on and try to make the finishing point within seven days. We did.

But before doing anything we had to walk the six kilometres up to the Dunbar homestead and arrange for a plane to land at the station. And we had to sort out the gear. For the three of us going on there were complications, in that each of us would have to take turns at paddling the second 5-metre Canadian canoe solo. Our gear had to be kept to a minimum so that the weight advantage could be maximised.

We were greeted at Dunbar by Di Bird. She packed us off to the Kitchen, where we set about to demolish one of the biggest curries I have ever seen.

Bougainvillea at the Merluna homestead in Cape York Peninsula.

The author's Toyota Hilux four-wheel-drive stuck in the Mitchell River at the Dunbar to Koolatah crossing. The dog didn't give a damn!

Meanwhile she sat at the two-way radio until she had verification that a Bush Pilots (now Air Queensland) plane would land at the station.

Late that afternoon she drove us back down to the river where we worked out what gear was going to be left behind. The three of us going on to Kowanyama got in one hour's paddling before making camp for the night.

I next met Di in 1981 when I was covering the student graduation ceremony at the Burdekin Rural Education Centre, southwest of Townsville. Di and her husband Danny had come down to see their son Dan graduate from the college. Dan finished as one of the top pupils in his year and was going home to work on Dunbar.

Seven thousand square kilometre Dunbar has a ninety-six kilometre frontage to the Mitchell River. It boundaries the stations of Kowanyama, Rutland Plains, Inkerman, Van Rook, Dorunda, Koolatah, Drumduff and Highbury. The latter two properties are out-stations of Wrotham Park.

The Birds have lived at Dunbar for the past five years. Before taking over the management of Dunbar, Danny had managed Van Rook, Rutland Plains and Glencoe stations in the Gulf. The Birds have four children, all of whom have had part of their education by correspondence.

Dan was Di's first pupil and she taught him herself until half way through his first year of schooling. But, like most station mothers who take on the teaching of their children, Di found the job too much. She was being called away too often to help out on the station and as a result Dan's education was suffering. A governess was employed and Dan's education was able to continue without interruption.

The Bird children have all had lessons over the radio from the School Of The Air (SOTA) in Cairns. This has been a major breakthrough in the education of bush children. Talking on the radio provides these isolated children with a great sense of togetherness, even though their nearest class mate might be 500 kilometres away. The radio also teaches them to think quickly. For thirty minutes each day, children of each grade sit by their radios and talk to their teacher in Cairns. The 'classroom' is thousands upon thousands of square kilometres. And all over it, in mining camps, cattle station homesteads and professional fishing camps, young children sit with microphone in hand. The answers to questions like four plus three and six multiplied by four crackle across the lonely distances.

When learning entirely by correspondence, children tend more to work at their own pace. The School of the Air puts them in a 'classroom' situation, albeit a scattered one, and they learn to compete and to compare themselves with the other young students on the radio link-up.

They are classes typified by voices only. A student might complete her primary education without ever once meeting any of her classmates.

The School of the Air does have social functions once in a while so that the children can meet each other. The shy bush youngsters learn to play with others their own age and it helps them adjust to the company of other children. But for children on stations like Dunbar, more than 300 bad road kilometres from Cairns, it is impossible to attend these functions. The children grow up with the ringers and other men working on the station. They learn to ride horses early and to handle cattle and they learn to live in the bush. These children have a different concept of the world from that of their counterparts in the city. Ask a bush kid what the colour of grass is and he will invariably answer 'brown'. Ask a city kid the same question and he will answer 'green'.

After Dan Bird finished his primary education, he was sent away to a boarding school on the Atherton Tableland. He was at the time a typical bush kid—independent and already hardened to physical work. He came from a place which did not have television, nor were there any picture theatres, fun parlours or shops filled with bright displays. His was a world of horses, cattle, rivers and creeks, and dry, brown grass. After a year he left the boarding school and enrolled at the Mareeba High School. His time at the high school was not considered a great success by either Di or Danny. They suggested boarding school, but young Dan was against the idea. There were tears and fights. In the end Di brought him back to Dunbar to do his Grade Ten schooling by correspondence.

A trained teacher was employed to coach Dan through to his junior examinations. He was confronted with a great deal of work, no competition and a shortage of reference material. Text books were plentiful, but library facilities were non-existent. Despite the dire predictions of failure, Dan passed his junior examinations with fours and fives. But Di Bird vowed that no more of her children would do any secondary schooling from home.

'These are important years of development. Living on a station like this they miss out on too much sport, competition and social activity. At that age they need to be around other children. They have to learn how others their own age behave,' she said.

After finishing his junior, Dan was sent to the Burdekin Rural Education Centre. The underlying reason for this was that Dan wanted nothing more than to come home and work on Dunbar. He wanted to spend his life on the land, and sending him to the rural-based college seemed the natural thing to do.

When he came home on his first term holidays he was bitter about the college. He was bored, he said, and had nothing to do. He wanted to stay at home. Di and Danny put up a fight and insisted he at least finished the year. 'If you still feel the same way at Christmas then we'll talk about you leaving,' they told the upset Danny.

Di and Danny decided they would have to try and keep Danny busy at the college for the remainder of the year. When he left they gave him orders to make as many saddle bags, quartpot holders and dinner hobble straps as he could. They would sell the equipment for him to the ringers on the station.

But not one saddle bag, quartpot holder or dinner hobble arrived in the Dunbar mailbag. Dan was having the time of his life down at the college and simply couldn't find the time for leather work. In 1981, his final year, he became president of the college's rodeo and rifle clubs and was a member of the horse club. The icing was put on the cake when, at the graduation ceremony, he was named runner-up to the dux in the final year. He was also the college's most improved student and winner of its grain crop award. Dan Bird jnr, it seemed, had come to grips with life on the outside. The shy bush kid who didn't want to leave home had thrown himself into the system and come out on top.

At home now on Dunbar, where he wanted to be all those years, he is one of the station's most valued employees. His education at the Burdekin Rural Education Centre taught him the importance of versatility, and now he can turn his hand to anything from welding and motor repairs to horse breaking.

Despite the problems of correspondence education, Di Bird insists that all her children stay at home until the eighth grade. Once they leave home at the end of seventh grade they come back rarely. 'You never really get to see your kids once they leave home. It's not so bad with boys because they usually come home to work on the station, but with girls it's different. They have to leave the bush to find a job once they have finished at school,' Di explained.

Bush children doing correspondence are now the recipients of advanced communications technology. A lot of their lessons are on prerecorded tapes, and in 1983 it is anticipated that video lessons will be introduced. This is a far cry from the old days when the bag of written lessons arrived at the homestead every five days from the Primary Correspondence School in Brisbane.

Di Bird has no criticism of either the School of the Air or the Primary Correspondence School. They both supply a terrific resource to the bush and are always available to help out with specific learning problems. Despite the geographic isolation of the students, Di Bird said it is a personalised form of teaching. Both the School of the Air and the Primary Correspondence School go out of their way to ensure no student is left behind. Both organisations have an extensive library system from which children can borrow books. Di's two children currently doing correspondence, Wayne, seven, and Jenny, five, are avid readers, and books are borrowed for them from libraries at Kowanyama and Normanton. All books are posted to the station, as Dunbar is 265 kilometres north of Normanton and 104 kilometres east of Kowanyama. Getting to either of these two places involves bouncing over some of the worst roads in Queensland. Any special learning problems that young students have can be handled by itinerant teachers. These teachers perform an invaluable task in the outback and much of their work is directed at helping mothers and governesses with teaching problems.

Governesses are a problem at times, in that not many girls want to live on a station as isolated as Dunbar. Once there, they are virtually prisoners of the environment. The closest town to the south is Normanton, and at the best of times it is a five to seven hour drive. The nearest town to the east is Chillagoe and it is an eight to ten hour drive. It might be remembered that neither of these communities offers the sort of charm or gaiety which might appeal to the romantic mind of a southern maiden. The fact that the roads are cut for six months every year does not help the situation.

Di prefers to employ governesses who live in north Queensland, so that if they do get homesick they can go home for a while. At least then there is a chance of their coming back. It is expensive to travel to the south and girls from Brisbane and outlying areas usually never return after they have left for a holiday.

The Dunbar schoolroom in one corner of the cool homestead kitchen is the same as schoolrooms anywhere. Posters are on the wall and paintings by Jenny and Wayne hang from the old hardwood rafters. It is run along strict lines. If Wayne wants to go and help Dad with the mustering during school hours, he has to catch up on his school work in his own time. School gets under way every morning at 8.30. At smoko time they trot off to the roomy men's kitchen beside the house where they share tea and homemade biscuits with the mechanic and cook and the rest of the permanent homestead-based staff. Then it's back to the schoolroom until the books are closed at 3.30 pm. Anyone behind in their school work has to stay behind or have a short lunch hour.

In the summer months when the sun beats into the kitchen and young minds wander into drowsy oblivion, Di finds that it is better to fit as much work into the morning session as possible. No one, whether it be teacher or student, can be expected to operate at peak efficiency through the appalling afternoon heat.

Di copes well with the isolation, but laughs gaily when she mentions how much she enjoys their four weeks' annual leave. Holidays have to be taken over the wet season when there is little activity on the station. The normal station routine gets under way again in March, when the cowboy and cook return and the ringers begin to drift in for the commencement of the mustering season. And the action is on for another six or seven months.

As well as supervising the running of the house and homestead kitchen, Di can be called on to perform almost any duty on the station. Her bright smile flashes as she talks about the times she has had to deal with men in delirium tremens, commonly referred to as the horrors. After a heavy drinking session a man might begin to see terrible things: monsters, snakes, murderers stalking him with axes and knives. A man goes out of his senses and sometimes wanders off. In the vast bush this can be tantamount to signing a death warrant. A man in the horrors at Dunbar once walked away from the station and became lost. A search was organised with the help of the Normanton police and the man was found beside a waterhole where he had 'come to'. If he hadn't come out of the horrors beside that waterhole the story would probably have ended on a different note.

Sometimes, Di said, people had to be put on roster to watch over a man in the horrors during the night so he didn't walk away or injure himself. Victims of the horrors have been known to cut their own throats. Di Bird recalled having to lock one such individual inside a horse crate after it became apparent he was hell-bent on self-destruction.

The danger time for the horrors is when a man has come back to the station after spending a week or so in town. Di Bird knows the pattern. He will have had nothing to eat while away and will have drunk enough liquor to pay for the local publican's next holiday at Surfers Paradise. When he returns to the station he will be okay for two or three days and then it will happen. He will be hit by the horrors. Green and yellow serpents will chase him out of his room and outside hidden snipers will fire at him from the tree tops.

Across the river at Koolatah Station, David Hughes told me how he found a contractor who was doing some work for him sitting on the back of his burned-out truck holding a rifle. When David and another man approached him he sang out to them to be careful:

'There's someone trying to murder me.' David and his companion overpowered the man and were able to get him into a vehicle and into Chillagoe.

All during the long drive into town the contractor happily listened to Slim Dusty playing through his wrist watch. His truck back at the station was a burned-out wreck. Apparently he had set fire to it in an attempt to flush out his imaginary killers.

Koolatah

David Hughes reckons he was born at Cunnamulla on a Black Friday in 1953 in the middle of a dust storm. If so it wouldn't be the only storm Hughsie has kicked up in his day.

David and I were good friends going right back to our junior school days at a Gold Coast boarding school. We were both pretty dab hands at working the wrong side of the law as far as school life was concerned. We got up to the sorts of things which breed a natural jungle cunning and a profound understanding about the foibles of school authority.

One sunny Saturday towards the end of our Grade Nine year we were skilfully camouflaged in some long grass munching on carrots and other edibles we had scored from a raid on the headmaster's vegetable garden. It was a blissful scene. Hughsie, I remember, had just lain back in the grass with a Log Cabin cigarette hanging from the corner of his mouth when all of a sudden a shadow loomed over us. We jumped to our feet, ready to cut the breeze, but it was too late. The shadow, to our visible disappointment, belonged to Gus, the crusty old school headmaster. All around us were green carrot tops and orange peels. Our fingers were in the till, so to speak.

Gus, at the time, was lacking in the qualities of sympathy and humour, and ordered one of his lackeys to deliver upon our respective backsides six of the very best with ye old whippy cane. Not satisfied with this close relation of capital punishment, he then ordered that all our leave be cancelled for the following year. This meant no Sundays or weekends away from the school. Now that *was* a blow.

When I arrived back at school the following year there was no Hughsie. His father, I later learnt, had received one of those letters advising him that 'young David' might be better suited to some other school. In other words, 'we don't want the little bugger back'. Hughsie's father packed him off to All Souls at Charters Towers. It so happened that some time later a bloke arrived at The Southport School from All Souls after his father had got one of those same letters from the All Souls' principal. In a sense the two schools had executed a kind of swap.

At school Hughsie was a tough, freckly-faced little bloke with a fringe of straight brown hair and a cowlick. He was pretty handy with the 'dukes' and wasn't above bringing them into action when the occasion warranted.

Oftentimes he had one or the other hand in plaster after cracking a knuckle or two on some opponent's head.

He had come straight into boarding school at Grade Six level from Nocatunga Station in the Queensland Channel Country. He was used to the wide, open spaces and the company of men more than twice his age. Petty school officials and the day-to-day discipline of boarding school life were a long way from the stretching horizons and knockabout ringers on Nocatunga. Like most kids from the really geographically isolated areas, he was independent. And independence is not a desirable characteristic in an institution that dotes on conformity.

There was a time in our Grade Nine year when grizzly old Jack Fitzgerald, the Nocatunga head stockman, drove up to the school gates and left David with two cartons of Red Rothman cigarettes and some biscuits. Jack was on his way to Moray Downs in the Clermont district, where he was going to run the mustering camp for David's father, Bill Hughes, who had taken over the management of the property.

That same year I went out to Moray Downs with David on school holidays. We were both looking forward to it, as we were going to spend a week out in the mustering camp with the ringers. We reckoned this was pretty tough stuff at twelve years of age—spending a solid week in the saddle and sleeping in a swag. It was to prove a memorable sojourn for reasons other than the above.

One afternoon Hughsie and I arrived back early to the camp with the ringers. Jack Fitzgerald was still out tracking a mob of cattle and was not expected back at the camp until after dark.

Two of the ringers produced a bottle of OP rum from the depths of a swag and poured two very generous nips in a couple of tin pannikins for the 'young fellers'.

Every man in the camp, including old Norm the cook, crowded around as we threw the lethal brew down straight without water. For a full minute I didn't know if my eyes were going to burst from their sockets first or if the top of my skull was going to blast into space. The ringers thought it a huge joke, and for the remainder of the afternoon Hughsie and I lay on our swags and watched the sun retreat slowly over the gidyea trees.

It was just after dark when Jack brought the cattle back and we all raced to our horses, which we had left saddled in the shade of a clump of trees. I remember fumbling madly with the Bates fastener on my saddle girth as I tried to cinch it tight. Nearby, Hughsie sat between the front legs of his horse, giggling wildly as he tried to undo the leather hobble straps. In time we both made it into the saddle and set off in rather awkward pursuit of the cattle which had broken at the yards and headed for the timber. My horse, in control of the situation, paced through the scrub after the mob while I grabbed with my hands and legs as much leather as I could in order to stay on. That night the sparks flew in the camp when Jack Fitzgerald tore strips from the ringers who had given us the rum. Jack, by the way, can now be found on Augustus Downs, in the Gulf country, which is managed by Philip Hughes, David's younger brother.

David's first job after leaving All Souls in 1969 was as a stockman on Fort Constantine Station, north of Cloncurry. David's father, Bill Hughes, was and still is the manager of 'The Fort', and is pastoral supervisor over the eighteen stations owned by the Stanbroke Pastoral Company in Queensland.

Jack Fitzgerald was the head stockman on the station at the time and was charged with the responsibility of moulding the young David into a bushman. 'Fitzy', as he is called, had been a part of the Hughes family for a long time. Over the years David had become a kind of surrogate son to the tough old bachelor stockman. Jack was going to make his young charge into a 'good man' or he was going to break him in the process.

David recalled a day when they were drafting horses at 'The Fort'. In an atmosphere of swirling dust, heat and nervous horses, Jack screamed out what seemed an impossible order to David. The young sixteen-year-old, in a fit of temper, glared back at his tough taskmaster through the rails and yelled at him to 'get fucked!' Jack spun where he stood and charged towards the rails to get at David, who by then was nothing more than a blur across the flat, travelling as fast as his high-heeled Williams boots could carry him. When in a fighting mood, Jack Fitzgerald is said to be a good man to stay away from.

David left Fort Constantine after being broken-in by Jack and went to work on the 3108 square kilometre Abingdon Downs Station, north of Georgetown.

One of the first things a young bloke learns when he lives and works in a mustering camp is to get on with the cook. This has to be done no matter how nasty, snakey or vindictive that particular individual may be.

Camp cooks, as a rule, are not an easy lot to get along with. Whether this has something to do with the hardships involved with their particular calling to the culinary art, or whether it is to do with plain orneryness, is a matter for speculation. Like most who dedicate their lives to the preparation of food and beverage, they are a most unpredictable lot. Manoeuvreing oneself into a position of favour with a camp cook requires immense tact and better than a layman's knowledge of the intricate workings of human psychological processes.

But in all fairness, theirs as a rule is a hard road to hoe. They fight a never-ending battle with the elements. Branches pulled from trees are used as windbreaks around the fireplace where the bread and damper is made, and where the interminable curries and stews boil in blackened pots. They are at perpetual war with ants, possums and other creatures of the bush interested in the contents of their tucker boxes.

David once spent an afternoon fishing with a camp cook at a waterhole on Abingdon Downs. The cook, in a mood of festive merriment, called David over to complain of a snag which had caught his line deep in the pool. Would David be a good bloke and swim down and release the line? David, seizing the opportunity to get in the cook's good favours, stripped off and dived into the waterhole. Hand over hand he followed the line down into the depths. The line ran into a clump of moss-covered branches and he followed it along carefully, thinking the hook would have snagged on one of the twigs. He worked his finger along gently, probing into the darkness as a surgeon might when searching for an appendix in the intestinal maze. Then his fingers closed over something soft. He felt again. This time it squirmed and wriggled at his touch.

He didn't try it again. He flailed his arms at his sides, kicked his feet and shot out of the water like a Polaris missile. The old cook was rolling around on the bank, clutching his sides in helpless mirth. David, white faced and dripping, wasn't laughing. What had happened was that the cook had hooked a file snake, which is a large water snake found in the Gulf. When caught on a line, these snakes invariably entwine themselves around a snag and cannot be pulled free without breaking the line. The cook, of course, knew what he had on his line all the time.

In mid-1972 nineteen-year-old David was sent to Beresford Station in the Clermont district, where he was placed in charge of his first mustering camp. In 1973 he was appointed head stockman on 2330 square kilometre Donnors Hill Station in the Croydon district. In 1974, looking for a change from the bush, he went and tried a variety of jobs, including horse breaking and bricklaying in the Northern Territory, washing ceilings in Brisbane after the 1974 floods, and working as a deck hand on a Yeppoon-based charter boat. In 1975 he returned to the bush to look after Koolatah, which is owned by Bill Hughes and his two brothers Cec and Herb. The brothers also own Dixie Station in the Peninsula, which is managed by Herb. In 1976 David left for the Northern Territory to run a mustering camp on 10 360 square kilometre Elroy Downs for the Australian Agricultural Company. He was at the time one of the youngest head stockmen ever to have worked for the AA Company. In 1977 he was transferred back to Queensland to manage Drumduff, a 3108 square kilometre out-station of Wrotham Park in the Peninsula. In July 1981 he took over the management of 5700 square kilometre Koolatah Station for his family.

After calling in at Dunbar on the way to Koolatah, Di Bird warned me against trying to drive across the river at the crossing. 'No worries,' I said. 'I'll leave the vehicle on this side and walk up to the homestead.' Di said that in the meantime she would try and get Koolatah on the radio and let them know I was on my way. I had Danny Mortison, a Townsville based reporter, with me at the time and we had a swim at the crossing before starting the long walk up to the house.

We had just breasted the northern bank when a Toyota appeared coming down the track. It was David. 'What sort of vehicle are you driving?' he asked.

'A Hilux four-wheel-drive,' I replied.

'Oh, shit,' he said, 'you'll get across easily in that.'

So back we went and I drove the Hilux across the sand to the edge of the water. The river at this particular point is about 550 metres wide from bank to bank. But the actual width of water is about 140 metres. The water at the crossing at its deepest is about a metre deep, but it is fast flowing and runs over very soft sand. We prepared a run-up for the vehicle over the dry sand and covered the engine with my swag wrap to protect the electrics from the spray. Everything was as ready as it could be.

'You're going to think I'm a real bastard if you get bogged in there,' David said, pointing to the fast, clear water.

I looked and told him that bloody oath I would.

I reversed back over the packed sand, stopped, and accelerated forward. The Hilux hit the water at about 20 kilometres per hour, ploughed on gamely for another fifteen metres and died. Gradually it sank down into the soft sand, and the mighty Mitchell River, the river I have loved the most out of all rivers, started to run through the cabin of my brand new Hilux.

David looked sheepishly sideways at me and I could see a faint smile tugging at the corners of his mouth.

'The bastard,' I thought.

After two hours of swearing and heaving we managed to tow the vehicle out to the Dunbar side of the river where we left it. As we walked across the river to where the Koolatah Toyota was parked, David looked up and down the Mitchell and remarked:

'This is God's own country, isn't it?'

'Yes,' I said. 'It really is.'

Away at all points the wild Peninsula bush scrambled towards the horizons. Towering fortresses of rubber vine, the choking exotic vine pest, hung from the riverside gums. The metallic glint of the sun burned down from a royal blue sky. And as if following a snake's trail from the east, the Mitchell River, one of Mother Nature's most extravagant gifts to a wilderness, flowed silently towards the Gulf.

I wasn't surprised to hear David speak of this part of the Peninsula as 'God's own country'. It was in his blood as a nine-year-old schoolboy. His infrequent visits had been made with his father from Nocatunga, but there had been enough of them to fire the pulse of the Gulf in his blood. At school he regaled us with stories about crocodiles, sawfish, barramundi, and Old Spud, the ancient black man who lived in the Koolatah black's camp. Old Spud had fathered countless children and his wrists were badly scarred from handcuffs which were roughly removed by sympathisers after he escaped from troopers some time in his youth. The Koolatah black's camp, like all station camps, was disbanded soon after the Act changed giving Aboriginals equal rights. The Hughes family, like nearly all other station owners, could not afford to feed, clothe and pay the large numbers of blacks who made Koolatah their home. Old Spud has long since joined his ancestors, but the corrugated iron shed where he lived with his wife and people still stands a few hundred yards distant from the Koolatah homestead.

As a thirty-year-old cattleman today, David Hughes still loves that virgin bushland. He accepts its crushing seasons and its pitiful isolation with equanimity—a casual 'such is life' attitude. But at the same time he has not grown blasé to its wild beauty and its savage charms.

As far as cattle country goes he accepts that it is not as attractive as some areas. He sees this as a challenge.

'Just about everything up here is a challenge. Things like reading the country, mustering the cattle, getting and holding on to good men. They are all challenges. The biggest one of them all is reading the country and being able to get the cattle out of the scrub,' he explained.

Koolatah is blessed with water. The 12 000 cattle it carries have a run which includes a 100 kilometre frontage to the Mitchell River and a 112 kilometre frontage to the Alice River, and there are numerous lagoons and creeks.

Finding and getting their cattle to the yards and ultimately to the market place is the eternal problem faced by Peninsula cattlemen. A helicopter has been used on Koolatah the past two seasons to help with the mustering. But David believes this system of mustering carries its own inherent problems. One of these is ground-to-air communications and another is pilots who don't know how to read country or handle cattle.

The communications problem means that ground stockmen often have to try and guess what the pilot is going to do and vice-versa. And a pilot who does not know the country he is supposed to be mustering will inevitably push cattle in the wrong direction, resulting in lost time and, often, lost cattle. Despite his misgivings about chopper mustering, however, he does believe it is a 'good thing'. On the other hand he does not want to get into a situation where he has to rely on helicopters indefinitely. Once all the rogue cattle are off the station he would like to dispense with the helicopters.

'I prefer ground mustering because it's better for the cattle and it's better for training men,' he says. By 'training men' he means teaching ringers how to read country and how to handle cattle. Put simply, they stand a better chance of becoming good bushmen.

Shotguns have been used for some years on Koolatah to get the wilder cattle out of the thick scrub and the rubber vine which chokes the river country. Old cleanskin cattle and rogue bullocks learn after a short time that the chopper cannot hurt them. It can make a lot of noise and hover over them, but it cannot actually touch them. But the situation changes when a shotgun is poked out of the bubble and a few pellets of number seven duck shot sting their hides. This is not a practice which might appeal to animal liberationists. It is, however, a necessary one. The fact remains, too, that towards the end of the 1980s all these wild cattle may have to be shot to comply with the Queensland Department of Primary Industries tuberculosis and brucellosis disease eradication programme.

There is also a lot of noogoora burr, berry bush and freshwater mangrove scrub country on Koolatah. All this makes an ideal sanctuary for the wild cattle. Towards the mouth of the Mitchell, the river breaks into numerous large islands covered in jungle and is intricately hard to muster. The helicopter has proven useless in this country, and usually it takes two rounds of the full mustering team of ten men to get a sixty-five per cent muster on these islands. This is dangerous work and involves the throwing of wild cattle by the tail either from the ground or from horseback. Not long ago a ringer was badly horned by a scrub bull after he had thrown it. The horn ripped the man's stomach open, exposing his intestines. He was taken back to the homestead and a call was made to the Royal Flying Doctor in Cairns. Noting the urgency of the situation, the Flying Doctor had a commercial charter flight which was flying in the area at the time diverted to the Koolatah airstrip. The injured man was carried into the plane and an elderly male tourist was requested to keep pressure on the ruptured stomach with his hands to prevent the total dislodgement of the intestine. During the flight back to Cairns the elderly tourist suffered a heart attack, but it was reported that both men survived their respective ordeals.

A matter which might interest some is that a Peninsula identity, whom David quoted as a reliable source, vows and declares there is some sort of manlike monster living on the islands down near the mouth of the Mitchell.

Another method used to capture wild cattle on Koolatah is described as 'blood bagging'. This involves either putting blood in bags or simply dropping the intestines of a dead bullock or cow near a cattle pad leading from a scrub. When the wild cattle leave the scrub just on sundown to feed out in the more open country, the bulls especially are attracted to the gore. Most people have probably seen on television how elephants behave when one of their herd is killed. They prance around the corpse, smell it and generally carry on with much ado. Cattle, and particularly bulls, do much the same thing.

While the herd of wild cattle is dancing around the blood bag or the pile of intestine, the ringers move in from behind with a herd of quiet coacher cattle. The wild cattle cannot retreat to the scrub, and being caught more or less in the open makes it easier to round them up. Once they have settled down in the coacher mob they are quietly driven back to the yards. The use of coacher cattle is common on nearly all stations with a rogue cattle problem. Wild cattle are almost impossible to muster back to the yards without losing some of the more desperate ones to the bush and exhausting men and horses in the process. Usually a coacher mob will contain a quiet lead bullock which the herd will follow faithfully back to the yards. It is interesting to note that most meatworks use these Judas bullocks to lead the cattle to be slaughtered up to the killing ramp. Once near the top the Judas is drafted off and his followers go through to the killing floor. During a single season the Judas will lead thousands upon thousands of his kind to their death at the hands of the slaughterman.

'Moonlighting' wild cattle was occasionally practised on Abingdon Downs when David was working there as a young stockman. This involves a team of men riding out at night to catch the scrubbers feeding out in the open. Cattle are, as a rule, a lot easier to handle at night and it was a fairly successful form of mustering. However the dangers for a man galloping around in the bush at night after cattle are numerous and 'moonlighting' was not a favourite occupation among the Abingdon ringers.

This 'moonlighting' can also take another form. An old Channel Country stockman told me years ago of how he and a team of men would throw wild cattle at night and tie their horns with wet greenhide. After the horns were tied they would leave the beast free to walk around. The next day they would return and usually they would find the cattle rubbing their heads against the trunks of trees not far from where they were thrown. His theory was that the agony of the contracting greenhide pulling in their horns was so great that the animals could not stand to walk any distance.

Eventually David Hughes plans to breed his own bulls on Koolatah. This, he said, would involve buying two good-quality bulls and putting them over a selection of his best cows. The biggest male calves from this association will then be used as sires on the station. He believes this will lead to a herd of cattle better suited to the harsh Peninsula environment and will bypass the need of having to buy bulls from studs.

The Koolatah cattle herd consists basically of Brahman stock but David is looking towards the day when he will be running a Droughtmaster herd. This line of thinking towards a 'softer' *Bos indicus* line is not unique in Cape York. A common complaint among cattlemen is that their Brahman cattle have become too wild and too difficult to handle. Some station owners admit that they have not even got the horses to catch the long-legged Brahmans once they are in full flight.

The Droughtmaster, they say, with its Brahman and Santa Gertrudis bloodlines, will make for a more manageable herd.

Brahman cattle have been the mainstay of the Gulf and Peninsula cattle industry for many years. Without the breed David Hughes reckons that Koolatah would have been a 'broke' station long ago. No one disputes the fact that Brahman cattle are a tough, resourceful breed and that they can thrive in the sort of country that starves the softer British breeds such as Hereford and Shorthorn. But the fact remains that, until a strong, long-term docility characteristic is bred into the Brahman breed, its future in the far north Queensland cattle industry will be uncertain.

Koolatah is spread across the sort of country which titillates the more adventurous strings of the imagination. It has all the ingredients of a *Boys Own* classic—deep and mysterious waterholes, crocodiles, barramundi, wild horses and cattle and those sensual, jungle-clad islands. A fiction writer looking for a wild Australian background could find no better place. At a spot called The Lakes on Yanco Creek, a tributary of the Mitchell, a large stingray was caught. When it was put on the back of a Toyota Landcruiser, the flaps touched the ground on either side.

The Lakes waterhole is some twenty-five kilometres long and has an estimated depth of twenty metres. It is assumed, of course, that salt water crocodiles inhabit it and no one would dream of plunging in for a swim.

Occasionally horses disappear on the station and the blame for this is nearly always laid at the jaws of the crocs. Only days before I arrived at Koolatah a horse had one of its back legs ripped open at a waterhole called the Jewfish Hole on Eight Mile Creek. The only safe place for swimming on the station is at the Dunbar-Koolatah crossing, where the water is shallow. But this is not considered 100 per cent safe, as crocodiles have been sighted short distances downstream from the crossing on several occasions.

Freshwater lagoons, which are numerous all along the Mitchell River, are said to be the most likely places in which to encounter a saltwater crocodile. Usually a lone croc will stake out a lagoon for himself at the end of a wet season, particularly if it has an adequate supply of barramundi.

On a canoe trip I did down the Mitchell in 1978 with friends, we took precautions against crocodiles and sharks after a series of waterfalls on Gamboola Station. These falls roughly mark the river's pass through the Great Dividing Range and are some 500 kilometres from its mouth. The first night we camped just below the falls. We were woken in the early hours by stingrays feeding in the shallows on food scraps we had tossed into the river. Not far downriver at the junction of the Walsh and Mitchell Rivers I caught two sawfish on live catfish bait.

Being on the northern bank of the Mitchell, well away from the main Peninsula track, puts Koolatah in a very isolated position for most months of the year. It is nearly impossible to get to the station by vehicle from November through to July. The Dunbar-Koolatah crossing is nearly always out of the question, and another crossing well up-stream on Wrotham Park is passable only for a few months each year. This road leads through Drumduff and across the Palmer River to Koolatah.

Wet season supplies are brought in every October and these may have to last for as long as seven months. Fuel supplies for the station are bought once a year, and to cut transport costs David has the fuel unloaded at the

Dunbar side of the river. He floats the forty-four gallon drums across to the Koolatah side. Heavy transports have no way at all of getting across the river and all cattle taken from Koolatah have to be walked over to Dunbar and yarded before they can be trucked.

But even more isolated than Koolatah is Sefton, an 800 square kilometre station owned by Norman 'Nugget' Finch and his wife Pam. Sefton joins Koolatah on the latter's northern boundary and runs through what is known as the 'forest country'. This is mainly ti-tree timbered country and does not rate highly as cattle land. But it is home to Nugget and Pam and their 700 cattle and they work it and love it and lavish almost every second of their lives upon that desperate, unyielding country. Side by side they work, day in and day out, fencing, yard building, tending to their stock, looking to the day when Sefton will become a viable cattle operation. Nugget envisages the day when Sefton will carry 1200 cattle.

Nugget was born in the Gulf country township of Georgetown, the son of a sleeper cutter. At ten years of age he was out in the rugged Newcastle Range area around Einasleigh, working shoulder to shoulder with his father, pushing a crosscut saw through ironwood and box trees. In five years he cut thousands of sleepers for the Queensland Railways Department.

When he was fifteen his father took him off to Mt Surprise, where they established themselves as stockyard building contractors. A typical set of yards would take six months to build, and the hundreds of post holes which had to be sunk were dug through the hard basalt with a crowbar and a long handled shovel. In the slamming heat of the north Queensland sun this was hard work at its awesome best.

Nugget eventually drifted away from yard building and into stock work on the stations. He worked as a ringer and drover through the lower Gulf country until he bought Sefton in 1967. There is no proud old two-storey station homestead on Sefton to signify past eras of quiet affluence. This is a young, sixteen-year-old station that in its brief life has been assailed by drought, depressed cattle prices and a flood of almost biblical magnitude. Nugget and Pam's homestead is a tin hut with a dirt floor. Almost hermit-like in their isolation, they rarely travel to the 'outside world', much preferring the solitude of Sefton and the fight they share together against Mother Nature and her bitter elements.

I met Nugget and Pam at Koolatah, when they arrived with a mob of cattle they had been driving for three days from Dixie Station. Pam had acted as the cook on the three-day trip for Nugget and the team of Aboriginal stockmen.

I mentioned that I would like to talk to them about their operation at Sefton. And could I use the information in a book I was going to write? Pam laughed and Nugget shuffled his feet in the dust and muttered that they wouldn't have anything to interest me. Nugget spent the next two days dodging me at every turn, but I eventually trapped him in the cattle yards on the third day and the two of us squatted in the dust as horses milled about and had our talk. Nugget answered my questions quietly and shyly as Pam walked restlessly in the background with one ear cocked for what the damn pesky reporter was saying.

Their only communication with the outside world from Sefton is a two-

School's in at Dunbar Station in Cape York.

One-armed cook on Koolatah Station.

Action on Batavia Downs.

way radio. On this they can send telegrams to the Cairns Royal Flying Doctor base. They have no mail service, and any mail sent to them goes to either Dixie or Koolatah where it is collected every one or two months.

Like Koolatah, Nugget and Pam get in a year's supply of stores every October before the wet season starts. This usually involves the purchase of about six bags of sugar, a carton of tea, several drums of flour and enough packets of Flagship tobacco to last Nugget the year. They are cut off by road from civilisation for six months of the year. If they want to get out in this time they have to do so on horseback, and this involves swimming numerous creeks and rivers. Their saving grace during this period should they have an accident is the Royal Flying Doctor Medical Kit, which is provided free of charge to all isolated stations on the network.

The continual battle of life on the land has been alleviated somewhat by tin scratching excursions to the Chillagoe area during the wet season. But in recent years, with falling tin prices and the monopolistic hold on land by big mining companies through 'Authority to Prospect' leases, tin scratching has yielded minimal profits. A reduction in tin quotas announced by the Government in mid-1982 delivered the final crushing blow to this enterprise as far as small operators were concerned.

But in past wet seasons Nugget and Pam have collected their two young children from school at Mareeba on the Atherton Tableland, and taken them into the wild limestone mountain country around Chillagoe. The children spend their holidays in the makeshift camp helping to look for the grey metal along the rocky creeks and boulder-strewn hills.

Nugget and Pam's one regret about living at Sefton is that they rarely see their children. It is a bone-jarring twelve hour drive over rough bush tracks from Sefton to Mareeba. Weekend visits to see the kids are out of the question. And when they are home on holidays, Nugget and Pam are usually working at one corner of the property mending a stock yard or building a fence line. The education of their children is one of Nugget's and Pam's main expenses, but it is one they are prepared to live with. Despite the fact that they both had little access to formal education when they were young, they want their children to stay at school and finish their secondary education. Nugget is not sure if he wants them to come back to Sefton and help with the work when they finish at school. 'I'd want the young feller to knock around a bit first and see how the other half lives,' he explained as he rolled a smoke in the stock yard.

Seeing how the other half lives is important to Nugget. Through his days cutting sleepers in the Newcastle Range, his ringing and droving in the Gulf, up to his ownership of Sefton, he has never travelled out of the Peninsula or Gulf. He has never been to Townsville or Brisbane, but said with a smile that he spent two days in Cairns 'a couple of years ago'.

On his last night at Koolatah before heading back to Sefton, Nugget, with a cold beer in his palm, stretched out in a squatter's chair on the wide station verandah. Pam sat close beside him. Someone strummed a guitar and sang the words of a country and western song. Nugget mouthed the words of the song softly to himself. He looked the most contented man alive.

Van Rook

There was a song which tickled the funny bone of most Australians in the late 1950s called 'The Pommy Jackeroo'. It poked all sorts of fun at a hapless young Englishman who had come out to Australia for the great adventure of working on a cattle station.

We got the picture that he was a gawky, bumbling youth who had nought in his favour except boundless enthusiasm and derring-do. He was the target for all sorts of pranks and the sole perpetrator of all sorts of blunders. But apart from the misfortunes that went hand-in-hand with his new chum's inexperience, we got the feeling he was a likeable sort of bloke, and that one day the area behind his ears would dry up and he would become a 'good man'. In the meantime he had to endure all the taunts which are part and parcel of trying out a new job in a tough land.

Peter Fox-Linton is one such pommy jackeroo. An ex-public schoolboy and son of a retired civilian lecturer from Sandhurst Military College (Captain Mark Philips' alma mater, no less), he was polishing a saddle with the seat of his Levis on Van Rook Station, north of Normanton, when I caught up with him in 1982. Fox-Linton has found out with some measure of displeasure that the mirth surrounding the concept of the pommy jackeroo is alive and well in this country. Not long after he carried his swag into the Van Rook jackeroos' quarters, he was forced into defending his right as an Englishman to work on an Australian station. Fox-Linton, 20, put up the 'dukes' and gave his chief tormentor, a tousle-haired scallywag, a good healthy drubbing. From that moment on there was a marked improvement in the treatment accorded the Englishman by the young Australian stockmen on the station.

Fox-Linton is tall and dark haired, and when I met him he was burnt a ruddy brown from the Gulf country sun. Searching the ti-tree scrubs and kunai grass country of Van Rook for cattle is about as far removed from life in Surrey as an Eskimo selling life insurance in Alice Springs.

After finishing school at Eastbourne College on the English south coast, Peter travelled to Australia and found work on a sheep property near Orange in New South Wales. He left after two months and travelled to New Zealand and toured the North Island on a 10-speed push bike. 'A bit lonely at times, but good for you,' was his only comment on the trip.

104

When he returned to Australia he travelled straight to the Northern Territory, where he had a pre-arranged job on Ban Ban Springs—a cattle and buffalo station 193 kilometres south of Darwin. Fox-Linton thought he was going to be right in the middle of a professional outfit. What he got was a run-down station. The main preoccupation on the property was buffalo catching. Helicopters would muster the beasts towards portable yards, and the buffaloes would be forced into the yards by men in four-wheel-drive vehicles.

Fox-Linton kept his eyes open in the Territory. It was, as it would be for any young Englishman with a yen for action, a rich experience. 'The Territory,' he told me, 'is supposed to be a civilised place since the cyclone. But you can still find trouble there if you look for it. You can get tied up with illegal pet food operations and that sort of thing without too much trouble. There are plenty of blokes running around towing horse floats behind their Landcruisers. But what's in those floats? Not horses half the time but deep freezers filled with illegally shot meat.'

Sitting on his bunk in the Van Rook quarters, Fox-Linton explained how 'you could still feel the shadow of the past in the Territory—all these misfits and money makers lured to the frontier'.

He left Ban Ban Springs after five months, but said with the benefit of hindsight that he should only have stayed five days. There was little money being invested in the property, and scant opportunity to learn about the nuts and bolts operation of a cattle station.

After leaving Ban Ban Springs he was granted an extension to his travel visa, and accepted a job bull catching on Tipperary Station south of Darwin. But when he arrived at Tipperary he found there was no bull catching in progress and was assigned to general duties on an out-station.

On 10 December 1981 he returned to England and stayed for three months. Returning to his homeland, he was not without some misgivings. The green pastures and careful English manners were a far cry from the spinifex and rough and tumble ringers on the Territory stations. He went home, he said, to clear his head on what he wanted to do with his life. He wanted to make sure he was doing the right thing staying in Australia.

While in England he went and had an interview with a recruiting officer of the Gordon Highlanders, a Scottish regiment. Fox-Linton was offered a regular commission providing he passed the entrance examinations.

He explained to the recruiting officer that he wanted to spend some more time in Australia, working on the stations, before he made any commitment to the regiment. This was agreed to, and the offer still stands for him to return to England and sit for the entrance examinations. It seems that the British military establishment views with considerable favour any young Englishman swashbuckling around the antipodes.

'Most people at home, especially in the villages, believe that one of the greatest adventures left today is to work on an Australian cattle station. When I went home everyone wanted to know about it. You feel like a bit of a hero,' he said.

While in England he made up his mind that Australia was the place for him. He wrote to John Stewart, the general manager of Queensland Stations, for a job. A letter came back advising Fox-Linton he could have the position of second-year jackeroo on Van Rook. He packed his western shirts, blue jeans and R. M. Williams boots and caught the next plane back to Australia.

Of Normanton, Fox-Linton said he wasn't impressed when he first saw the place, but then again he wasn't surprised either.

'I'd seen it all in the Territory before,' he explained. Once again he had to cope with the culture shock. 'Seeing Normanton, the dissipated blacks roaming the streets, the hardness of it all, and then spending days in the saddle, I just thought "Oh my God".'

He is not blind to the fact that he is different to the other jackeroos and ringers on the station. In most cases their backgrounds are vastly different and he is an Englishman. But despite any initial trouble at settling in things soon settled down. The pommy jackeroo had slept enough nights in his swag out in the mustering camps and had ridden enough rough horses. He had proved himself.

There were, though, some things he could not accept. One of these was the young ringers' liking for the grog.

'It puts me off. I'm not a big drinker and I can't do what these young blokes do. I might have carried on like that when I was sixteen, but not now,' he explained.

Before going to Van Rook he had worked mainly with men who were out of their teens. He found their attitudes towards him different from those of the young eighteen- and twenty-year-olds on Van Rook. 'I got into a scrap soon after I was here. You have to let someone know when to stop. Things can only go so far. I don't like to polarise the other blokes, but then I'm not going to mimic their behaviour either. They have to realise that. You have to get used to irritating people and learn how to handle them. I learnt this at boarding school and it's not all that different in the mustering camp.'

Even though he said he has found the professionalism he was looking for on Van Rook, he still might return to England and take up the commission with the Gordon Highlanders. 'I'm English and I want to go home, but if things didn't work out there then I would come back here. If I came back I would probably try and get a job with the Department of Primary Industries or I might even try and work my way up to station manager. I don't know.'

It is the lifestyle, the reliance on one self, the danger, the skill, and the sheer romanticism of it all which keeps Fox-Linton in the saddle on Van Rook. It is a life, he explained, that really has no place in the latter part of the twentieth century.

'I like working with animals and the adrenalin buzz you get when something happens in the line of action. There is a fantastic feeling of self-reliance about it all.'

The jackeroo system has now changed radically from what it was ostensibly designed for in the early days of the industry. Then, and up to about a decade ago, a jackeroo working on a large cattle station was trained in everything from stock work to windmill mechanics to bookkeeping. Because they were inexperienced they were paid less, but it was anticipated that in most cases they would go on to become leaders and managers within the industry. Indeed, a jackeroo today is still basically a trainee manager. But it is the amount of training he gets to equip him adequately for this task that puts the whole ideological base of the system in question.

Pommy jackeroo Peter Fox-Linton giving his saddle cloth the tenderising treatment.

An Aboriginal stockman watches as the horse-tailer brings in the horses on Van Rook.

In years gone by there was also a distinct social demarcation between the stockmen on the station and the jackeroos. Today this is probably just as pronounced as it ever was on smaller properties in southern Queensland and New South Wales. But today in the Gulf country and on the big stations in the Northern Territory and the Kimberleys—the home of so-called egalitarianism—every man is equal from the crown of his dusty cowboy hat down to the soles of his cuban heeled boots.

On the big northern stations today the jackeroos do the same work as the stockmen. They spend the interminable months of the mustering season camped out in swags, living a day-to-day existence in the saddle. It is only in rare cases that they are provided with a wide spread of station experience. In reality, a jackeroo today might go from his first to his fourth year without ever taking the head from a windmill or pulling a bore. One thing he will do plenty of is mustering cattle. There is no question at all about that.

There is, too, the suspicion that some of the large pastoral houses are deliberately exploiting the archaic jackeroo system as a cheap labour source. John Stewart of Queensland Stations, a former jackeroo himself, claims that despite the obvious criticisms there is still a place in the industry today for the jackeroo. He does concur, however, that some large grazing companies might be taking advantage of this system and its meagre award wages.

In 1983 a first year jackeroo grosses $94.23 for a forty hour week spread over five and a half days. A second year jackeroo is entitled to $103.53 while a third year jackeroo receives the award payment of $140.53 a week. A station hand working the same hours is paid a gross wage of $188.45.

Unprecedented financial pressures in the cattle industry today force with an even heavier hand the old business maxim that profits must be made. One way to do this is to reduce labour costs and one way to reduce labour costs is to employ jackeroos.

Another problem associated with the training of jackeroos on large area stations today is the shortage of good bushmen to act as their tutors. Good bushmen, or 'good men' as they are simply called in the back country, are one of today's endangered species. In terms of skills they encompass all that is done in the bush. A 'good man' can fix an engine, diagnose the ailment of a sick horse, and ride forty miles in darkness through trackless bush and come out on target. He can in effect do just about everything that is asked of him.

Every station I visited lamented the passing of 'good men'. Jackeroos and young trainee stockmen are now, in the main, gaining what experience they can from head stockmen who as often as not have only been in the industry a few short years. How then do stations employing a high percentage of 'green' labour manage to muster their cattle successfully? It must be remembered that on some stations cattle are spread over hundreds of square miles of unfenced country. How can an inexperienced labour force be expected to comb these large areas without getting lost and without riding past large numbers of cattle? The answer is quite simple. According to John Stewart, the ground stockmen employed by Queensland Stations are no longer expected to muster these large areas. Nowadays these large areas are mustered by the grazing industry neophyte—the chopper pilot. He covers the large areas involved, pushes the cattle to a central spot where the jackeroos and ringers are waiting and from there they are walked back to the yards.

According to John Stewart, Queensland Stations will continue to use choppers for as long as the company can afford to keep them in the air.

What, then, will the situation be like in ten years' time? Will the labour situation have reached a standard of such gross inefficiency that large area operations might find themselves floundering? Will they, like the dinosaur, fall victim to their own unwieldy size? The answer to all these questions, according to John Stewart, is 'No'.

'In 1970 I probably thought the situation was going to be drastic in 1980. But it has not happened. We haven't yet got to the stage where we are unable to operate any of our properties.'

He does not see the situation becoming extreme in the ten years to 1993. Instead he believes that technological advances will enhance the operation of these stations and contribute favourably to the quality of life for people working on them. The communications satellite will bring untold benefits. The most obvious at this stage will be in the fields of education, television and telephone communication. Political pressure has been brought to bear on the Federal Government to stop the launch of the satellite in 1985. In July 1983 its future was in serious doubt.

Until this satellite becomes operational, most people living in the Gulf and Peninsula will have to be content with their radio telephones and two-way radios. Television is an almost unheard-of luxury in most parts of the Gulf and Peninsula.

The industry lost a lot of its most experienced staff in the 1970s beef recession. This was a time when many station owners were forced to stand down labour. This labour drifted into the towns and cities and found alternative employment. The burgeoning mining industry in Queensland absorbed many of them.

When the cattle prices stabilised in the late 1970s, this labour force did not return. It stayed in the coastal centres, the cities, and the mining towns. Why then didn't this labour market return? Weren't these the bushmen who loved hard riding? The men who never feared a spill? What were and what are they doing off-siding for boiler makers in Townsville, selling cars in Cairns and mining for nickel at Greenvale? They're making pretty good money, that's what. And they are experiencing a quality of life a lot of them never had before.

Most of these men, after they left the bush and started working in the factories and the mines, became aware of a strange phenomenon called Unionism. It got them good wages, tolerable working conditions and overtime payments if they worked longer than a forty hour week. 'Holy boon boon,' they said. 'We've been living in an industrial relations dark age.' No more did they have to spend months at a time living out of a swag in some isolated mustering camp where the staple diet was curry and rice and salt beef. No longer did they have to take their turn at running in the horses, climbing out of the swag at 3 am to catch the night horse. No more did they have to ride from sunrise to sundown, looking ahead to the horizon for the glimpse of a windmill and the hope of a drink of water. And no longer did they have to work on Saturday mornings. The weekends now were their own.

The plain fact is that the grazing industry has failed to keep pace with the sophisticated happenings in the arena of industrial relations. It has maintained

Paul and Flo Beard and their daughter Cynthia with a 'fair' haul of barramundi taken during a morning's fishing on Van Rook.

Parky Atkinson outside the shack where he lives on the bank of the Clarke River.

a conservative 'quartpot' mentality not conducive to enlightened thinking. In an age of industrial psychology, 'I'm OK — You're OK' awareness and militaristic union demands, the bulk of the grazing industry plods on as though in another world.

John Stewart believes that one thing which might relieve the labour situation in the future is the establishment of more married accommodation on stations. The lack of this type of accommodation is a factor contributing to the labour drain on the large stations, he said. In most cases, under the present preoccupation with single mens' accommodation, once a bush worker decides to get married, he has virtually no alternative but to move to a town or city. John Stewart's rationale for moving more towards married accommodation is that good men can be kept on the stations, and the children of these people will grow up on the properties learning about bush life right from their early years. 'They learn to ride and handle cattle at an early age and they become an important attribute to the industry.'

Rod Dixon, a former Territorian and manager of 7800 square kilometres Van Rook, sees the labour situation as a sensitive issue. The jackeroo system, he believes, has outlived its usefulness. The reason for this is that the majority of the workforce is made up of inexperienced young men. 'When a group of them are expected to work together they are like a mob of uneducated pups,' according to Dixon. They have little bush sense, get lost easily and are more prone to injury because of their inexperience. That they have no one to learn bush skills from is of paramount importance.

He maintains that the object today is still to give jackeroos special attention, grooming them for the day they might have to take over the management of a station. But, he says resignedly, they do not get this 'special attention' because they cannot be spared out of the mustering camp. Like John Stewart he believes that some pastoral companies are now viewing jackeroos as a cheap labour source, using them as a hedge against the inflationary wage spiral.

But what does the future hold for those young jackeroos who wish to make a career out of the cattle industry? According to Rod Dixon, their long-term futures within the industry are limited. Only a very small percentage of jackeroos in Queensland go on to become station managers. This figure is even less in the Northern Territory.

Most station managers, he said, come from the better class of stockman; a stockman who has come up through the ranks and who is familiar with most aspects of station operation. It is more important today in this era of staff shortages and budget cuts that a manager be familiar with all working components on a property. The duties of a manager in the 1980s are far more extensive than they were fifteen or twenty years ago. Those were the good old days when the manager was Lord over all he surveyed, and had an array of staff specialising in all phases of station activity.

The single most noticeable lack of specialised staff on large company-owned stations today is that of a bookkeeper. Rod Dixon's wife Val, like many managers' wives, spends four days a week in the office looking after the books. She does not get paid for this work. Dixon explained that, if Val didn't do this work, he would be unable to spend the time he does supervising the on-going operations on Van Rook.

On some company-owned properties, the manager's wife might also be expected to undertake the cooking for the home station staff. This workload is even further compounded if she is teaching children. A situation such as this, according to Val Dixon, ultimately leads to unhappiness and family breakdown.

Constant staff turnovers on a station like Van Rook mean that new men have to be trained continually. Helicopter pilots and head stockmen have to learn the country before they are of any use. Until they know the country and can effectively work it, Dixon says, they are as handy as a back pocket in a singlet.

He is proud of his ability to handle Aboriginal stockmen. Van Rook operates three permanent mustering camps: one from the home station; another at the out-station of Stirling; and another at the out-station of Macaroni on the coast. The Macaroni camp is an 'all black' camp and is made up of one Aboriginal head stockmen and six Aboriginal ringers. They are all experienced stock handlers and he claims they can do twice as much work in half as much time as the other two camps.

Dixon first started working with Aboriginal labour in 1955, when he commenced work in the cattle industry in the Northern Territory and the Kimberleys. One of the cardinal rules for a white man supervising bush Aboriginals is to maintain a high moral standard. He cited examples of young white head stockmen going to town and getting drunk with Aboriginals with whom they worked. Aboriginals, he said, viewed this sort of behaviour in a white man as a weakness and would exploit it in a mustering camp situation.

It is important, too, that a white man be able to do every task he asks his Aboriginal labour to do. And he must be fair. Once Aboriginals sense any discrimination against them, especially if it is in favour of a white man in the camp, they will lose interest in the job.

There is also a pecking order in the Aboriginal hierarchy which must be observed. Usually one man, through either ability or age, is the recognised leader of the group. Any approach to the group must be made through this man. If this man is getting on in years the smart head stockman will call him 'old man'. This is a term of respect. If, in turn, that Aboriginal respects his white supervisor, he might call him 'old man' or use the native word 'maluka'.

A young head stockman, ignorant of these different forms of simple protocol, can easily make blunder after blunder. He becomes frustrated and the Aborigines become frustrated. The system breaks down. It is not uncommon to hear of young white men who have left stations in the Northern Territory and parts of Queensland because they have been unable to manage Aboriginal labour.

There is even a protocol to observe when giving something to an Aboriginal. Giving is seen as a weakness by Aboriginals. Rod Dixon said the best way to give something away was to be seen throwing it away in a dump or handing it to a child. Either way the Aboriginals do not have to lose face by accepting a gift directly.

Dixon extends this 'giving' philosophy further to the grants made to Aboriginals by the Federal Government. He sees this form of 'giving' as a serious mistake, one which humiliates and alienates the recipients. Bush Aboriginals in the Northern Territory commonly referred to this money as 'sit down money'. It is money they know they are getting for doing nothing, and as a result have scent respect for it or for the Government giving it to them. Likewise, young Aboriginal children at boarding schools who are provided with pocket money by the government call this money their 'coon cheques'.

This latter demonstration is a sore point in many isolated communities in north Queensland. Aboriginal children living in these areas have their fares to and from school paid, their uniforms provided and their fees paid. Whites living in these same areas, particularly underprivileged whites, have to pay all the costs associated with sending their children away to boarding school. In communities such as Normanton and Burketown, resentment towards this bias is running dangerously high and, as a result, racial unrest is at an all time high.

No one can ever say there are too many dull moments on a cattle station. Excitement is always just around the corner, whether it be a young horse which might buck or bolt through the timber or wild cattle which have to be thrown or worked in the yards. There is usually something happening and each night around the mustering camp fire the men will laconically discuss the day's dramas. 'Close shaves' are talked about, but because they are so intrinsically woven into the pattern of everyday life, very little is usually made of them. A horse might fall with its rider at full gallop. This is a close shave. A man working in the yards might make it to the rails just in front of the speary horns of a rogue bullock. This is a close shave. A team of musterers might have to eat a curry which has been sitting in the camp oven for three or four days. This too can be a close shave.

But whatever the case, it's not the done thing to turn misadventures into stories designed to show a glint of personal heroism. Old timers usually keep their mouths shut. It's like being thrown from a horse. Most ringers will be loath to admit they have been thrown. Very rarely, it seems, do ringers get thrown when they are by themselves. If they have to walk back to the camp it's usually because the horse fell with them, or it pulled away from its hitching tree during dinner camp, or something like that. When there are no witnesses, few men worth their salt will admit to being thrown. And if he does get thrown in front of his mates, well, it's because the saddle slipped or the stirrup leather twisted or his hat fell over his eyes. Admit the horse was too good for him? That's like the admiral of the fleet confessing to sea-sickness.

Ringers, too, have their own individual styles when it comes to getting on a horse in the morning which they think might buck. Some put on a great show of pulling the horse's front legs forward so that all the loose skin is pulled forward from beneath the girth. Then they check the tightness of the girth and the setting of the saddle before leading the horse around the yard to let him get used to the feel of things. When satisfied that every possible contingency has been taken into account, they swing aboard.

Then you have the casual types. These are the old timers who like to give the impression that they've been on so many rough horses that one more isn't going to make any difference. They saddle up quickly, inspect everything at a glance and, as the horse prances around them with its tail jammed between its hind legs, they pull out the tobacco tin and roll a smoke. This sort of ringer doesn't put up with too much in the way of shenanigans. If the horse plays up too much he is just as likely to draw the near-side rein up tight, take the near ear in the same palm and twist it savagely as he swings aboard. The horse is too busy thinking about the dizzying agony coming from its ear to worry about bucking. And when he is seated firmly in the saddle he lights the smoke. It is a study of movement that would impress any choreographer.

All sorts of things happen on stations. Even guns come into play now and again. Paul and Flo Beard of Van Rook told of the time a young ringer from a neighbouring station went berserk at the Macaroni camp with a .22 rifle.

It was in 1973. At the time Paul was head stockman at Macaroni and Flo was doing the cooking for the men. The mustering team was bringing in cattle from the Van Rook Creek area. Paul asked the ringer to check for cattle around a dam. He rode off and Paul didn't see him again for several hours.

Instead of riding around the dam, the ringer rode back to the Macaroni house where Flo and her children were. The excited ringer told Flo that the old male cook out in the mustering camp was sick and coughing up blood. 'I'm going to shoot him and put the poor bugger out of his misery,' he said.

He caught a fresh horse, tied a semi-automatic .22 rifle to the saddle and rode off again. Flo and her eldest daughter, Cynthia, followed him as far as they could on foot but eventually lost him in thick timber. Later on the ringer met Paul, who was on his way back to the homestead. He rode up with the gun levelled at Paul and shouted: 'I was sent here to shoot all you bastards, but first I'm going to finish off that old cook.' He galloped off, but fortunately for the 'old cook', Paul and the men had shifted him away from the camp and propped him up in the shade of a tree. The cook was apparently suffering from ulcers, hence the coughing up of blood. But Paul said he doubted that he felt so bad he wanted to be put down by the gun-slinging ringer.

Paul and the rest of the men galloped back to the house and radioed the Cairns police. The police said: 'If you have to shoot him (the ringer), shoot him in the legs.'

They had a mini-arsenal at Macaroni which included two .303 rifles, a .308 rifle, a shotgun and two .22 rifles.

A quick plan was formulated for their defence. Flo, her four children and an old Aboriginal man and his wife barricaded themselves in the house with a .303 for company. The men took the rest of the weapons and positioned themselves in sheds and behind vantage points around the house. An innocent bystander walking in on the scene might well be excused for thinking he had walked onto the set of High Noon.

An hour went by and then a rider appeared in the distance. He cantered up to the house shouting out that he had shot Pat Rice, the cook. With the .22 in his hand he leapt from his horse and made for the barricaded house. He jumped the garden fence.

Paul called out to him from the cover of a shed: 'Stop. Put down your gun.' The man kept walking towards the house. Paul steadied his .303 on a support, took aim and fired. The bullet missed and the gunman kept walking. One of the other men took aim and fired. The bullet hit a stump just behind the surprised ringer. He threw down his rifle and pointed his arms skywards. He was unceremoniously tied up with dog chains and rope and placed under guard in a small shed until the arrival of the police.

Paul Beard has lived his share in the Gulf country. Born at Croydon in 1923, he was off on his first stockman's job at the age of twelve. He was given his first head stockman's job at the age of eighteen and since then has worked in that capacity on stations all over the Gulf. Among them have been Delta Downs, Maggieville, Abingdon Downs and Van Rook.

But it was Van Rook which captured his imagination most, and he has spent many years working as head stockman in both the Macaroni and station camps. The Macaroni block is prime crocodile country because of its deep salt-water channels and coastal frontage. Crocodiles and sharks can be found right up in the freshwater stretches of creeks such as Van Rook Creek. 'You had to be pretty careful in that country when you were swimming cattle. You'd put a mob in the water and the next thing a cow would go down. You had to be careful yourself too,' he reckoned.

When it came time to swim a mob across a salt-arm or deep freshwater channel, a lot of noise was made or shots were fired into the water to scare away any munchies. On occasion a man, too afraid of what was under the water, would refuse to swim his horse across. The crocodiles would and still do travel upstream in search of easy prey such as cattle which they lock onto at watering points. Even today Paul said the Van Rook coastal country is treacherous.

Paul told of the time Gulf country identity Les Henry was swimming a horse across Van Rook Creek. The horse went down and when it came up its head had been torn off. Les Henry swam to shore at what must have been a very clicky pace. The next day he found the carcase of the horse and its head jammed under a log in shallow water. Thankful for small mercies, Les removed the saddle from the animal's distended body and the bridle from its severed head.

Paul now lives at the Van Rook station headquarters. Too old for full time stock work, he now does odd jobs. Flo is employed as the station cook. The couple started living together in 1953, and decided to make the arrangement legal and proper by getting married in 1972. They were married at Macaroni, where they were living at the time. The best man was John Stewart who was then the manager of Van Rook.

They were good years down at Macaroni, according to Flo. There was plenty of barramundi and other fish, and no shortage of ducks and Magpie geese. It was a good existence.

The one bugbear was the windmill which was supposed to pump water to the house. Most of the time there was not enough wind to turn the mill and Flo would have to bucket water from the creek. She had a phobia about crocodiles, and spending any more time than she had to around their chosen habitat sent shivers up her spine. 'You had to keep an eye open around that water,' she said with a laugh.

Paul and Flo were on their annual leave when the full brunt of the 1974 floods hit Van Rook. The low Macaroni country was inundated by flood-water coming down the myriad coastal creeks and channels. An estimated 19 000 cattle were drowned in those floodwaters at Van Rook. Aerial photos at the time showed cows, their heads barely above water, swimming feebly thirty kilometres out in the Gulf of Carpentaria.

The company, which also owns Miranda Downs and Strathmore Stations in the Gulf, lost an estimated total of 65 000 cattle in those floods. At the time of the floods, Van Rook Creek between the Gilbert and Staaten Rivers was sixty-four kilometres wide. Van Rook is not expected to get back to pre-flood numbers until 1985. By then it should be running a herd of about 38 000 cattle.

When Paul and Flo returned to Macaroni after the flood, they found that their chooks had all drowned but their ducks, dogs and cats had survived the deluge.

The isolation of Macaroni was never a great problem for Flo. She had grown up in the bush and was used to the privations imposed by the elements and the long distances of the outback. The Macaroni camp was cut off from the Van Rook homestead, eighty-four kilometres away, from December until May. During these months the road to the head station was cut by the swamps and creeks.

Necessary food items such as butter were flown out by small plane but, because the airstrip was usually inundated, the butter had to be hurled from the plane as it passed low overhead. Individual lumps of butter were usually pushed into powdered milk tins before being dropped groundwards.

The suburban housewife who complains about feeding three or four mouths should take a leaf out of Flo's book. She had eight men in the mustering camp to cook for, plus her four children and Paul. A 32 volt generator supplied all the power to the house and all the food for the fourteen mouths was stored in one kerosene refrigerator.

And there were snakes. Once she opened a kitchen cupboard to be confronted with a two-metre tree snake. The reptile shot out and slithered into the oven of the wood stove. The whole show came to a steaming climax when Flo poured boiling water into the oven.

In the wee hours one morning, while Flo and Paul were sleeping soundly, their pet cat suddenly put on a pantomine. Flo woke up and straightaway felt a movement in the bed. While she was still in mid-air, a three-metre water snake popped its head up from beneath the sheets to see what all the commotion was about. It too fell victim to Flo's kettle of boiling water.

Mt Fullstop

The big white house on the bank of the Burdekin River loomed up a kilo-metre or so down the brown-dirt station track. It is the home of Mac Core, his wife Jean and their daughter Jennie. Further along the river bank, a long ranch-style home appeared — the home of Mac's son David and his wife Desleigh. As far as homestead settings go, these two, overlooking a grand sweep of the north's 730 kilometre long Burdekin, are hard to beat. The wide, sandy river bed, creased by a ribbon of running water in the dry season, is home to black duck and pelican, wood duck and egret. At dusk battalions of flying foxes wing silently across the blood-red sky to feed on the blossoms of the ti-trees which curtain the river banks. At sunrise they take wing again through the morning's orange light to their camp further along the river. At this time of day, all is activity in the Core households. Levis are pulled on over saddle-bowed legs and snap fasteners are clamped on western shirts. Another day in the saddle is about to commence for the Core clan.

Family patriarch Mac Core is something of an institution in the upper Burdekin grazing country. At sixty-three years of age, dressed in Lee check jeans and wearing a yoked cowboy shirt tied at the throat with a string tie, he looks more like a hard-bitten American cowboy, on his way to the Fort Worth rodeo, than a Queensland cattleman. A kind of Queensland Jimmy Stewart, drawl and all.

Now and again Mac moseys down to Townsville and holes up at the Hotel Allen, where he puts away his share of Scotch on the rocks and conducts a bit of business. He looks like a grizzly old hellion who wants to whoop it up after being on the trail for a long time. North Queensland is his home range. Around the upper Burdekin he knows the gullies and the timbered ranges, and how the passions of the country change with the passing of the seasons. He'd be a bad man leading a posse if you were working the wrong side of the law.

After leaving the Scots College at Warwick in 1935, the fifteen-year-old Mac returned to the then family property of Blue Range on the Burdekin River, not far from the present site of Mt Fullstop. Two years later he was running the mustering camp and supervising the branding of 4000 calves a year. This was before the spaying knife was brought into play and the calving percentage was lowered to a reasonable level.

Mac's mother, Mary Ada McDowall, was the daughter of pioneering Scotsman William McDowall, who, at one time and another, was the owner of several stations in northern Queensland. In 1902 William McDowall skilfully circumvented one of the greatest calamities ever to strike northern cattlemen: the arrival of *Boophilus microplus*, the Australian cattle tick, into the north Queensland cattle country. At the time McDowall owned Greenvale Station and had witnessed the decimation by the tick of the Kangaroo Hills Station cattle herd across the Burdekin River. Astutely, he sold Greenvale Station before the ticks crossed the river. He then bought Kangaroo Hills, retaining the balance of the herd which had proved resistant to the ticks.

During his career as a pastoralist, McDowall owned Christmas Creek Station, which was also in the Greenvale district. It was on this station that an event once occurred which changed the face of the cattle industry in north Queensland and indeed in northern Australia.

In 1910 a Zebu cow with a bull calf at foot was imported from India as an exhibit for the Melbourne Zoo. McDowall got wind of the arrival and something must have prodded his instincts. He began to wonder if the Indian cattle would be better suited to the harsh conditions of north Queensland than the British cattle, which were the only stock then available to northern graziers. McDowall had a contact, an official at the Melbourne Zoo, who was only too willing to help his friend bring to fruition the idea of introducing a hardier breed to the dry tropics. The finer details of how the bull calf eventually came to be estranged from its mother have been lost in the telling of the story over the years. There appears to be a hint of truth in the rumour that a certain amount of fancy footwork was executed in removing the bull from the zoo. But, whatever the case, the bewildered Zebu, on whose shoulders lay the future of the northern cattle industry, was soon ensconced on Christmas Creek. There must have been a twinkle in the young monarch's eye as he surveyed the rolling acres dotted with sloe-eyed Shorthorn cows, for he bent to the task at hand with a reckless will.

In no time at all . . . yes, it was announced the Zebu was a success. His offspring *were* tougher and better suited to the dry tropical northern conditions. Gradually a revolution took place as the predominant British breeds of Hereford and Shorthorn were phased out of the north to make way for the Zebu and his more refined cousin, the Brahman.

Southern cattlemen expressed concern and accused many of the northern graziers of trying to sabotage the entire Australian cattle industry with the strange-looking Indian cattle. Some wondered if they were really cattle at all and not yaks or some other creatures from a lost corner of the globe. Today Brahman cattle, or extractions thereof, constitute almost the entire north Queensland cattle herd, though there are still some cattlemen who refuse to budge from the British breeds. Most of them are adamant that they wouldn't have 'one of them bloody stupid looking yaks' on their properties.

When McDowall died he left Christmas Creek to his spirited daughter Mary Ada McDowall, who married English engineer George Eugene Core in 1913. The couple's only son, Mac, took his name from his mother's initials, M.A.C. Mary Ada died in 1980 and still retains a strong position in the hearts of all who knew her. She was a true bushwoman, and before she died she left with her family a written reminiscence which shows, to a tee, what

Jack Gould, bull catcher and part-owner of Westmoreland Station.

Helicopter mustering pilot, Heather Mitchell.

Sunset over the Gulf of Carpentaria, Cliffdale Station.

Goose Lagoon on Van Rook Station.

life was like on a Queensland station in the earlier part of the century. But more than that, it shows what a truly remarkable woman she was. Her story commences when she was eight years old, just after her father, William McDowall, had sold Greenvale Station (then known as Lake Lucy) and purchased Kangaroo Hills.

Leaving Lake Lucy was quite a picnic. We had a five horse dray on which was loaded our piano (we were a musical family), my mother's prize possession — a hand operated sewing machine, and all our bits and pieces. We all rode on horseback, my mother side-saddle. Everyone was carrying something — a cat, hen, parrot, a box with chickens in it. I was carrying a pup. My pony objected to the pup and bolted with me. I lost my hat but held onto the pup and rode all the way for two days to Kangaroo Hills without a hat.

When I was about seven I went to the Ingham Show with all the family riding on horseback from Lake Lucy. It was the first town and first show that I can remember seeing . . . The last night before getting to Ingham we camped at a station called Colo Water which was managed by Ted Blackman. He was schooling his horses, getting them ready for the show and as it was early afternoon we joined in the fun. Fred, my brother, who was always my friend and adviser, said to me:

'Put Masher over the jumps.'

I had ridden Masher all day and besides, he was a baulker, but Fred handed me a whip and so I knew what I had to do.

I gave Masher a few good cuts and he cleared the jumps easily . . . Then it was: 'let Mary ride Masher in the ring tomorrow.' I was really bewildered when I got into the show ring as I'd never even seen a show before, let alone ridden in one and I was afraid Masher would baulk and send me over the hurdle instead of jumping himself . . . But armed with the whip and Fred's instructions to 'hit him hard when I came to a jump to make him take off' off I went. It must have been a wild ride but I didn't let him baulk and got first prize. When the judge put the ribbon on Masher's neck the crowd threw their hats in the air and cheered and I said to Fred, who was holding Masher: 'what are they doing that for?' And so ended my first but not the last of my rides in the show ring.

This is one of the rare occasions when I disobeyed Fred. He took me for a gooseberry when he escorted our governess for a Sunday ride. We got to a creek and he said to me: 'You wait here until we come back, we are going around the bend there.' So I waited and waited, looking at the sun and thinking it must be dinner time and that they had got bushed. So finally I went home and was peacefully eating my dinner when Fred walked in. He took off his belt, grabbed me by the back of the neck and I got one of the best hidings of my life. All the time Fred kept saying: 'when I tell you to wait, I mean wait. You wait there. Wait even if you die there.' So I learned to wait when left (even if I died there). But I never lost faith in Fred, he was really one of the kindest and most generous persons I have ever known. In those days we seldom went to town and if Fred went and we didn't he would always bring back something even if it was just a bag of lollies.

Just before we left Lake Lucy I was invited by Mrs Fenwick, then staying at the Valley of Lagoons, to go over to the 'Valley'. For some reason Mrs Fenwick had taken a fancy to me and wanted me as a riding companion. She went for a ride every afternoon on a groomed horse which had shining buckles on her saddle and galloped all the time, bringing her horse back white with foam. This went against my grain and I didn't like her much for it. I tagged along behind and nursed my horse, taking short cuts. At nights she'd sing and dance for us, and she could dance too, all sorts of fancy dancing. One night she broke her pearls and they scattered all over the floor. The room was locked and I was the one on hands and knees all over the floor next morning picking up the pearls. I didn't like staying there and fretted for my family. I didn't like their 'nice food' because my sisters and brothers couldn't share it and I wouldn't drink their 'rain water' for the same reason and used to take a cup and go down to the lake and drink the lake water. My sisters and brothers only had lake water to drink. So finally I was 'taken home'. Evidently Mrs Fenwick's riding companion had failed her, but I was happy to get home even though we ate off tin plates (not china plates like the Valley) and drank lake water and used 'fat' lamps and not kerosene lamps like the Valley. My mother was a good cook and we always had plenty of food to eat. We were a very happy family.

It was while we were at Lake Lucy that Fred, who was the eldest of the family was sent to boarding school in Herberton. He ran away from the school after a few months. It was during a heavy wet season. He walked to the nearest station, swimming a creek on the way, borrowed a horse from there and rode it to the next station, swimming more creeks and so on until he got home . . . Unseen, he let his horse go and hid in the saddleroom where we found him. We were afraid of what father would do and say and so got mother and after a long discussion between all of us, she was sent to Bell the Cat. Things were not as bad as we thought and Fred was not thrashed as had been expected nor was he sent back to school. Fred was an exceptionally good rough rider and old hands always said he was one of the best in the district.

It was also at Lake Lucy that I went out with Fred gathering firewood. We used a team of five goats to cart the wood. Fred loaded the cart and said: 'You stop here, I'm going to take this load home, and don't, I say *don't*, touch the axe.'

As soon as he had gone, I picked up the axe and put my foot on a log, and bang—it came down on my big toe and split it almost in half. I ran all the way home, fascinated by watching the blood spurting out.

When I got home they could not stop the bleeding. So my mother saddled her horse, took me up front and rode 25 miles to Walters Plains where my father was camped out mustering. I amused myself on the way by watching the blood from my toe run down the horse's shoulder. When we got to the camp they were yarding a big mob of cattle and they had 'rung up' and somehow we got caught in the middle of the milling cattle and got pushed around but the horse stood on his feet and all was okay. My mother wanted father to take me to Herberton to the doctor but he sent the men out hunting for cobwebs and bound my toe up with the spider webs and flour which partly stopped the bleeding. The next day we were sent back home, it was not 'necessary' to take me to a doctor. I still have a deep scar the full length of my toe and half way up my foot, the full length of the axe blade.

Kangaroo Hills was a straggly bit of country with lots of cleanskin cattle in the Oak scrubs around Mt Fox. Father and Fred were good cattlemen and after many exciting adventures they had Kangaroo Hills cleaned up. Bull Hill is named after a wild cleanskin which used to run there but was eventually thrown and yarded. All that country was mustered from the old Mt Fox outyards and hut and many a night we kids camped there. I remember it well as it was notorious for fleas which bred in the ground there and feasted on us at night. One day my younger brother Bob and I were sent to tail some horses about two miles away. We found this monotonous and decided to have a race, picking a tree some distance away as the winning post. Away we went, and both of us hit the winning post together, knocking it and both our horses down . . . The horses ran away, I got up but failed to catch one. Bob lay very still. I dragged him into the shade and ran all the way home. By the time we got back Bob had gone from where I'd left him. So, we had some tracking to do. Fred, who was an expert tracker (being taught by a half-caste Charlie Burdekin to track on the oak leaves at Mt Fox) found Bob quite a distance away walking down a creek quite unconcious of where he was, or what had happened.

While I was at Kangaroo Hills, a good looking brumby had been seen at the Two Mile. Fred was determined to run him in. He fed our old racehorse Apple Jack and he and I went to get the brumby. I was given all sorts of instructions. I'd never been running brumbies before and Fred decided I was so light that I was to ride Apple Jack and do the wheeling, and he would manoeuvre the coachers. We spotted what we thought was the horse in a mob and I went as instructed to 'work wide', but as the horses moved away Apple Jack took off after them. The pace was fast and the wind got between me and the saddle seat, and my legs and the flaps of the saddle were flying out, and all I did was hang on to the pommel like a monkey. Old Jack galloped slap into the horses which luckily belonged to some drovers. These horses were very tired after a long trip and the drovers were taking them home. I got a terrible scolding from Fred and a threatened hiding, and was pulled off Jack for 'not being fit to ride a decent horse'.

Gee, I'll never forget that ride, it was a thriller though I didn't appreciate it as such at the time. Some weeks later we did run the brumby in. But this time Fred was on Apple Jack and I handled the coachers.

While at Kangaroo Hills we young ones were invited to the wedding of Mary Johnstone, of Stoneleigh Station. She was marrying someone who was taking her on a honeymoon 'around the world'. We rode down in one day, starting very early and taking our wedding 'togs' in front of us in a valise which was strapped to the front of the saddle. We each caught and saddled our horses and Hetty, my sister, who was always most particular about her appearance, discovered when daylight broke and we were miles away, that she still had her 'yard boots' on and the ones she had polished and intended to wear at the wedding were still on the verandah at home. I can't remember what she wore at the wedding, but there were a few tears shed on the way down.

When Kangaroo Hills was cleaned up Father bought Greenvale Station. One day Father was driving the four in hand and Lizzy (my sister) and I were with him. We went over a bad rut and Father's foot must have slipped off the brake. He took a header out of the buggy taking all the reins with him, and both Lizzie and I jumped to our feet — with an exclamation unprintable! I, being on the outside jumped out, grabbing the near-side poler's trace with my right hand and worked my way up to his collar where the leader's reins ran through the hames.

I gradually pulled them to one side and finally with Lizzie's help, for she had followed me, to a stop. It was near changing time and the horses were tired and only travelling at a slow trot. Father at this stage had caught us up, gathered up the reins, climbed back onto the seat and no one spoke a word then or at any other time about the affair. We dared not put Father at a disadvantage. I'm sure no one ever found out about that little incident. The next day Father was busy in the blacksmith's shop welding a bar on the outside of the brake, to prevent his foot slipping off again.

One day at Greenvale Station Bob and I were supposed to be tailing goats but instead we were on the roof of the shed playing. About 9 am we suddenly saw Father riding home and we both took fright. Bob was jumping up and down on the roof saying: 'quick, quick, what will we do now? Here he comes.'

I said: 'jump down and go for your life after the goats.' So away we went without any dinner or even some matches to cook a goanna. We dared not bring the goats back before sundown.

While we were at Greenvale Father bought Cashmere Station and we, Mother and girls, moved there. Fred remained at Greenvale and Father and Mother went between the two places. One night when we girls were alone at Cashmere someone threw a stone, a big one about six pounds, through our bedroom window. We jumped up and barricaded ourselves in, but we could hear some-one walking around outside and he kept trying the doors. We spent a restless night, but in the morning he was gone. We kept close to the house all day hoping Father would come home. But he didn't and the man came again that night, banging around with rocks and trying the doors. He was gone in the morning and we never found out who or what he was. Probably a swagman.

This reminds me of something I should have told about the old Lake Lucy days. We all slept in a home made galvanised iron shed divided into three rooms. We girls had one room. One night just after getting into bed and lying awake, we saw a man lying along one of the rafters high up in the unsealed roof. We never stirred, but Cissie called out in a loud voice: 'father, bring the gun, there is something up in the rafters.' The man was down and out of the room like a shot. Father was miles away camped out, but Mother brought the gun and let off a few shots, just to let him know we had a gun. A few nights after that Hetty woke and saw, leaning over the head of her bed, the head of our old white donkey who had wandered in looking for bread. That frightened us all more than seeing the man in the rafters.

About this time of the scare of the man in the roof, Father had gone to Brisbane on business and he told Mother to always have the gun handy. He gave Fred a whip handle which was loaded with lead and told him to keep it by the door and use it if the occasion warranted it. We had a governess, who was evidently a bit silly, and who planned a joke not letting Mother or anyone else know of it. She told us all just about sundown that she had seen a man standing up on the ridge, and when he saw her he had ducked behind a tree and hid. So after supper she went and blackened her face, and put on an old dirty pair of trousers and shirt that Father had been killing in, and walked into the dining room where we all were, with a tomahawk in her hand. Fred jumped straight for his whip handle and gave her a good hit on the side of the head and she dropped like a stone. Mother had run into the next room and hidden the baby under a bed, thinking the blacks had come to kill us. When she came out we all crowded around to look at the dead blackfellow. After a minute Fred cried out, 'Good god I've killed Miss Hamilton.' But a bucket of cold water soon brought her around and she didn't get any sympathy from anyone.

Father was always one for giving you something to do that he thought, perhaps, you couldn't quite manage. One day at Christmas Creek when we were in our middle teens, he said to Lizzie and I: 'I have brought a thoroughbred mare. She was bred at Maryvale and was run in from a brumby mob. She is now in the Clarke River paddock and is said to be roughly broken in. If you can ride her home from the Clarke you can have her.'

Lizzie and I gave this some thought and laid a few plans. We rode down to the Clarke next morning, yarded the mare, and in due course caught her and got her saddled. She could strike like lightning and was very touchy. There was no question as to who would ride her. Lizzie was a really good rough rider, and would beat me any day. When Lizzie finally got on to the mare she didn't buck but pig jumped and raced around the yard striking at the bit. We realized she didn't have any 'mouth' at all. So we had another confab and a smoke and a drink of water. We finally decided that I would have to drive the mare home with Lizzie on her back. We put Paul, the horse Lizzie had ridden down to the yard, in with the mare and then Liz got on the mare. We made the mare follow Paul around the yard. After a while of this, I got onto my horse, and opened the gate.

Paul knew where home was and set off at a fast pace. Luckily the mare followed him and of course I brought up the rear. I could hardly keep them in sight, for the faster I went, the faster the mare went ahead of me with Liz on her back and Paul didn't need any excuse to put on the pace. It was a really wild ride and a fast one. Paul kept to the road and went straight home. I blocked them up in a corner and got the rails down and then we were safe and sound in the home paddock. Paul went straight to his mates and I ended up yarding a dozen or so horses with Lizzie still on the mare in the thick of it. She was a really nice mare, a bright chestnut with markings, and looked a thoroughbred. We put her straight to breeding as we had Braw Laddie, a five furlong Brisbane record breaker at the time. The mare had many foals and we called her Quality. Some of her foals were Grey Quality, Big Quality and Young Quality and they were all good useful mares. They broke in quietly and were good lookers too. Quality herself really had very little vice, and had only been half broken in when she got away with the brumbies.

It was past midnight. The unexpected winter rain was still slapping away at the corrugated iron hut on the banks of the Clarke River, some sixty kilometres southwest of the nickel mining township of Greenvale. Outside it was black—as black as the tall Northern Territory-born Aboriginal sitting beside me in the small hut.

The black man, known in the district by two names—Parky Atkinson or Parky Wollogorang—paused at times to stroke his thick grey beard and to let his long dark fingers play at the protuberances of his slender hips. He was casting his mind back to when he was a child on Wollogorang Station in the Northern Territory. He was searching for a day, a date, sometime in the early 1920s, when a motor car pulled to a halt beside where he was playing in the black's camp, and a white man asked if he wanted to go for a drive. It was on that day that Parky was taken from his home and driven to Greenvale Station, 1500 kilometres away. He has not seen Wollogorang or his mother and father since.

'I said, yes sir, I would like to go for a ride very much. I got in and was it a motor car ride . . . whoooo! We kept going and going and didn't stop until we got to Greenvale Station. It was a motor car ride all right,' he said.

The white man in the motor car was Henry James Atkinson, a pioneering pastoralist and owner of Greenvale Station. He had driven to Wollogorang soon after buying it in the early 1920s.

A small cooking fire burned in the iron-covered galley adjacent to the room where we sat. At about 2 am the fire would be used to heat a can of baked beans and a tin of herrings in tomato sauce. This was about when the combined effects of cold and rain began to knuckle down on our appetites. A bottle of Bundaberg rum was doing its best to keep out the cold. Outside, the lonely Mt Fullstop bush stretched away in its fantastic monotony of ironbark and dry, yellow grass. Now and again the black man's chestnut brumby stallion snorted outside as he faced away from the rain.

For some years now Parky has lived alone in the bush with his horses and a multitude of birds which descend each morning for whatever food he can give them. They are mostly lousy jacks, soldier birds, magpies and butcher birds. His horses are his people, and he holds lengthy conversations

with them about the state of the world. The brumby stallion, though, is his
real pet and he lavishes flour and sugar on the wild-eyed, unbroken chestnut.
The horse is 'one man'—no one else can get near him.

The hut where he lives is owned by the Core family, owners of Mt
Fullstop Station. They use the hut occasionally throughout the year as a
mustering camp base and allow Parky to live there. When the team arrives
with its retinue of ringers, Parky moves out to camp beneath a strip of
tarpaulin set up beneath a straggly ironbark.

Parky is illiterate. Like most blacks brought up on cattle stations he was
given little, if any, formal education. His education had to do with horses,
cattle and the ways of the bush. At this he was a top student. One of the
best, some of the Greenvale bushmen say today.

As we talked the rain softened and the wind whipped up a fury, running
its naked breath along the hanging timbers and rusted iron of the hut. Parky
droned on. Now and again he would ask me to switch off the cassette
recorder when he wanted to tell me something confidential, such as how to
kill a bullock without leaving a mark.

Parky Atkinson today looks upon the descendants of H. J. Atkinson as
his protectors. He refers constantly to Henry Atkinson of Lucky Downs
Station at Greenvale, and explains that there is a home for him there
whenever he wants one.

'All those children at Lucky Downs, they all call me uncle. You know
that? They all call me uncle,' he said, running his fingers through his beard.

Parky thinks he was about seven years old when he was taken from
Wollogorang. While he was still a young boy, he was learning the ropes on
Greenvale Station under bushmen such as Arthur Furber, who was head
stockman on the station for a number of years. Parky can only guess at his
own age, but he thinks he is about seventy. Local cattlemen like Mac Core of
Mt Fullstop say he would be younger than this—in his mid to late sixties.

Parky did not work on Greenvale Station all his life. At times he struck
out on his own and worked for other graziers in the region. But always
Greenvale Station was home. It was the place he made for when a job was
over—or when he was in trouble, like the time a policeman at Hughenden
tried to gaol him for the shooting of a Mt Sturgeon Station bullock. (Parky told
me the name of the man who actually shot the bullock on the station and
butchered it for his own Christmas dinner.) Parky, though, had been working
alone on Mt Sturgeon while the owner was away, and all the evidence
pointed to him. He was arrested in Hughenden, but before he was shown the
interior of the 'Crossbar Motel' he pleaded with the policeman to let him go
back to the station and unhobble his horses and collect his belongings from
his open camp out in the bush.

The policeman gave Parky permission to go, but told him to return to
Hughenden immediately after so he could appear before a visiting magistrate
over the slaughter of the bullock. Parky hightailed it for Mt Sturgeon, ran in
his horses, packed all his belongings on his pack-animals, and made a non-
stop 200 kilometre ride through the bush to Greenvale Station and the safety
of the Atkinson enclave. The Hughenden policeman was left scratching his
head and kicking himself for a fool. And that was the last, apparently, that
was ever heard of the slaughtered Mt Sturgeon bullock.

Parky wants one day to have his own hut somewhere out in the bush. He doesn't want to die in Mac Core's mustering camp shack. He doesn't think it would be fair on the Cores to have an old Territory Aboriginal die in their hut. If he can't die in his own hut he wants death to come to him in the open bush. It can come to him then with boots on and both hands clapping. But not in the Core's hut.

The wind had about dropped. I rolled my swag out on the floor and listened to Parky mumbling something about having to buy more beds for visitors. Outside the brumby stallion snorted and pawed at the earth. Parky began to outline his plans for the day.

'We go into Greenvale for a beer and then you go to Rosella Plains and I go to Lucky Downs. I told you all those children call me uncle? Yes I did. And then I go and find woman in Greenvale.'

He had a good belly laugh.

'You know I got woman in Charters Towers, yes, I got woman in Charters Towers. She like me that one . . .'

The wind began to howl again, and outside, the Fullstop bush moaned softly in the black night.

Note: 'David [Core] found Parky dead in his bed in the hut. Looked like he'd been dead for a month. He seemed to have died peacefully as he still had his thongs on' (Mac Core's station diary, 21 February 1986). Parky was buried in the Lucky Downs Cemetery. He was home again with the Atkinson family.

Rosella Plains

Heather Mitchell, thirty, thin, and blessed with a Jane Fonda face, grips the joystick and throws the Hughes 300 into a spin towards a group of cattle hiding beneath an acacia.

Heather Mitchell is a helicopter mustering pilot — the only such female in Australia. She is one of the new breed of Aussie stockmen known simply in the game as the 'chopper pilots'. As a female, Heather is an enigma in the macho world of chopper mustering; a world that demands a 'thumb-in-the-belt-loop' type of attitude. She is the puppet mistress pulling the strings on an 'Avgas'-charged marionette which swings like a pendulum, dangerously close to the lower Gulf country tree tops. The joystick is the string which holds her act together.

On Rosella Plains Station near Mt Surprise this former primary school teacher, from the then African nation of Rhodesia, each day takes control of the Hughes 300. It is a job she loves and one that is not without that delicious spice of adventure. She does not take for granted the fact she is the only female helicopter mustering pilot in Australia — and is grateful to Gerry Collins, part owner and manager of 1295 square kilometre Rosella Plains Station, for the job. Mr Collins, a former president of the Cattle Council of Australia, is one of the leading voices in Australian agropolitics today. He has had the trust and foresight to employ a woman to do a job which most of his industry counterparts believe is the sole domain of men.

But why the resistance to females in the chopper mustering game? Why is it that swaggering males chortle when they hear a female has broken their ranks? One explanation could be the Viet Nam war where the chopper pilot came into his own as a combat agent. Indeed many of the male pilots flying station choppers today cut their teeth above the jungles of Viet Nam. Some say that excitement-wise, chopper mustering runs a pretty close second to dodging sniper fire and machine gun bullets.

Since then the tough guy image has been reinforced by movies such as *The Deerhunter* and *Apocolypse Now*. Each of these celluloid epics, to a certain degree, used choppers to portray the inherent savage he-manliness of warfare. No place for a pretty woman.

Meanwhile, as Heather goes about her job on Rosella, there are some who say she should be in the kitchen doing women's work. At Rosella Plains she

126

Drought-stricken horses feeding on molasses in the Gulf country.

Yarding cattle with the help of a helicopter on Rosella Plains.

has been accepted by the stockmen, but at neighbouring Spring Creek Station, which she also musters, there are small pockets of resistance.

'There is some uncertainty, some reluctance to do what is suggested by the chopper pilot,' Heather admitted. She knows of only one other female who has broken the male-held ranks of chopper mustering. This woman went to massive Victoria River Downs Station in the Northern Territory but only stayed for three weeks.

'I don't know if it was pressure which pushed her out or if she just couldn't take the flying on VRD,' Heather said.

The few female helicopter pilots in Australia work mainly as commuter pilots flying executives hither and thither. On a chopper pilot's macho scale of one to ten, this rates pretty well near zero and is not sought after as work by the majority of pilots. Women, though, are locked into the system and find it difficult to get any work apart from commuter flying.

The top flyboys are either in turbines doing geosurvey work, mustering cattle, or working amidst the clouds and mountains of New Guinea. According to Heather, anyone who has mustered in Australia and worked in New Guinea can boast what is considered the top flying reference in this country. Both places offer unique experience, much of it being work that is carried out in the presence of trees and cloud-swathed mountains.

Chopper mustering requires lightning reflexes and a cool head. The pilot often works only inches from the swaying treetops. The brain has to take note and store information about tree location in regard to the tail rotor, the location of ground stockmen and the whereabouts of cattle. One slip-up, one forgotten moment when the pilot is working on a mob of cattle, and the tail rotor can be mangled in the foliage. Co-ordination, Heather explained, is the key to flying a chopper. Unlike a fixed wing aircraft which is stable in the air, a chopper has to be flown all the time. You have to have your hand on the stick every second. Take it off for a moment and the machine lurches. Leave it off for too long and you're in big trouble. Heather skims over the treetops at Rosella Plains at speeds that reach 75 knots. Most of the work is done at treetop level but occasionally she ascends to 160 metres so she can have a wide view of the countryside.

Chopper flying over the basalt-strewn ground of Rosella Plains has its exciting moments, but they are moments common to pilots who work in country that is fairly thickly timbered. Wind is a major consideration for any chopper pilot. The helicopter generally faces into the wind especially when hovering or working at a slow speed. If this cardinal rule is not observed and a chopper travels downwind without sufficient forward speed, it can simply fall away like a stone. As Heather said, she gets a scare every now and again, especially when the wind changes and the machine is working at a slow speed. When she was first learning to fly in the bush she used to terrorise herself on a regular basis, she said.

Helicopter pilots live with the very uncomforting thought that they are much more prone to accidents than their counterparts in fixed wing aircraft. But they can be comforted by the statistics which tell them that if they do 'come down' they have a much better chance of walking away from the prang than the fixed wing pilots. Heather quoted Australian figures taken over an eighteen month period ending in 1981 which detailed seventeen separate helicopter crashes. Out of those seventeen accidents two pilots were seriously injured. None were killed. Even if something goes wrong at 160 metres the pilot can execute a safe, slow rotation. In thickly timbered country which is characteristic of much of Rosella Plains, the blades might be wrecked on the descent but the pilot would have a good chance of walking away. She added as an afterthought that the likelihood of a back injury was extremely high. Fire is also a major consideration in a crash.

Insurance companies do not go out of their way to be bosom buddies with the harum-scarum chopper brigade. The premiums are so high as to be unaffordable, and in Heather's case Gerry Collins has taken out a special policy which has her covered.

Nearly every station I visited had stories to tell about choppers coming down. The common causes were either engine malfunctions or pilots flying the machines too close to trees and clipping branches. On one Gulf country station a pilot hovered over a waterhole to look for barramundi. Intent on his search for the fish, he didn't realise the tail rotor was dipping towards the water. In moments the $200 000 machine was slowly sinking in the lagoon. The spotter panicked and tried to get out but was hauled back into the cabin by the pilot to prevent his decapitation by the blades which were swishing only a few metres above the water level. The chopper had to stay in the waterhole for some time before it could be inspected by Department of Aviation officials, and in that time a mustering camp cook nearby, who was in the horrors from the grog, thought he was hallucinating. After several days of viewing this apparition, the blades draped with water lilies, he broached the subject with the stockmen and was apparently much relieved that it was actually a helicopter and it was in the water. Back to the bottle. Everything's okay.

When the machine was towed from the lagoon by a tractor a large barramundi was taken from beneath the pilot's seat. It was the first barramundi that pilot had ever caught.

Heather Mitchell, being worldly-wise and intelligent, observes with some humour the antics of her male counterparts. A certain amount of insight into the male pysche leads her to the observation that some pilots think they virtually have to fly the machine upside down. This, she reasons, is more a demonstration of their flying ability for the benefit of the ground stockman than of their ability to muster cattle. Handling cattle from a helicopter requires special skills, and Heather, like most people who have anything to do with the subject, believes that the best way is to keep the chopper as far away as possible from the stock. Put too much pressure on the cattle and they will become stubborn, often refusing to budge.

On several occasions during the short muster I did with Heather, she had to fly the Hughes 300 in beneath the treetops to scare cattle which had taken shelter under the branches. Several times we hovered at a height level with the cattle, staying there until they moved out. Some choppers are equipped with sirens which are played to keep cattle moving. Often the pilot plays his favourite music over the system, and one pilot in the western Gulf has claimed that nothing shifts cattle like Linda Ronstadt's special brand of country melodies.

In some cases when cattle absolutely refuse to budge from beneath a tree

Heather will give a blast on the siren and one of the ground stockmen will come across. But in some cases, she said, you can see a line of cattle galloping for thick scrub as soon as they hear the chopper. Once inside the jungle they are impossible to see and many of the cattle which specialise in this sort of escape live to a ripe old age.

Hundreds of brumbies roam across Rosella Plains and are a threat to fences and the tame station horses. Brumby stallions in particular are a special menace and they are not the noble wild animal that the Marlboro Man would have us believe. In most cases, if a stallion wants to get to station mares through a fence, he will force his own herd over the fence and then he will go through last when the barbed wire has been flattened. An old timer near Burketown told me a tale of how a crocodile had taken several horses at a waterhole. This old fellow observed a brumby herd come to drink one day. The stallion pushed the weakest mares down to the water's edge and would not drink himself until satisfied there was no danger from the crocodile.

At Rosella Plains brumbies are often shot from the air, and usually it has been the duty of the chopper pilot to fly the marksman around the station while he thins out the wild horses. Heather Mitchell is a horse lover and cannot stand the idea of being involved in any plan to shoot horses, no matter how much trouble they cause. Well into her second season at Rosella Plains last year, Heather had not been asked to take part in a brumby hunt. That she had not been asked to do so was purely out of deference to her by Gerry Collins. But she was anxious about the day when she would be asked and would have to make a decision.

Heather was granted permanent residence in Australia in 1982 and to ensure that her status is maintained, she cannot leave the country for any length of time until the end of 1983. She is, she said, interested in remote places and enjoys the feeling of living on frontiers. Naturally her next step is to work in New Guinea, flying turbines. There is, though, one 'frontier' where Heather will never be able to work—off-shore oil rig work. Men have a strange superstition of women being on rigs. They simply don't let them on.

Spring Creek and Rosella Plains Stations, on the Basalt Tableland near Mt Surprise in the lower Gulf Country, are owned by the Collins brothers— Gerry, David and Bruce. David manages Spring Creek and Bruce is in charge of Daintree, a fattening property owned by the family near Winton in Central-Western Queensland. They are the great grandsons of the pioneering pastoralist Thomas Collins, the man who followed Leichhardt's track up the Burdekin River to settle on what he named Spring Creek Station. When the party arrived at the head of the Burdekin River it was confronted by a basalt tableland, and while they were crossing this tangle of scrub, a bullock was lost. The animal was tracked through the lava flow and was found by a waterhole in a spring-fed creek. The country around looked promising and Spring Creek Station was born. The year was 1862.

A partnership then developed between Thomas Collins and his brother Charles. Thomas married Mary Jane Firth in 1873 and their daughter Lelia Elizabeth, born in March 1875, was the first white child born on the Gulf watershed. The couple had two more children, both sons, who were named Noble Victor Collins and Thomas Bramwell Collins. The three children attended boarding school in Brisbane, and when travelling to school they had to go from Spring Creek to Port Douglas, north of Cairns, by horseback.

In those less than halcyon days, when Aboriginal tribesmen still roamed the area, the journey was not without some measure of adventure. The children were always accompanied by at least one station stockman during the trip. At Port Douglas they would be safely deposited upon a Brisbane-bound lugger.

Thomas and Charles Collins took up Brooklyn and Ambo Stations in the Mt Surprise district in the latter part of the last century. In 1901 they bought Rosella Plains. Brooklyn is now part of Mt Surprise Station, which in those infant days of Queensland's pastoral history was a sheep station. The blacks, it is said, had a field day with the sheep and one of their favourite tricks was to break the leg of a fat wether and leave it near a waterhole so it could graze on the sweet grass on the bank and drink at its leisure. The doomed sheep, though, could not travel any great distance from where it was left and when the natives were hungry for meat they would simply return and knock it on the head. Leg breaking was a common method of restraint used by the Aboriginals to ensure any prospective meals did not wander too far away from the cooking fire.

Gerry Collins, one of Australia's most articulate analysts of cattle industry affairs, was launched into the agropolitical arena in 1968 when he joined the Upper Burdekin branch of the Association of Central and Northern Graziers. After this he had what some might describe as a meteoric rise through the ranks. After serving on several committees and delegations he was appointed chairman of the United Graziers Association Cattle Committee in 1980. In the same year he was appointed UGA delegate to the Cattle Council of Australia. Prior to this he had been a member of the Producers Consultative Group which had been instrumental in the setting up of both the Cattle Council and the National Farmers' Federation.

Today, he claims without hesitation that the establishment of the National Farmers' Federation was the single most important step ever taken in the history of Australian agropolitics. It was the first time a unified federal primary industry organisation had been set up in this country which represented all persons associated with primary industry, whether they be a poultry breeder or stud cattle grower. Today, supported by a highly professional public relations network, the National Farmers' Federation is considered one of the most powerful lobby groups in Australia. Representing some 170 000 primary producers, it is comparable to the enormously influential Australian Council of Trade Unions.

In 1981 Gerry Collins was elected to a three-year term of presidency of the Cattle Council of Australia, and in 1979 was appointed representative from that body to the National Farmers' Federation. His crystal ball tells him that the future holds some dark days for the Australian cattlemen. He sees the future of the industry as essentially tied up with the Australian government's ability to manage the economy and the ability of the industry as a whole to compete on international markets.

The handling of the economy will determine if Australian beef is to remain competitive in the international marketplace. If the rural industry does not remain viable, producers will quit beef and switch to some other form of enterprise which provides a safer and better economic return.

The sad epitaph to a family pet that ate 1080 dingo bait on a Gulf country station.

Lower Gulf country cattleman Alan Furber hamming it up at the homestead gate.

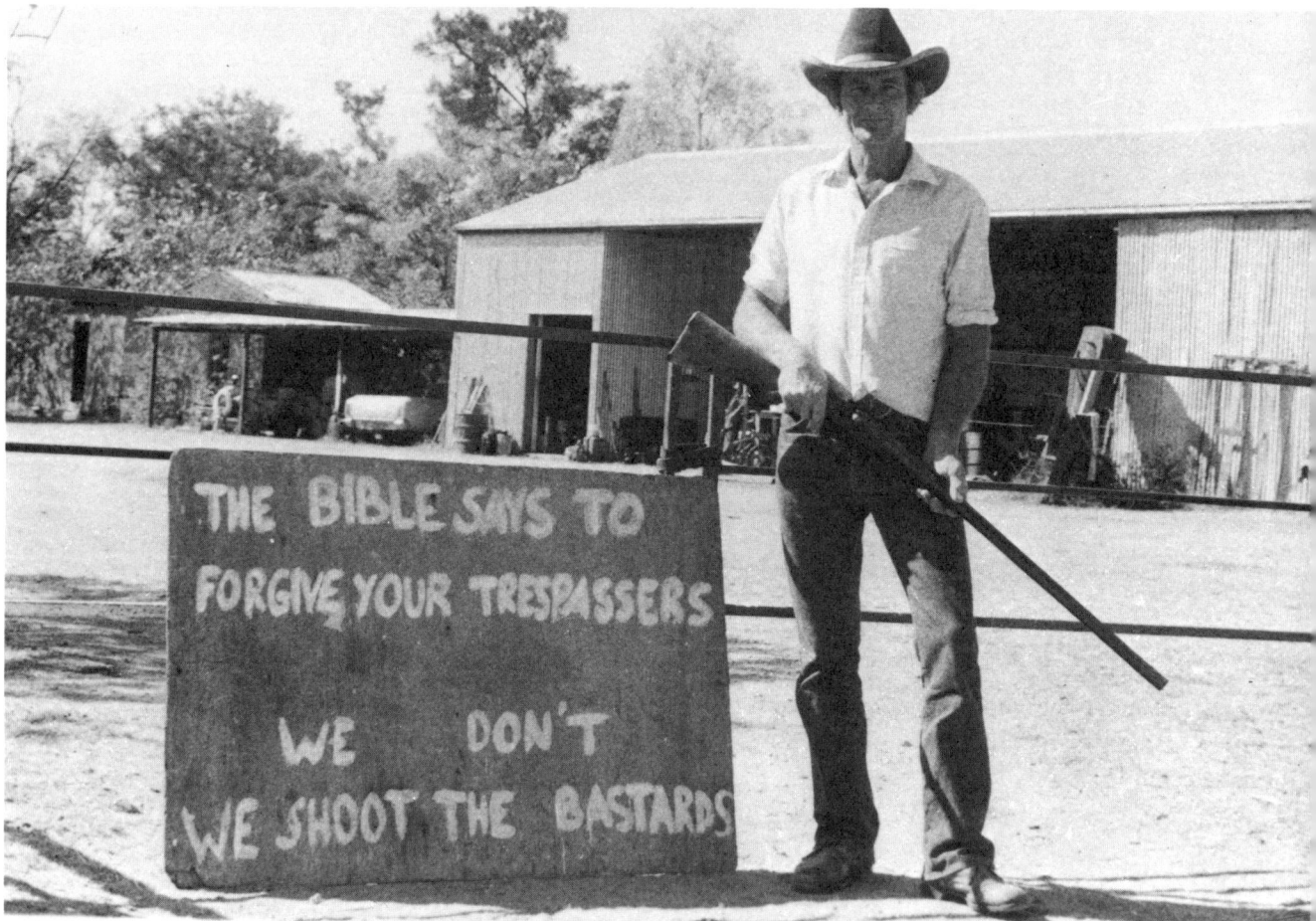

Unions, too, particularly transport and waterfront workers, are doing nothing to enhance the image of Australian meat exports, and unless an attitude change occurs in these departments repercussions could be felt.

But it is the European Economic Community which largely pulls the strings that will steer the destiny of Australian meat overseas. The EEC, often painted as the 'bad guy' in world trade, has a critical overproduction problem which allows it to dump commodities such as beef on the world market at greatly reduced prices. Gerry Collins sees this over-supply problem getting worse and its effect, he said, is deleterious to the whole free world trade price. The EEC drops about 600 000 tonnes of surplus beef on the world market annually—the Australian export total is 600 000 tonnes, so the effect is obvious.

Collins sees the problem in the EEC countries as being more of a social security blanket. The European farmers are subsidised by their Governments through a value added tax. The Governments give the growers more money for their product so they remain viable as farmers. So naturally the farmers maximise production. Mr Collins would like to see some other mechanism used to maintain financial equilibrium within the European farming community. He has made two trips overseas to meet with EEC officials since 1981 to discuss the problem, but as yet has received no encouraging signs from them.

Meanwhile, back at Rosella Plains the cattle are still being mustered and Heather Mitchell is darting about like a humming bird with her chopper. The flailing entanglements of the EEC and agropolitics are miles and miles away.

Note: Heather Mitchell's body was found on a lonely hillside near Lae in New Guinea on 6 July 1987. She had been raped and murdered. Heather had achieved her ambition to fly jet helicopters in New Guinea and was regarded as one of the best. Her lifestyle, her grit and determination to make it in a man's world, remain an example to women everywhere.

Kilclooney

Dinny Sheahan has come a long way since he drew 269 square kilometres West Creek in a ballot in 1953. He threw his worldly possessions on the back of an A-Model Ford and nursed it up the steep, winding track of the Seaview Range, west of Ingham, to Mt Fox. He was cold stony broke, with the seat out of his pants, but upstairs he had a notion that in the long run he would make a go of things. His friends told him he was crazy, that he would get into debt and become bankrupt. Dinny didn't hear that sort of advice too well. He borrowed money from Dalgety's, the pastoral agents, and slowly built fences and put together a cattle herd. During the initial hard years he lived in a small stringybark hut virtually cut off from the rest of the world.

Dinny was the son of the late Dan Sheahan, a celebrated north Queensland bush poet, the author of 'A Pub Without Beer', which was later rewritten and added to by song writer Gordon Parsons and called 'The Pub With No Beer'. The song was written after Dan rode into Ingham during World War II for a beer. All the pubs were out of beer, and during the thirsty ride home he composed the words to the song. It became a hit for Slim Dusty in Australia and England. Dan Sheahan owned a sugar cane farm at Trebonne in the foothills of the Seaview Range, not far from Ingham. As a boy, then as a young man, Dinny worked on the cane farm, cutting the crop by hand and ploughing the fields.

'I used to sit on the tractor and look up into the mountains and just dream of the day when I would have my own cattle property,' Dinny said in his easy drawl. In 1953 it all came true when he drew West Creek.

In 1960 Dinny married Nancy Scott from Ingham and they settled into a small tin house on West Creek. Nancy mustered with the men and camped out with them as they mustered the unbroken mountain country. Jones Yard, a camp and cattle yard complex nestled in amongst a gloomy she-oak forest, was her home on many occasions. She laughs now when she remembers how she had to cart water from the creek to the camp by hand so that she could have a bath in privacy before the mustering team arrived back at camp. In 1961 Jim Mercer, a noted Ingham district bushman, came to work for Dinny and has been on the station ever since. He lost an arm in a vehicle accident in 1972 and since then has been on a pension. He chose to live by himself at Jones Yard and in 1982 moved into a house he had built beside the mustering camp.

134

Bath time out in the mustering camp on Kilclooney.

In 1964 Dinny bought Ryeburn, a 539 square kilometre block, which had been part of Kangaroo Hills Station. When the land came on the market Dinny had no money and the asking price was £18 000 ($36 000). But Dinny had a friend in Bunty Allingham, the owner of Kangaroo Hills and an established grazier. Bunty told him to borrow what he could and he would lend him the balance at three per cent interest.

Dinny borrowed £10 000 ($20 000) from the Agricultural Bank, and Bunty lent him the £8000 ($16 000) balance. He was now the owner of a large, viable station. The days spent sitting on a tractor gazing up into the mountains were long gone. He called the station Kilclooney, 'the meeting place'.

In 1967 a homestead and men's quarters was built at the site of the present Kilclooney head-station complex. Not long after, something happened which made Nancy's life a whole lot easier. Dinny bought a 32 volt generator. Now she could have a washing machine and other electric gadgetry, and she could throw away the carbide lamps and the hurricane (larrikan) lanterns. Early in 1982 the Sheahans moved into a new homestead—a two storey, $250 000 monolith of brick and wrought iron which rears from the rolling hill country like a liner on a gently swelling ocean.

Just before the 1970s beef slump, Dinny bought Glendhu, a fattening block across the Burdekin River from Kilclooney. With the onset of the slump, the trouble began to pay off the loan for the 220 square kilometre property. But Dinny rolled up his shirt sleeves and battled through the recession, resisting offers along the way of $1·3 million for Glendhu. During the slump he went on the road with 1000 fat bullocks which, in good times, might have been worth $400 000. He walked the cattle to a railhead on the Atherton Tableland and trucked them to a Cairns meatworks where they sold for $48 per head. To keep his head above water during the recession, he once again had to borrow money from the Agricultural Bank. He readily admits today that without the Agricultural Bank, not only he but also a lot of other cattlemen would have been rolling up to the dole office a long time ago.

Travellers stranded on Mt Fox by impassable roads or a flooded Burdekin River know only too well the hospitality handed out by Nancy and Dinny Sheahan. They are the Good Samaritans of the High Country. I visited there, broke and busted after four months constant travelling and research, and I would vouch for that any day.

Nancy tells the story about a young labourer who worked on their new home. When the house was finished, Dinny threw a party for all the carpenters and workmen. During the course of the celebration, the young workman walked up to Nancy.

'Y'know,' he said, 'when I came up here to work, I was prepared to hate you and hate this whole turnout. I thought, these graziers, these cattlemen, they're all rich snobs, they've got everything. I hated you and everything about you before I even got up here. But now, after living here and seeing the way you live and the way you work and how you treated us, I think you're the most beautiful people in the world. I just didn't know before what it was like'.

'That's the trouble,' Nancy explained. 'So many people from the towns and cities don't have any idea what life is like on a station. They think we're all rich toffs who sit around all day and don't do any work. So many people talk about wealthy grazier snobs and it's so wrong. They think we're all millionaires. If we are, we're bagmen millionaires. They just don't have any idea what the life is really like or what the people are like.'

Mum, Dad, and the kids all join in the fun at the Oak Park Races.

Kilclooney homestead.

Oak Park

Each year around the beginning of July a strange disease takes hold of the station folk in the Einasleigh area and other parts of the lower Gulf country. The women wangle some excuse to make a trip to Townsville or Cairns, where they dart from one boutique to another trying on dresses and hats and having their hair styled. Meantime, the honourable hubbies have been concerned with matters close to their hearts: matters like grog supplies, horseflesh, and the vital organisation of camp gear.

This is *the* time of the year: bigger and better than Christmas and of infinitely more religious significance than Easter. This is the time for the Oak Park Amateur Picnic Races. Hold on to your hats, ladies, and buckle up your girths, gents! This is the best little wingding turnout of a bush bash that ever hooted and honked among the ironbark and spear grass.

'Oh!' the Danish wife of an EEC official said to me as we shivered around the blazing Oak Park Station camp fire. 'It is so cold, just like at home, but here everyone is still outside. They are having such a good time. At home by now we would be inside rugged up in our pullovers and blankets.'

The Danish woman was having the time of her life; loving every minute of seeing how the other half lived in the Wonderful Land of Oz. Before being invited up to Oak Park and rolling out their swags in the Rosella Plains camp, the woman and her husband had been following the well-trodden trail of the Sydney and Melbourne cocktail circuit. Now at Oak Park she was experiencing some fair dinkum, heady Australianism. It was change at its best.

'This,' she said as she looked around at the men in their cowboy hats and riding boots and the children playing in the semi-dark, 'is how I always imagined Australia'.

And indeed this was Australia as it was always meant to be; friendly, hospitable and with no frills or pretensions. There was a carefree warmth which soaked through every pore, every atom, and it was savoured by everyone from the tiniest tot to the oldest hardcase cattleman.

They come from miles around, the station folk. They pitch their marquees along the bank of the Copperfield River and establish the most elaborate camps complete with power generators, deep freezers, and enough turkey, steak and ham to placate the fierce appetites forged over the racing festival.

And they bring their supplies of grog—champagne, rum, whisky and beer—enough to see them through the heat of the days and the cold of the nights, and then some.

Each year about fifteen of the local stations set up their own camps, the focal point of each being the marquee that houses the booze, food and eating tables. Set up in calvary precision in line with this main 'tucker tent' are another fifteen or twenty smaller tents and marquees which house the host and hostess and their invited guests. It stretches in a three deep tier along the bank of the river: a static procession of billowing canvas and taut guy ropes leading from one camp into another.

For many of the bush people the Oak Park Races is their annual holiday. Some arrive ten days or more before the races start to supervise the training of their horses or to add extensions to their camps. But there are other reasons too: this is when they can get together at a casual pace, renew old friendships, and just take things nice and steady before the hurly-burly of the race days and the evenings of dance.

There is something which attracts the isolated bush folk to Oak Park races like moths to a flame. Club stalwart Mary Dixon of Bagstowe Station explained it like this: 'The races are so special to everyone around here for different reasons. I think that one of the reasons is that everybody camps in close proximity and everyone knows just about everyone else. Anyone who isn't known is soon made welcome. Even the town visitors soon forget they belong to an urban society and begin to enjoy the freedom of the bush.

'Even though the local people all live within a radius of a hundred miles we seldom see each other. The races offer the opportunity of a once a year reunion, of being able to forget the trials and tribulations of running a cattle property. It means being able to welcome old friends.'

Oak Park is also a time for children. They laugh and they play and they get up to mischief, but most importantly, they learn to mix together. These are the bush kids who talk to their teacher over a two-way radio and rarely get the chance to join in with others of their own age. At Oak Park each year a school room is set up a week before the races get under way, and lessons are supervised by itinerant teachers Frank and Colleen Simms. Games are played and mothers and fathers join in racing with their children in the egg and spoon race and other novelty events. At first shy little boys and girls peer curiously at the goings-on from behind their mothers' skirts. The gaiety, the unleashed exuberance finally becomes too much and one by one they run out on to the playing field in front of the bar. They laugh and they squeal and they fall on the ground with their sides splitting at the sight of their big, tough dads coping with the indignity of a three-legged race. And at the centre of all the pandemonium are Frank and Colleen Simms, the teachers whose home is a Toyota Landcruiser and whose backyard is the entire eastern Gulf country and Cape York Peninsula.

The Simms are an institution in the north. They are the saints who travel from one homestead to another, from one camp to the next, helping mothers and governesses who are teaching children by correspondence. There is no one in the Gulf, from the roughest prospector to the wealthiest cattleman, who would not set a place for Frank and Colleen at his dinner table. I asked

Mary Dixon what she thought of the two teachers. Her reply was typical: 'The bush people welcome Frank and Colleen as they welcome the first storms after a long and severe drought.'

In the afternoons during the two days of racing people drift from one camp to another along the river, calling in here for a beer and there for a yarn. In fact it is impossible to walk the entire distance of the camping area without having seven or eight total strangers call you in for a drink at different points along the way.

'Hey mate! Ya lookin' a bit dry on it. You better come over and 'ave a snort!' They shout out along the way.

It doesn't matter if 'mate' has been imbibing at a steady rate for the past twelve hours and is about as 'dry on it' as a sponge in a bath. He has to go and have a snort. It's the done thing after all. And when in Rome . . .

At Oak Park, coats and ties are the order of the day for the gents, and the ultimate faux pas is to go to either the ball or the dance devoid of these sartorial symbols. Do so and you will be ostracised like a hell's angel at a debutante's ball.

The one thing to remember at Oak Park is that you're not at the Birdsville Races. Ya don't walk around in thongs and T-shirt, mate, and ya don't vomit down the front of a lady's dress, and ya don't urinate on the ground around the bar. That's okay at Birdsville when the hordes of city slicker yobbos gather for the fray. Try it at Oak Park, and you're mighty likely to wind up with an XOS fist planted fair square in ya dial. At Birdsville now most of the locals bolt for cover when race time comes around. They leave the dusty oasis to the angry mob. No one at Oak Park wants that to happen. The Oak Park race committee is well aware of the price they would pay for prolonged publicity. Inevitably they (the 'angry mob') would descend and this small, happy gathering of bush people would be facing a replica of the Birdsville debacle.

I remember in 1981 the ABC was going to send a television crew up to film the races. The prospect excited mixed feelings among the committee, but the overriding thought was, 'Oh well, it had to happen one day'. But two weeks before the races Aunty decided against sending a crew because of a belt-tightening exercise. There was an audible sigh of relief from the Oak Park regulars who could take solace once again in the relative obscurity of their race meeting.

The Oak Park Races first got under way in 1904 and, tradition-wise, very little has changed since then. The winning jockey and horse are each still given three cheers as they enter the saddling enclosure after a race. And on the evening of the final day's racing there is a sit-down presentation dinner which Mary Dixon has described as an 'emotional ceremony'.

'The atmosphere in the hall on Saturday night is one of complete friendship, loyalty, and respect for those who have worked so hard for the club. And there is a feeling of keen and dear hope for the future welfare of the club.'

My wife and I stayed in the Oak Park Station camp run by husband and wife team Jim and Wendy Nimmo and Jim's sister Alice. The Nimmos are the owners of 429 square kilometre Oak Park Station where the race meeting is held. The Nimmo family has been connected with the meeting since it was first run in 1904 on nearby Lyndhurst Station. In 1929 the meeting was moved to its present site at Oak Park and has been staunchly supported by generations of the Nimmo family ever since.

I went there as a rank outsider; a 'townie' and a journo to boot. After a couple of hours I realised I was in the middle of something special. Maybe it happened one of those times as I was walking back to my tent when a voice sang out: 'Hey mate! Ya lookin' a bit dry on it. You better come over and 'ave a snort!' Maybe it was then that the thought struck me about that timeless masterpiece, bush hospitality. It's not dead. Not by a long shot. You only have to go to the Oak Park Races to see that.

Esmeralda

At 2.02 pm on 22 January 1974, at Esmeralda Station, 120 kilometres south of Croydon, a family of six bravely looked death in the eye. It was at this moment that the watercourses of Esmeralda Creek and the Yappar River, swollen with 2500 millimetres of flood rain, burst into the isolated station homestead. The family of six included Frank Vicary, who had managed 414 000 hectare Esmeralda for thirty years, his wife Mary, and their four daughters Veronica, 20, Alice, 17, Tricia, 13, and Francis, 9.

For fourteen days the family had watched the flood waters swirl past the stockmen's quarters not far from the house. Being the wet season, no men were employed on the station; the family was alone. Frank Vicary had lived at Esmeralda for forty-four years. He had gone there as a toddler when his father, Frank Royal Vicary, took over the management of the station in 1930. In all that time and in all of his conversations with old timers he had never seen or heard of a flood such as this. This was the one-in-a-century history maker which all but drowned the eastern Gulf.

During those fourteen days while the family watched the water rush past the quarters, no one dreamed it would threaten the house. And then, with nowhere else to go but sideways, the brown, carcase-filled water, which might have been from hell, turned towards the old two-storey station homestead which had been brought from Croydon in 1940. Like a tidal wave it swept away the neat garden fence surrounding the homestead and spewed its savagery inside the house. A row of oleander trees in the garden helped break the monster's force. The Vicarys, taken by surprise, could do nothing but salvage whatever survival items they could find before retreating to the top floor. With the water swirling around their feet, they began to gather items which might help them through the ordeal they knew lay ahead. High powered rifles were taken upstairs; fresh water, a gas stove, blankets, foodstuffs, and the radio transmitter. Thirteen-year-old Tricia heaved a thirty-kilogram bag of sugar over her shoulder and carted it up the flight of stairs. In normal circumstance, Tricia could not even budge a bag of sugar from the floor. It was Tricia, too, who in the bedlam of frantic activity ran to a room to salvage some valuable books. No one knew she had gone. The water slammed the door shut behind her and its force held it closed. She was trapped just as effectively as if someone had turned the key in the lock. Her yells for help were eventually heard and it took most of Frank Vicary's powerful strength to open the door.

The chaos of those frightful minutes was made worse by the fact that Frank still had a leg in plaster after being kicked by a horse two years previously. Francis, a victim of cerebral palsy, was in a wheel chair. Mary Vicary could not swim. Those three would have to stay behind even if the opportunity to swim to high ground presented itself.

The day before Frank had shifted a herd of domestic goats to high ground away from the station complex. But the goats came back and climbed a firewood pile which held enough wood to last the station three years. The flood water took the woodpile and washed the goats away. The family in the house heard the cries and thought for a while that people were being washed down in the flood. The frantic cries from the drowning goats sounded like human beings in distress. The morning after the flood hit the house, Frank found two of the goats, which had managed to escape the water by swimming into the cabin of a blitz truck. No matter how hard he tried he could not force the terrified animals from the truck.

A pet cattle dog, which had come into the house while the family was packing the items to take upstairs, was tied to a bed to prevent its being washed away. But, as the family worked, the bed was washed towards one of the doorways. The dog, powerless to stop the bed, was dragged towards the savage current outside. With only a fraction of a second to spare someone cut the leash which tied the dog and carried the terrified animal upstairs. The next morning when it seemed safe to go downstairs, the dog could not be moved. No way was it going to set foot downstairs.

As the last of the survival gear was taken upstairs, the family took one last look at the water outside. It was a scene of utter and total destruction. Carcases of kangaroos, cattle and brumbies, bloated with death, washed silently past. Some of the animals struggled feebly in the muddy water in vain attempts to beat inevitable death. Birds, soaked through and starved as a result of the twenty-one days of rain, fell from their perches into the horror below. Cockatoos and galahs, for once silent and beaten, floated like chips of pink and white ice on the surface of the hissing water. It seemed that Mother Nature, that benign sovereign of strict orderliness, had turned upon herself in a frenzy of hate.

The family, too, saw the 150 station horses crowded on a patch of high ground only a few hundred metres from the homestead. The next morning when they looked again the horses were gone, the high ground smothered by the whipping water. For months afterwards Frank Vicary would see the carcases of horses high in the branches of box and bloodwood trees. They hung there in the forked limbs until the bones bleached white and the driving Gulf winds shook them to the ground. Brumbies, bogged to the withers in sucking mud, perished while the crows picked at their eyes and the hawks tore at the soft hide at the butt of their tails.

While the Vicarys watched the picture of death washing past the homestead, they wondered if they, too, would be joining the hopeless animals in the flood. They prayed that the pilot of the rescue helicopter they had radioed would reach them before it was too late. All that afternoon the water rose through the house as the family closeted themselves in the bedrooms upstairs. All that afternoon no one knew if they would be washed away or not. Just before dark, with water running more than a metre through the house, it stopped rising. All through the night they listened to the roar of the flood outside. In darkness, its magnificent horror multiplied. The sounds of drowning goats came again from across the slapping waves. All through the night they sat and talked among themselves, but every ear listened to the turbulence below. No one complained even though the desire to express fright must have been overpowering. They sat, they listened and they talked. No one panicked.

It was Francis in her wheelchair who typified the fighting spirit of the family. As she was being carried upstairs, she turned and said to her mother in her soft voice: 'This is good, Mum. Between us we can't swim a stroke.'

The family had decided early in the piece that they would stick together. No one would try and swim for high ground. This would have been suicidal, anyway, as the current was so powerful that not even the strongest swimmer would have been able to battle it for any distance. The only choice was to allow yourself to be washed away with it in the vain hope that it would pass high ground. The chances of a swimmer staying afloat long enough for this to happen were about the same as those of a shipwrecked sailor climbing on to the back of a whale in the middle of the Atlantic.

As day broke over the brown seas outside, they could see that the water had dropped. Inside the house the water level, which had risen to about a metre, was beginning to recede. That afternoon the rescue helicopter from Magowra Station arrived and took the family out to safety in three lifts.

Esmeralda was not the only station threatened in this flood. Along the Gilbert River homesteads were swept away as the mighty Gulf-bound river broke its banks. Isolated station people sat on roof tops praying for one of the few rescue choppers to arrive before the flood waters covered their homes. On a station outside of Normanton, a lone woman waited on her roof, frightened half to death that at any moment a large crocodile would emerge from the water, which was level with the guttering, and crawl on to the roof. The crocodile had been living in a waterhole near the homestead and the woman had been feeding it regularly for some months before the floods. Now, she feared it would come for her. The crocodile, though, stayed away and the woman was rescued.

Only miracles—and the bushmen who co-ordinated rescues over their two-way radios, and some fearless policemen—prevented lives being lost in those terrible floods. Helicopter pilots, like Ken Ware from Magowra Station, were the real unsung heroes of the dramas which were played out during the floods. These pilots broke every rule in the book to save lives. They ignored official directives to ground when their daily flying hours were exhausted, and stayed in the air travelling from one emergency to another. They knew that only by keeping their machines in the air during every minute of daylight would they save lives. At night when he couldn't fly, with every nerve in his body jumping, Ware would swig from a bottle of booze until the early hours of the morning until he collapsed in an exhausted heap. Then at daylight he would be back at the controls again, day after frantic day.

People who were going to die were saved—people like Robert McFarlane of Lake Carlo Station, who was plucked from the roof of his homestead and strapped to the skids of an already fully-laden chopper.

'I'll come back and get you. The chopper's full,' the pilot had shouted down to McFarlane.

'Leave me here and I'll be gone when you come back,' McFarlane shouted back as he cast his eyes over the rapidly rising water. The chopper descended and he was strapped to the skids and taken out.

There was an Aboriginal woman at Prospect homestead on the Clara River who had to be knocked unconscious before Ware could get her into the chopper. He had already taken out her six children and returned for her, landing on a flimsy skillion roof. The woman, in her panic, with the water raging all around, believed Ware had killed her children.

'No,' she screamed. 'I'm not getting in with you. You have killed my children.'

Ware, with no time for niceties, clipped her squarely on the chin and loaded her aboard.

Most Gulf country flood victims today have few kind words to say about the officials who were supposed to be organising the rescue operations in the north. These officials, many of the victims say, sat in offices in Cairns and had no idea what the real situation was like. Eventually they were largely ignored and the isolated station folk, using their two-way radios, established a network of rescue communications. When the floods hit Brisbane, the plight of the Gulf was virtually forgotten, and then and only then did the inland residents of the Far North realise they were well and truly on their own.

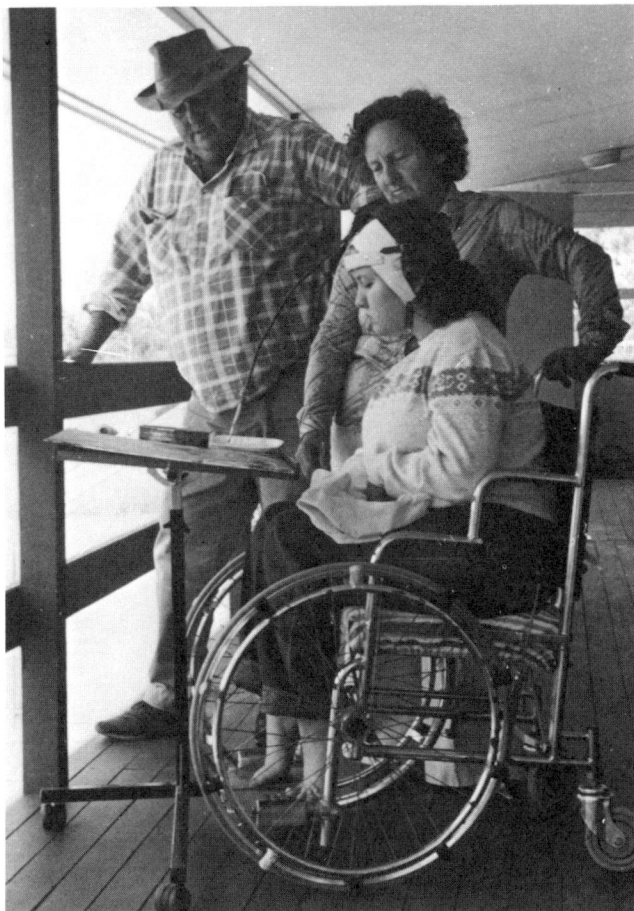

Frank and Mary Vicary watch as their young daughter Francis paints with the aid of a head piece.

Upper Burdekin River identity Earl Robinson.

Robin Hood

Sprawling through the rugged Newcastle Range south of Forsayth, in Queensland's lower Gulf country, is the 1295 square kilometre cattle station known incongruously as Robin Hood.

Incongruously, because the terrain is characterised by the rolling, sometimes angular, slopes of the ranges and the panorama of dry, dull eucalypt vegetation which camouflages a myriad of kangaroos, wallabies, horses, and probably some wild cattle.

It is a far, far cry from the green, shaded, twilight world of Sherwood Forest known to the archer supreme, Robin Hood. That fellow would surely have shuddered to have found himself extradited to the property named after him in the Gulf.

The jolly laughter of his merry men would certainly have held a note of despair as it resounded from the craggy cliffs and spinifex ridges which jolt and tear down to form the banks of the Robertson River.

Friar Tuck's parish would have held few religious men, and his gluttonous appetite might have been appeased by voracious feastings of kangaroo stew, complemented by the occasional black bream hauled unceremoniously from the depths of the river. No doubt he would have become homesick for venison and wild duck and dainty meals prepared by the hand of Maid Marian. Johnstoni crocodiles might have frightened him.

Robin Hood was bought by Cob Terry and his wife, Mary, in 1962. They also own another property, Lucerne, outside of Richmond. They stayed on Lucerne until 1970, and then moved to Robin Hood.

Cob Terry is the archetypal bushman—a ramrod straight torso topped by a craggy, at times fierce, face which reflects the gullies, gorges, ravines and scant plains of this station he loves.

There are some eerily haunting corners on the station, not the least of which is Gorge Creek, a black slash which cuts through the hard acres of the arid Conglomerate Wall. The view looking down into the creek from the top of the Wall is one which sends a tingle up the spine. The sheer rock walls plummet down into the black water. When standing at the lip, it is difficult to resist a feeling of almost overwhelming vertigo. The Wall, with its crisscrossed surface, which gives it a textured flagstone appearance, and its crevices and caves, is said by the Aboriginals to be the haunt of the Greasy Man—a hostile dreamtime figure who still strikes fear today into the hearts of local blacks. Aboriginal stockmen, it has been said, are loath to camp anywhere in the vicinity of the Wall.

Whether there is a Greasy Man in attendance or not remains to be proved, but there is the distinct likelihood that there could be at least a generously proportioned saltwater crocodile in Gorge Creek. Some years ago a crocodile skull, as long as a man's arm, was found on the bank of the creek. The broad snout and the width of the tooth cavities ruled out any possibility of the skull's having belonged to a fresh water Johnstoni River crocodile, of which there are many in the area. It is a long, long way to the sea from Robin Hood, but it is conceivable that a salt water crocodile could travel up the Gilbert River from the Gulf and into the Robertson River which runs through Robin Hood. Gorge Creek, like nearly all of the watercourses on the station, is a tributary of the Robertson. In 1982 Cob Terry discovered a freshly dead fifteen kilogram barramundi which had died in Fish Hole, a permanent waterhole on the station. If a barra can get there from the coast, there is nothing to suggest that a saltwater crocodile couldn't do the same.

A kilometre or so upstream from where Gorge Creek runs into the Robertson River is the grave of John Corbett, a teamster who was apparently murdered by blacks in 1871. Corbett was on his way from the nearby Percyville goldfields to Georgetown when he was speared in the back. But there are those who say that Corbett was, in fact, done in by a white desperado who first shot his victim and then jammed a spear into the bullet hole to direct the blame onto the Aboriginals. Probably no more than a dozen people stumble upon the lonely grave each year but even so, in 1981, vandals found the grave and splashed the headstone with blue paint. Some years before this, sections of the cast iron balustrade which surrounds the grave were stolen, and have never been recovered.

A kilometre or so from the grave is Stone Yard—a natural amphitheatre which penetrates deep into the Conglomerate Wall for a distance of about seven hundred metres. Towards the end of the amphitheatre is a keyhole-shaped yard surrounded on all sides, except at the opening, by steep cliffs and protruding ledges. At one time cattle were mustered into the amphitheatre and driven into the yard, where they were drafted. The stockmen worked in bare feet and, whenever an animal charged, they would leap for one of the protruding ledges. The amphitheatre, with its soaring sides and one way out, was said to be a favourite haunt of the Greasy Man.

At another end of the property is Agate Pocket on Agate Creek, a gem-hunting field popular with rock hounds from all over Australia. This is an isolated area and seems an unlikely spot for a tourist enterprise to take shape. But there, sure enough, is a camping complex built and run by erstwhile Sydney union organiser John Barron and his wife Claudia. The Barrons have created an oasis, utilising a wide variety of fruit trees, and have what must be the only vegetable garden in Australia fertilised with bat manure. Claudia guides tourists to a nearby cave which has a resident bat colony. On the floor of the cave a thick layer of manure has built up over the centuries. The tourists who want to see the colony have to pay a price: Claudia hands each one a bucket to fill with bat manure and carry back to

Trucking cattle at Doncaster Station in northwest Queensland.

Richmond district station manager Doug McGrath.

Twenty-year-old Richard Terry, part owner of Robin Hood Station.

Time passes slowly at the rail head of Forsayth in the lower Gulf country.

the camp. The flourishing vegetable garden testifies to the fertile goodness of the manure.

Cattle duffing has at times been a headache, as it proves difficult for the Terrys to police their extensive, largely unfenced boundary. But now that Cob and Mary spend much of their time operating from the homestead, they are able to maintain presence around the boundary. Up until 1982 the couple camped out in the mustering camp with the boys and helped with the mustering of the cattle. Peter, who has his pilot's licence, bought a light plane in 1980, and he and Richard, who also has a licence, are able to fly over the station periodically. This is enough to deter all but the most determined poddy-dodgers.

The station was turned into a fauna sanctuary in the late 1970s, largely to deter the people who used to go there and indiscriminately shoot brumbies and other wildlife. It was not unusual to see a brumby with its entrails hanging out days after it had been gut shot by a 'hunter' using a high powered rifle. Now, with the protection offered under the auspicies of the National Parks and Wildlife, this sort of thing has become extremely uncommon. One old-timer, apparently disgruntled by the tightening up of things at Robin Hood, was heard to grumble in the Forsayth pub that 'now ya can't shoot the wallabies, ya can't shoot the pigs, ya can't shoot the kangaroos, and ya can't even shoot ol' Cob'.

When the Terry family first moved to Robin Hood they stocked it with Hereford cattle. In 1974 disaster struck. After seventy-six consecutive days of continual rain, a redwater epidemic caused by cattle ticks swept through the herd and 2000 cattle died. The family rolled with the blow and since then they have been gradually increasing the amount of Brahman blood in the herd to give the cattle a greater resistance to ticks and tick-associated diseases. Cob Terry is wary of the Brahman infusion, and is attempting to achieve a level that will maximise docility. Too much Brahman blood, he says, and you can't catch the cattle.

'When you first sight them they're not there for long. All you get is the hair where the bastards have been,' he said.

When Cob and Mary first moved to Robin Hood, they employed Aboriginal stockmen to help them on the station. Then, in 1973, Peter came home from boarding school to work on the property. Gradually the rest of the sons finished their schooling and returned home to work on Robin Hood. In 1980 Richard, then seventeen years old, gave up studying for a Surveying degree at the Darling Downs Institute of Advanced Education to help out on the station. Only Simon, who in 1983 is in his final year of schooling at a Toowoomba boarding school, is not connected directly with the running of the station. At school holiday time, though, he is bustled out into the mustering camp by his brothers and put to hard work.

Simon is no stranger to mustering camps. When the family first moved to Robin Hood he was five years old. For the first two years he attended school in Georgetown, eighty kilometres from the station. He boarded in town during the week and returned home on the weekends. After two years he returned to live at Robin Hood, where Mary taught him by correspondence. These were the days when Robin Hood was being turned into a viable station, and Cob and Mary spent nearly all of their time out in the mustering camps with the native stockmen. Simon, who was not yet eight, spent his days on horseback, following his mother and father around the property as they mustered the cattle. In the evenings he did his lessons and sometimes, when chores around the camp demanded it, Mary would take a day off from mustering to bake bread and such while Simon caught up with his lessons.

In 1976 Simon went away to boarding school, but already he had served a worthwhile apprenticeship on the land. Cob and Mary's two eldest children are their daughters Fran and Robyn, who are married and not directly involved with the station.

It took some years before the family was accepted into this isolated Gulf community, and it wasn't until the boys were working at home and mixing in the district that the local population began gradually to accept them. The boys are all keen rodeo enthusiasts, and have supported many of the local rodeos extensively, not only with administrative input, but with competitive prowess in the rodeo arena. In 1977 Peter travelled to America to follow the rodeo circuit and stayed for six months. He was an accomplished steer wrestler and calf roping exponent, and for a time considered taking up rodeo on a professional basis. But he was faced with the choice of either spending a lot of time away from home on the circuit, or giving his undivided attention to Robin Hood. Robin Hood won and now Peter never competes in a rodeo, but remains a staunch supporter of the local Forsayth rodeo along with the rest of his brothers.

Driving to Robin Hood is a trial. The road is rough, long, studded with tricks—no harbour for a continental sedan. Despite this, Cob Terry says the isolation is minimal.

'We are not really isolated, particularly with the Flying Doctor,' he says.

Cob Terry has plans for Robin Hood—more fences, additional water. It all takes time, money and hard work. Patience too, is a virtue of the building cattleman: patience to endure the droughts, the fires, the floods and the other poisoned arrows in Mother Nature's quiver.

Robin Hood has already progressed to the stage where it is a monument to this family's dedication. Who knows? Perhaps the real Robin Hood might feel at home there. Friar Tuck, though, might still have trouble gathering a pious parish.

The Terry family line-up.

The terrible 1982–83 drought. This poddy calf on Robin Hood Station was taken back to the homestead and reared as a pet. Note the calf's dead mother in the background.

Old and new homesteads on Woodleigh Station.

Blencoe Falls on Kirrama Station.

Woodleigh

The homestead of 173 square kilometre Woodleigh Station sits atop a high bank overlooking the cool, green waters of Millstream Creek. Several hundred metres downstream the Wild River joins the Millstream and at the confluence the Herbert River is born. The Herbert then commences a spectacular journey through forest, gorge, and jungle until it cuts through the sugar cane lowlands at Abergowrie, forty kilometres west of Ingham. The Herbert, in its upper reaches and particularly in the fifty kilometre long Herbert River Gorge, is a true wilderness area. The inhospitable nature of the country through which the gorge runs means that few people have seen this rampantly beautiful river at its soaring best.

Woodleigh Station is owned by Pat Williams, a descendant of Henry Sydney Williams, who arrived in north Queensland in the days of the Palmer River gold rush. Henry Williams was the man responsible for the construction of the Lake Eacham Hotel at Yungaburra on the Atherton Tableland. The hotel was an architecturally ambitious project and remains today one of the finest structures of its type in the north.

Henry Williams had a son named Jack, who over the years cultivated something of a 'wild man' image for himself. One of his better-known feats occurred when he was bookmaking at a steeplechase race at the tin mining town of Herberton on the Atherton Tableland. Seconds after the starter's gun barked, a girth broke on one of the runners, sending the jockey tumbling to the ground, saddle and all. As the riderless horse bolted down the track towards where the bookies were plying their trade, Jack Williams threw down his bag, vaulted the fence, leapt upon the back of the runaway horse, and rode it to first place. There was much fierce debate around the track as to whether a win should be paid out on Jack's splendid ride to the finish. Those who had backed the horse, of course, were much in favour of a payout. But those who had backed the second placegetter to win were unanimous that Jack and his mount should be disqualified. The debate raged and a fracas was only averted when the bookmakers sat down and discussed the matter. The upshot was that they paid out on Jack's horse as the winner, arguing that, as Jack was three stone heavier than the tumbled jockey, there was no advantage evident.

Jack Williams was held in high esteem in some quarters because of the fact that he was mighty handy in a bare knuckle scrap. He had the most conspicuous habit of riding a mule from a property he owned outside Mt Garnet into the bar of Lucy's Hotel in 'The Garnet'. Once in the bar, he would sit astride the complacent mule quaffing his ale until a bout of fisticuffs came his way. Only then would he alight to the boards, demolish his opponent, and then climb back up onto the mule and recommence his drinking. On an average night at Lucy's he might step down on to the boards three or four times. His prowess in a scrap was so well known and so formidable that he was barred from fighting in any travelling boxing tent shows which passed through the district.

Woodleigh Station was bought by the Williams Estate in 1913 and was managed by Jack Williams until his death in 1943. Pat Williams took over as manager in 1949. In 1976, 388 square kilometres was resumed from the station, reducing the property to its current size. Pat Williams believes that more land will be resumed in the future by the Lands Department for more intensive agricultural development.

Woodleigh is situated between the Atherton Tableland and Mt Garnet. This area was once thought to be only marginal land in terms of agricultural development, but now this idea is changing and more and more agriculture is being practised on what was formerly only cattle country. Grain sorghum has been grown on Woodleigh for the past fifteen years and corn is also grown with good results. Large tracts of land in the area are now being turned over for the production of peanuts, and in the future this could be the number one cash crop grown on the red soils around Mt Garnet.

Pat Williams holds an optimistic outlook for the future of the beef industry, and isn't about to sell off his 2000 cattle and change over to total agriculture. His philosophy is that the industry runs in thirty-year cycles, which in simple terms translates that when things aren't getting better they're getting worse.

'It's like the old timers say, you know: the cattle industry stays down for fifteen years and then spends another fifteen years climbing back up.'

Woodleigh has taken measures to cope with the unreliability of the beef market. Not only agriculture is practised, but tourism also plays a hand in the station's viability. The tourism sideline got under way during the beef recession in 1977, when a firm which conducts sight-seeing tours approached Pat and his wife, Clare, about using the property as a stopping-off point. At the time Pat and Clare had two children away at boarding school. Income from the cattle operation had all but ceased and, like most other graziers hit by the recession, they were looking for a way to ride the slump. The tourism idea sounded as though it might be the 'ride' they were looking for and they stepped aboard. Now, even though cattle prices have stabilised to some degree, they have continued with the project. On an average week during the tourist season, three tourist buses call in at Woodleigh. Tourists, many of them from Sydney, Melbourne and Adelaide, look around the property and marvel at the century-old buildings. These include the original slab homestead which has been decorated inside to appear as it was in the pioneering days. They see cattle being worked in stockyards, and have the opportunity to ask a multitude of 'hows' and 'whys' involving life on a cattle station. One of the commonest questions women ask Clare is what she does with herself all the time. They can't believe that a woman on a station can be kept busy, and cannot begin to comprehend the amount of cooking, organising and bookwork that is the woman's lot.

'No,' they say. 'It must be wonderful to sit out in a squatter's chair and gaze over that beautiful river all day.' Not bloody likely.

Kirrama

Up in the Kirrama Range west of Cardwell is a slice of the genuine, spur-janglin' Lone Star State. The rain forest and hill country of the Kirrama Range has become home to the Gunn family, formerly of Texas in the USA.

Patriarch over the three generations of Gunns living on 430 square kilometre Kirrama Station is eighty-year-old Roy Gunn, a self-confessed old time cowboy who likes nothing better than life on the range. He still puts in a hard day in the saddle, helping muster the 5000 Brahman cattle on the station. In his cowboy hat, chaps and vest, he looks more like a character out of a John Ford western than a Queensland cattleman. Also on the station is Roy's son Sam, Sam's wife Christine, and their two children, Bobby-Sam and Valerie. Roy's daughter Pat and her husband Jim, along with their two sons, Mick and Jack, also live on the station. Both Mick and Jack completed university studies in America before moving out to Australia. Jack studied Physical Education and Mick took a degree in Petroleum Engineering. When I visited the station in 1982, both men were working at a mill on top of the range which cuts sleepers for Queensland Railways.

Before moving out to Australia, Roy Gunn owned a 1600 hectare ranch near Austin in Texas where he grazed cattle, sheep and angora goats. The ranch was scheduled to be flooded by a government dam project and was bought by the federal administration. After getting compensation, he could not find another ranch he could buy. Ranch land is a scarce commodity in Texas now, and unless a ranch is inherited it is virtually impossible to get hold of one. Cattle land is rapidly disappearing down the gullet of real estate development and being turned into 'ten acre ranchettes' for weekend farmers. Roy had always been fascinated by Australia, especially the stories about its wide open spaces and its cattle stations. In 1972 he and his wife left America with the intention of buying Mt Mulgrave Station on the Mitchell River. But a prearranged partnership deal fell through and instead Roy Gunn bought Kirrama. His family followed him out not long afterwards and have settled into the century-old split log homesteads on the property. Roy lives in one of the oldest slab cottages, built more than a century ago. Sitting beside the blazing fireplace, built from antbed and surrounded by thick slabs of hardwood, the old cattleman really does look like a travel-weary trail boss.

Since being in Australia, the Gunns have found that running a ranch is vastly different from what it was back home in Texas. Kirrama, in parts, is very rough country—gorges, rain forest and steep gullies are the order of the day. Mustering the long-legged Brahmans in this type of country involves quite a bit of fancy riding, which is not without an element of danger. Galloping out into an abyss such as the Herbert River Gorge, which forms one boundary on the station, is not out of the question. Roy Gunn added wistfully that, in Texas, all he had to do to muster a paddock was drive out and toot the car horn and the stock would come running. Try that on Kirrama and the man-shy Brahmans hightail it for the nearest patch of scrub.

Mt Ravenswood

On 17 November 1976, after a University of Queensland English examination in the old Cloudland Ballroom (now demolished) in Brisbane, I stepped into a battered Holden driven by a friend and we drove non-stop to Battery Station on the Burdekin River. We intended to paddle kayaks from there down to where the Bruce Highway crosses the river near Ayr on the coast. We had estimated the trip would take around three weeks.

We made camp on the twelfth day out in a dry side channel shaded by overhanging ti-trees. Just after dark, lightning started to light the sky to the north and the cannon sounds of faraway thunder rumbled down the river. Less than an hour later the effects of the distant storm could be seen as, barely perceptibly at first, the river began to rise. While we worked to move our gear up the steep bank away from the encroaching water, the sky above us opened. The rain came down and lightning bolts lashed the sky over our heads. The flashes seemed so close that we crawled on our stomachs through the rising water, snatching gear before it floated away and then running hunched over with it up the bank. Away from the river we could hear whip crack after whip crack as the lightning exploded the ironbark and box trees.

The storm passed after thirty minutes and we erected our sodden tent and tried to get to sleep in waterlogged sleeping bags. The next morning we went hunting for food and shot two wood ducks on a dam. As we were walking back to the camp we heard a vehicle. After a minute or so a Toyota Landcruiser came into view and we could see it was being driven by a woman. She drove towards us and introduced herself as Betty Prichard from Mt Ravenswood Station. With her was her brother Fred Prichard and the station cook, Harry Masso.

After chatting about things in general for a few minutes, Betty told us to paddle downstream until we saw a pump. A pipeline running away from the pump would lead us to the homestead, where we could give our gear the once over and sample a bit of home cooking. We spent two days at the station repairing the kayaks, getting them ready for the descent of the Burdekin Falls about thirty kilometres downstream from the station.

We pushed off early on the third morning, confident we would be camping above the falls that night. An hour or so away from the station, we approached a fairly harmless looking grade two rapid at the confluence of

John Ramsay, old time bush publican and former head stockman on Dotswood Station, at his Mingela Hotel between Charters Towers and Townsville.

the river and a creek. It looked deep and there were no visible rocks. I charged into the white caps and was half way through when I saw the pointed snout of a black rock protruding from the froth and bubble of a pressure wave. It was too late. I was going too fast and the rock was too close. The nose of the kayak crunched and water flooded the cockpit. I swam to shore, pulling the canoe, thinking, 'Oh well, we'll be delayed for a bit while we patch the break, that's all.'

The nose was shattered for a full forty centimetres, serious but not disastrous. The same canoe had split into two clean halves once on the treacherous Nymboida River in Northern New South Wales, after it reared into the air in a grade four rapid and smashed down on the bank of a pressure wave. A broken nose on the placid old Burdekin was the least of its worries.

Disaster did strike, though, when we unpacked the repair kit and found that all the resin hardener had leaked from its container. Without it we would not be able to get the resin to harden the fibreglass.

Desperate, and looking for miracles, we carefully bound the nose with thin gauge wire, wound fibreglass around the unlikely looking mend and painted on the resin. We raised the kayak and built a small fire beneath the nose, hoping that the heat might act as a catalyst to make the resin harden. We kept the fire burning all day, but that evening the 'glass was still tacky. It was the old story of trying to nail jelly to the wall. There was nothing to do but walk back to Mt Ravenswood.

Early the next morning we were cutting cross-country through the bush with Betty at the wheel of the Toyota, trying to find a gap in the mountains to the river. We found one towards midday, loaded the canoes and drove back to the homestead. The next day Jim Prichard drove us into the old gold mining township of Ravenswood and lent us twenty dollars so we could get a bed at one of the local pubs and wait for our belongings to arrive from Townsville.

That was my introduction to the Prichard family. I have never forgotten their kindness and the way they went out of their way to look after two total strangers. I have been back there on fishing trips many times since, and the hospitality has always been the same.

Two hundred square kilometre Mt Ravenswood was bought by Jim and Fred Prichard in 1955. The two men worked together on the property until 1962, when Fred was injured in a horse accident. No one saw the accident happen, but it appears that the horse fell and rolled on top of Fred at full gallop. An Aboriginal stockman found Fred lying unconscious where he had fallen, and galloped seven kilometres back to the homestead for help. The injured rider was left lying in the paddock until he was examined by a doctor and pronounced safe to move.

Fred regained consciousness six weeks later in a Townsville hospital. His injuries included a fractured femur and a head injury which resulted in paralysis to the left side of his body. Eight months later, when he was well enough to be moved, Betty took him to Sydney for further treatment. He remained in Sydney until January 1964, and then returned home to the station in a wheelchair. This remained his only means of mobility for the next seven years. The big, powerful horseman was reduced to a life of inactivity. Gradually, he began to walk around the house with the aid of crutches, but even now his poor mobility and balance mean that he requires constant supervision.

Betty, who is a trained nurse and midwife, carried out wartime service on Borneo and on Horn Island in the Torres Strait. After the war, she gave up what many people believed was a promising career to nurse her ailing mother at Charters Towers.

In 1956 Betty moved out to Mt Ravenswood to cook and keep house for Fred while Jim remained in Charters Towers trying to sell an orchard belonging to the family. After Fred had his accident Betty made the decision to stay on at the station.

Now, as well as operating the Mt Ravenswood telephone exchange, which has its switchboard in the homestead, Betty is president of the Ravenswood branch of the CWA. In less than two years she boosted club membership from five to twelve, and adds with a spark in her always twinkling eyes that Fred usually accompanies her to town for the meetings.

'He sits at the bar in the pub until everything is over, that's all. I haven't been able to drag him in to a meeting yet, but you never know . . .'

Betty and Fred Prichard and station cook Harry Masso.

Time out for a nap at a Charters Towers horse sale.

Strathalbyn

Strathalbyn Station is on the southern bank of the Burdekin River, adjacent to the small sugar cane growing community of Dalbeg, which is on the agriculturally productive northern bank. Up until the end of 1980, Strathalbyn was owned by the Cunningham family. It was sold to the Dunn family in that same year.

My Strathalbyn story, rather than being about the contemporary operation of the station, deals with a little-known event which occurred there in 1871. It is a story of murder and brutal revenge.

It is the afternoon of 18 June 1871 at Strathmore Station, on the banks of the Bowen River, not far from the mass of water which marks the Bowen's union with the mighty Burdekin. Predictably at this time of the year, the sky is cloudless and deep blue, and beneath it at the Strathmore killing yard the overseer and several Aboriginals, after having a smoko of black tea and Johnny cakes, are butchering a killer.

In the background a group of myall blacks wait for the leavings—the intestine, the milk gut and other offal which they will eat in the camp that night; nothing will be left on the carcass of the killer. That night at the homestead there will be fried brains, liver, sweetbreads, skirts and heart. Tomorrow there will be fresh meats, steaks and roasts. Thereafter until the next killing there will only be the interminable salt meat . . . the stuff they say sticks to a bushman's gut through thick and thin.

Suddenly, without warning, there is a whispering among the blacks. One of the myalls, less timid than his fellows, walks quietly to one of the station natives who is cutting meat. The message comes forth in a torrent of Aboriginal dialect. They always speak fast and fluently. The station native stops what he is doing and speaks to the overseer: 'That feller myall he all the same reckon murray (blacks) killem migaloo (whites) alonga Strathalbyn.'

The killing is supposed to have taken place that same morning. The overseer dismisses the story because of the time factor—Strathalbyn is fifty kilometres from Strathmore as the crow flies, and most people know the crow flies an awfully straight course in this wild Burdekin country. The Strathmore whites cannot conceive how such news could have travelled so far, so fast, over such broken country.

The Bonnie Doon blacks on Strathalbyn were originally warlike. They speared the great uncle of Ted Cunningham (the present owner of Strathmore) while he was riding from Strathalbyn to Strathmore. His unmarked grave, known only to Ted Cunningham, lies beneath a leaning gum tree on Bonnie Doon Creek. Until 18 June 1871 the blacks had been peaceful for some time. Something snapped.

An Aboriginal named Mangrove and his wife were employed at the Strathalbyn homestead. With them was their son, whom the station manager, George Stanley Lampton, wished to make into a houseboy. The boy did not relish the work and ran away to the native camp on the station. He was followed by Mangrove and his mother. Lampton awoke on the morning of their retreat and found the trio gone. He roused his overseer, a man named Longfield, and together they rode out to where the natives were camped, demanding that the three return. Voices rose; the altercation was inevitable. One of the younger members of the tribe threw a nulla-nulla, which knocked Lampton to the ground, caving in his skull. A volley of spears then brought Longfield and the two horses to the ground.

It wasn't until several days later, when the six-in-hand mail coach rolled into Strathmore Station, that the story of the killings was confirmed. Two men at Strathalbyn, Lampton and Longfield, had been killed by the blacks. How the Strathmore Aboriginals knew only a few hours afterwards has always remained a mystery.

The mailman, known as 'Toms', was the first person to pass through Strathalbyn after the slaying. He was running the Ravenswood-Bowen mail. 'Toms' immediately sent a man who was with him back to Ravenswood to relate the news, and a black boy was despatched to Leichhardt Downs. 'Toms' proceeded to Bowen to relate the news to Sub-Inspector Fitzgerald. Fitzgerald started for Strathalbyn, and on arrival found the mutilated bodies of the two men. They were then buried on the banks of the Burdekin just below the station. Later, relatives erected a common tombstone over the grave. The native camp had since broken up and the blacks had dispersed, breaking into small groups.

At this time there was a native police contingent under the command of a sergeant and a constable, which was camped at the junction of the Bogie and Burdekin Rivers. This force was given the task of bringing the murderers to trial.

What follows is not recorded in the colourful chapters of Queensland's frontier history, nor was the chase reported by the *Port Denison Times*, the then newspaper at Bowen. The information was told to me by Ted Cunningham of Strathmore Station. The events had been chronicled over a long period of his family's history in the north, starting with Edward Cunningham's exploration of the Burdekin area in 1860.

Ted said: 'The main perpetrators of the crime had split from the tribe and were living in the hills between Strathalbyn and Strathbogie. Here the native police found them, but the fugitives fled towards the river and escaped. They then went up the river, pursued by the native police, and managed to elude them for several days. Crossing the Bowen above the junction, they doubled back to the Burdekin and headed for a mountain just south of the Burdekin Gorge. Climbing up this mountain, they reached a sheer cliff, and here they decided to make their stand and attack their pursuers as they climbed the

mountain. However, they were no match for the carbines of the police and all
nine were shot at the base of the cliff—their bodies left there.'

Ted Cunningham feels sure the bones of the nine dead could still be
found at the base of the cliff today. What happened to the two white men,
Lampton and Longfield, was certainly an outrage, and all evidence seems to
point to the fact that the attack on them was maliciously carried out without
any introductory threats being made by the pair. What is questionable is the
ensuing reprisal against the Aboriginals. Retribution, for sure, was swift and
harsh, and history shows that the native police took to their job as hunters of
their own race with a great deal of enthusiasm.

One-time station manager in the Burdekin area, Charles Eden, wrote this
of the native police. The report appeared in an 1871 copy of the *Port Denison
Times*:

> They are devoted to their officers and to their grog, their pay is very good and as
> they all have gins, they lead a very jolly kind of life. The gins are captive of their
> bow and spear, and are brought home before their captor on his saddle. This
> seems the orthodox way of wooing the coy forest maidens.

This is certainly not a sensitive appraisal of the situation, but it is one which
reflects 'white' thought at the time.

This way of thinking can be expanded upon with reference to an article
which made space in the *Port Denison Times*. The article, 'An Apology for
Killing the Blacks', tried to justify the ritual extermination of the Aboriginals
who threatened the expansion of the frontier. The story draws upon Divine
Providence as a justification for the eradication of the Aboriginals who were
a 'corrupt, godless, wicked people'. Part of the story had previously appeared
in a Melbourne publication, the *Christian Review*, where it was apparently
given a favourable reception.

> Thousands of our Aborigines have been shot down with calm indifference
> because they were troublesome on the runs, like kangaroos; they have been
> poisoned with strychnine in company with the dingoes; they have perished before
> our eyes from our loathsome diseases, and from our firewater. We have been
> accustomed to regard these things as a blot upon our Christianity. We learn with
> gratitude now that in our murders we were but executing the Will of Heaven.

Noted northern historian and senior lecturer in Aboriginal Education at the
Townsville College of Advanced Education, Dr Noel Loos, said the concept
of Divine Providence was later replaced with Darwinism towards the latter
stages of the nineteenth century.

Frontier folk and city-based moralists could then justify the slaughter as
'survival of the fittest', the fittest, of course, being those with the carbines
and the will to settle a new land. Dr Loos did say that the frontier folk were
not ones to intellectualise the killing of the blacks, and so Darwin's ideas
were probably lost on them in theory, but in practice it worked perfectly.

The grave which holds the remains of Lampton and Longfield still stands
its lonely vigil on the southern bank of the Burdekin River at Strathalbyn.
The ghosts of the two men might now be swirling through the craggy
Burdekin mountains, mixing with the nine who live in their own bullet-
riddled Dreamtime.

Strathmore

Ted Cunningham of Strathmore Station outside of Collinsville makes it clear that he doesn't like Brahman cattle. Being one of the 'old school' cattlemen, he has chosen to stick with his Red Devon herd and woe betide any man foolish enough to suggest he change his ways.

Mr Cunningham, as he is usually called in the north, is his own man and has been for a long time. Anyone who forgets is usually haughtily ignored. Once a young veterinarian, new to the north, was sent out to Strathmore by his employers to examine some cattle. During the course of his ministrations he made the fatal blunder of suggesting to Mr Cunningham that perhaps it would be wise if he got rid of his British cattle and went into Brahmans. Mr Cunningham, it was said, stalked from the yards and rang the upstart's boss, telling him never to send the impudent pup out to the station again.

There is probably an element of stubbornness tied up with his refusal to switch to the hardier Brahmans, but he firmly believes that British cattle were bred to be eaten, 'unlike yaks [Brahmans]', he belligerently points out, 'which were bred to be beasts of burden'.

He claims that the entire Queensland beef industry is under siege by the Brahman influence in that the end product lacks quality. The meat, he argues, is tough and of little value to the consumer, whereas the meat from the British cattle is tender and delicious. He has little time for the argument that British cattle cannot adapt to the dry tropics, and counters by saying that they handle the conditions just as effectively as the Brahmans. He admits that they are more susceptible to ticks, but this, he says, is easily counterbalanced by the quality of meat.

'Eighty per cent of the places which breed yaks now have to muster with helicopters and are shooting the ones they cannot get. In a few years even the helicopters won't be able to handle them,' he points out.

I asked him how he could justify running British cattle when the 'experts' (DPI and CSIRO) keep repeating that *Bos indicus* (Brahman and extractions thereof) are the only cattle for the north. In true Cunningham style he answered: 'By "experts" I presume you mean those bright young boys who sit behind polished desks and churn out screeds of technical detail that cannot be put to practical use.' As well as 'impudent pups', Mr Cunningham doesn't have much time for 'bright young boys'.

A fisherman luring for sooty grunter in the magnificent Burdekin River near Mt Ravenswood Station.

Beautiful Strathmore Station homestead.

Bringing the cattle to the yards on Strathmore Station.

The old Bowen River Hotel.

The Cunningham name goes back to 1860, when Edward Cunningham explored the middle reaches of the Burdekin River in north Queensland. Accompanying him were three whites and an Aboriginal named Jimmy. The four white men were interested in staking out pastoral leases in the area, and in the course of their exploration opened up some of the wilder country on the frontier. In the foothills of the Leichhardt Range they were attacked by blacks, and one of Cunningham's companions was struck from his horse and nearly killed. He was saved only when Cunningham galloped into the melee firing his pistol and scattered the attackers into the hills. At the end of the trip Edward Cunningham had selected Burdekin Downs (56 700 hectares) on the Burdekin River not far from Charters Towers. In 1902 he bought Strathmore in a partnership agreement, and gradually the Cunningham properties were amassed.

The Strathmore homestead, built in 1903, with its wide verandahs overlooking a sweeping expanse of lawn and well-tended shrubs, remains one of the finest of its type in the north. Peacocks strut through the garden and towards one end is Ted Cunningham's private zoo complete with buffalo, deer, monkeys, a camel and native Australian animals. Standing in the Strathmore garden at sunset one can close one's eyes and easily transport this picture of sculptured elegance to a Far Eastern setting, complete with Somerset Maugham characters wearing white topees and sipping cocktails.

Towards the end of 1980, Ted Cunningham began to supervise the sale of eight properties owned by the Cunningham family in north Queensland. These were the properties of Bilimba, Torwood, Woodhouse, Hidden Valley, The Eight Mile, Strathalbyn, Johnny Cake and Table Top. The stations sold for a total in excess of five million dollars and represented a total land area of 11 655 square kilometres. I covered some of those auctions as a reporter and can still see Ted sitting bolt upright at the auctioneer's table, his tie in place, eyes to the front and no emotion on his face save for the occasional hint of a smile.

Ted Cunningham has a reputation as something of a story teller; a teller, in fact, of unusual tales. One such story concerns a little-known raid carried out by Japanese paratroopers to blow up the important Haughton River bridge, south of Townsville, during World War II. The plan was, apparently, to demolish the structure to prevent troops and equipment getting through. The two parachutists were sighted during their descent by a Mrs Cadio, the wife of a man who worked on one of the Cunningham properties in the area. The American army had agisted Dingo Park, a paddock on the property, and were running 1300 horses there under the supervision of a detachment of Texans. Mrs Cadio jumped into an old Blitz and drove hell-for-leather for the American base. When she arrived she informed an officer about what she had seen. The officer sent out a detail to locate the Japanese, who were shot where they were found. The event was never made public.

Ted Cunningham is a keen amateur historian and has a considerable interest in the history of the Bowen River area. One of his pet projects over the years has been the preservation of the old Bowen River Hotel not far from the Strathmore homestead. The old slab-walled hotel, which became a sheltering place for thirsty travellers in 1889, has undergone a partial facelift in recent years. A local craftsman, paid by the National Trust, has slowly been replacing the original split slabs in the building with local timber. Using an adze and wedges, he is slowly restoring the building to its former glory. It has been many, many years since the last rum bottle was uncorked in the pub, but on a dark night they say the ghosts of murdered men and suicides can be heard moaning inside. I camped in the pub one night in 1977 when I was a member of a party which canoed down the Bowen River. No one heard any chains dragging or door knobs rattling; then again, you don't hear much when you've been dragging a Canadian canoe over an almost dry river bed all day.

When the pub was opened it became a popular haunt for adventurers and ne'er-do-wells heading west to the promised land from Port Denison (now known as Bowen). Stage coach drivers and peaceful settlers broke their wearisome journeys to imbibe the warm liquor and embrace the proffered hospitality. The dusty track from Port Denison gave rise to some raging thirsts, which were quenched in classic style amid the rowdy bonhomie and at times violent pulsings of the Bowen River Hotel.

According to Ted Cunningham, the pub began to acquire a reputation in the early 1920s. In July 1921 a man named Joe Marshall, who was in the horrors, took a dose of strychnine and died on the river bank a few hundred metres from where the road bridge crosses the Bowen River today. A party of Aboriginals was sent over from Strathmore with a dray to bring the body back to the station for burial. The corpse was badly decomposed, and when it was lifted up to the dray the head fell off and rolled back down the bank. That was it for the blacks. They returned home without the corpse. Joe Marshall's body was later buried in a shallow sand grave on the river and would have been washed away in the first flood.

Bushmen bent on suicide were for some reason attracted to the pub. Not long after Marshall swallowed his strychnine, an old traveller by the name of Hipworth threw himself into a heavy drinking session lasting several days. One evening he failed to return from a walk down to the river. Searchers later found him barely alive with his throat cut. Bull ants, sand and grass had made a gory mess but, still breathing, he was carried back to the hotel. Meanwhile Arthur Cunningham from Strathmore had been summoned, and with the help of an assistant he put nineteen stitches into the slashed throat using spaying twine and a needle. After the operation Hipworth was given a reviver of brandy and rushed by buggy to hospital. For a time he responded to treatment. Then a nurse found him dead. During the night he had unpicked the stitches and bled to death.

Ted Cunningham tells the story of an old swaggie who had spent all his money after a momentous bender in the pub. Still thirsty, he tried to borrow money so he could continue the spree, but no one would lend him any. Filled with anger, he sat at the bar, withdrew a blunt pen knife and tried to cut his throat. The knife was so blunt that he only managed to inflict a bad wound. The sympathy of the gathered drinkers was aroused, and they took up a collection to see the old swaggie on his way. After he had been handed the money, the swagman, with his throat roughly bandaged, decided to stay on and drink out the collection.

Late in January 1922 two young travellers arrived at the hotel while looking for work in the area. The lessee of the pub told them they could camp on the verandah free of charge for the night and told them they might find work in the area the following day. Jack Baron (Flash Jack), a stage coach driver, had driven in that day and was known to be a bombastic, overbearing man. He was a master of the 'king hit' and had acquired a reputation as being something of a fighter. He was drinking heavily and, right or wrong, he wanted the young travellers to tip a glass with him. A row developed and in the end Flash Jack hit one of the travellers, after which both men returned to their swags on the verandah.

Jack Faulkner, the Bowen mailman, came out to the verandah and started to urge the man who had been punched to shoot Flash Jack.

'You've got a gun, don't let him bluff you,' he kept saying. Some minutes later Flash Jack again came out on the verandah and tried to get the two men to drink with him. When they refused, he threatened to use his fists again. One of the men called out: 'Don't come any closer, Baron, or I'll shoot you.' Baron laughed and stepped towards the man. A shot rang out and at point blank range the heavy bullet ploughed into Flash Jack's belly and a rush of blood gushed out.

The impact spun Flash Jack around and he staggered back to his camp. Some time later, when things had been sorted out in the pub, some of the more concerned drinkers decided to go and see how Flash Jack was getting on. They found him sitting hunched over a hurricane lantern beneath his buggy. One of the men asked how he was, whereupon Flash Jack threw the light in their direction and told them to 'go to hell'. The next morning when they went back Flash Jack was dead.

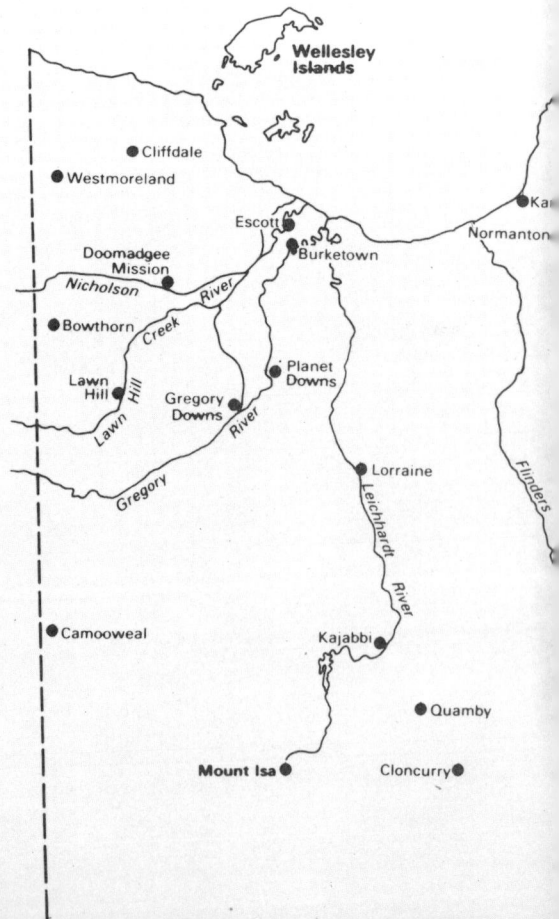

Gulf of Carpentaria

Wellesley Islands

● Cliffdale

● Westmoreland

Escott ●
● Burketown

● Ka...

Normanton

Doomadgee
Mission
Nicholson ●
River

● Bowthorn

Creek

Lawn
Hill ●
Lawn Hill

Gregory
Downs ●

River

Planet
Downs ●

Gregory

● Lorraine

Leichhardt River

Flinders River

● Camooweal

Kajabbi ●

● Quamby

Mount Isa ●

Cloncurry ●